P9-DJA-999

How Are We to Live?

How Are We to Live?

Peter Singer

Ethics in an Age of Self-Interest

Prometheus Books

59 John Glenn Drive
Amherst, New York 14228-2197

Published 1995 by Prometheus Books
by arrangement with Reed Consumer Books Ltd.

How Are We to Live: Ethics in an Age of Self-Interest. Copyright © 1993, 1995 by Peter Singer. Peter Singer asserts the moral right to be identified as the author of this work. All rights reserved. No part of this publication may be reproduced, stored in a retrieval system, or transmitted in any form or by any means, electronic, mechanical, photocopying, recording, or otherwise, without prior written permission of the publisher, except in the case of brief quotations embodied in critical articles and reviews. Inquiries should be addressed to Prometheus Books, 59 John Glenn Drive, Amherst, New York 14228-2197, 716-691-0133. FAX: 716-691-0137.

99 98   5 4 3

Library of Congress Cataloging-in-Publication Data

Singer, Peter.
    How are we to live? : ethics in an age of self-interest / Peter Singer.
        p.   cm.
    Includes bibliographical references and index.
    ISBN 0-87975-966-6 (pbk.)
    1. Ethics. 2. Social ethics. 3. Self-interest. I. Title.
BJ1012.S485   1995
170'.44—dc20   94-42598
                                                                    CIP

Printed in the United States of America on acid-free paper.

CONTENTS

———•———

PREFACE

Is there still anything to live *for?* Is anything worth pursuing, apart from money, love, and caring for one's own family? If so, what could it be? Talk of 'something to live for' has a faintly religious flavour, but many people who are not at all religious have an uneasy feeling that they may be missing out on something basic that would give their lives a significance it now lacks. Nor do these people have a deep commitment to any political creed. Over the past century political struggle has often filled the place that religion once held in other times and cultures. No one who reflects on recent history can now believe that politics alone will suffice to solve all our problems. But what else can we live for? In this book I give one answer. It is as ancient as the dawn of philosophy, but as much needed in our circumstances today as it ever was before. The answer is that we can live an ethical life. By doing so we make ourselves part of a great, cross-cultural tradition. Moreover, we will find that to live an ethical life is not self-sacrifice, but self-fulfillment.

If we can detach ourselves from our own immediate preoccupations and look at the world as a whole and our place in it, there is something absurd about the idea that people should have trouble finding something to live for. There is, after all, so much that needs to be done. As this book was nearing completion, United Nations troops entered Somalia in an attempt to ensure that food supplies reached the starving population there. Although this attempt went badly wrong, it was at least a hopeful sign that affluent nations were prepared to do something about hunger and suffering in areas remote from them. We may learn from this episode, and future attempts may be more successful. Perhaps we are at the beginning of a new era in which we will no longer simply sit in front of our television sets watching small children die and then continue to live our affluent lives without feeling any incongruity. It is not only the dramatic and newsworthy major crises that require our attention, though; there are countless situations, on a smaller scale, that are just as bad and are preventable. Immense as this task is, it is only one of many equally urgent causes to which people in need of a worthwhile objective could commit themselves.

The problem is that most people have only the vaguest idea of what it might be to lead an ethical life. They understand ethics as a system of rules forbidding us to do things. They do not grasp it as a basis for thinking about how we are to live. They live largely self-interested lives, not because they are born selfish, but because the alternatives seem awkward, embarrassing, or just plain pointless. They cannot see any way of making an impact on the world, and if they could, why should they bother? Short of undergoing a religious conversion, they see nothing to live for except the pursuit of their own material self-interest. But the possibility of living an ethical life provides us with a way out of this impasse. That possibility is the subject of this book.

Merely to broach this possibility will be enough to give rise to accusations of extreme naivity. Some will say that people are naturally incapable of being anything but selfish. Chapters 4, 5, 6 and 7 address this claim, in varying ways. Others will claim that whatever the truth about human nature, modern Western society has long passed the point at which either rational or ethical argument can achieve anything. Life today can seem so crazy that we may despair of improving it. One publisher who read the manuscript of this book gestured at the New York street below his window and told me that, down there, people had taken to driving through red lights, just for the hell of it. How, he was saying, can you expect your kind of book to make a difference to a world full of people like *that*? Indeed, if the world really were *full* of people who take so little care of their own lives, never mind the lives of others, there would be nothing that anyone could do, and our species would probably not be around for very much longer. But the ways of evolution tend to eliminate those who are *that* crazy. There may be a few around at any one time; no doubt big American cities shelter more than their fair share of them. What is truly disproportionate, though, is the prominence that such behaviour has in the media and in the public mind. It is the old story of what makes news. A million people doing something every day that shows concern for others is not news; one rooftop sniper is. This book is not blind to the existence of vicious, violent and irrational people, but it is written in the conviction that the rest of us should not live our lives as if everyone else is always inherently likely to be vicious, violent and irrational.

In any case, even if I am wrong, and crazy people are much more common than I believe, what alternative is left to us? The conventional pursuit of self-interest is, for reasons that I shall explore in a later chapter, individually and collectively self-defeating. The ethical life is the most fundamental alternative to the conventional pursuit of self-interest. Deciding to live ethically is both more far-reaching and more powerful than a political commitment of the traditional kind. Living an ethically reflective life is not a matter of strictly observing a set of rules that lay down what you should or should not do. To live ethically is to reflect in a particular way on how you live, and to try to act in accordance with the conclusions of that reflection. If the argument of this book is sound, then we cannot live an unethical life and remain indifferent to the vast amount of unnecessary suffering that exists in the world today. It may be naive to hope that a relatively small number of people who are living in a reflective, ethical manner could prove to be a critical mass that changes the climate of opinion about the nature of self-interest and its connection with ethics; but when we look around the world and see what a mess it is in, it seems worth giving that optimistic hope the best possible chance of success.

Every book reflects personal experience, no matter how many layers of scholarship the reflection may be filtered through. My interest in the topic of this book began when I was a graduate student in philosophy at the University of Melbourne. I wrote my Master's thesis on the topic 'Why Should I Be Moral?' The thesis analyzed this question, and examined the answers that have been offered by philosophers over the past two and half thousand years. I reluctantly concluded that none of these answers was really satisfactory. Then I spent twenty-five years studying and teaching ethics and social philosophy at universities in England, America and Australia. In the early part of that period I took part in opposition to the war in Vietnam. This formed the background to my first book, *Democracy and Disobedience*, about the ethical issue of disobedience to unjust laws. My second book, *Animal Liberation*, argued that our treatment of animals is ethically indefensible. That book played a role in the birth and growth of what is now a worldwide movement. I have worked in that movement not only as a philosopher but also as an active member of groups working for change. I have been involved, again both as an academic philosopher and in more everyday ways, in a variety of other causes with a strong ethical basis: aid for developing nations, support for refugees, the legalization of voluntary euthanasia, wilderness preservation and more general environmental concerns. All of this has given me the chance to get to know people who give up their time, their money and sometimes much of their private lives for an ethically-based cause; and it has given me a deeper sense of what it is to try to live an ethical life.

Since writing my Master's thesis I have written about the question 'Why act ethically?' in the final chapter of *Practical Ethics*, and I have touched on the theme of ethics and selfishness in *The Expanding Circle*. In turning once again to the link between ethics and self-interest, I can now draw on a solid background of practical experience, as well as on the research and writings of other scholars. If asked why anyone should act morally or ethically, I can give a bolder and more positive response than I did in my earlier thesis. I can point to people who have chosen to live an ethical life, and have been able to make an impact on the world. In doing so they have invested their lives with a significance that many despair of ever finding. They find, as a result, that their own lives are richer, more fulfilling, more exciting even, than they were before they made that choice.

Peter Singer
January 1993

CHAPTER 1

The ultimate choice

Ivan Boesky's choice

In 1985 Ivan Boesky was known as 'the king of the arbitragers', a specialized form of investment in the shares of companies that were the target of takeover offers. He made profits of $40 million in 1981 when Du Pont bought Conoco; $80 million in 1984 when Chevron bought Gulf Oil; and in the same year, $100 million when Texaco acquired Getty Oil. There were some substantial losses too, but not enough to stop Boesky making *Forbes* magazine's list of America's wealthiest 400 people. His personal fortune was estimated at between $150 and $200 million.[1]

Boesky had achieved both a formidable reputation, and a substantial degree of respectability. His reputation came, in part, from the amount of money that he controlled. 'Ivan', said one colleague, 'could get any Chief Executive Officer in the country off the toilet to talk to him at seven o'clock in the morning'.[2] But his reputation was also built on the belief that he had brought a new 'scientific' approach to investment, based on an elaborate communications system that he claimed was like NASA's. He was featured not only in business magazines, but also in the *New York Times* Living section. He wore the best suits, on which a Winston Churchill-style gold watch chain was prominently displayed. He owned a twelve-bedroom Georgian mansion set on 190 acres in Westchester County, outside New York City. He was a notable member of the Republican Party, and some thought he cherished political ambitions. He held positions at the American Ballet Theater and the Metropolitan Museum of Art.

Unlike other arbitragers before him, Boesky sought to publicize the nature of his work, and aimed to be recognized as an expert in a specialized area that aided the proper functioning of the market. In 1985 he published a book about arbitrage entitled *Merger Mania*. The book claims that arbitrage contributes to 'a fair, liquid and efficient market' and states that 'undue profits are not made: there are no esoteric tricks that enable arbitragers to outwit the system . . . profit opportunities exist only because risk arbitrage serves an important market function'. *Merger Mania* begins with a touching dedication:

Dedication

My father, my mentor, William H. Boesky (1900–1964), of beloved memory, whose courage brought him to these shores from his native Ykaterinoslav, Russia, in the year 1912. My life has been profoundly influenced by my father's spirit and strong commitment to the well-being of humanity, and by his emphasis on learning as the most important means to justice, mercy, and righteousness. His life remains an example of returning to the community the benefits he had received through the exercise of God-given talents.

With this inspiration I write this book for all who wish to learn of my specialty, that they may be inspired to believe that confidence in one's self and determination can allow one to become whatever one may dream. May those who read my book gain some understanding for the opportunity which exists uniquely in this great land.[3]

In the same year that this autobiography was published, at the height of his success, Boesky entered into an arrangement for obtaining inside information from Dennis Levine. Levine, who was himself earning around $3 million annually in salary and bonuses, worked at Drexel Burnham Lambert, the phenomenally successful Wall Street firm that dominated the 'junk bond' market. Since junk bonds were the favoured way of raising funds for takeovers, Drexel was involved in almost every major takeover battle, and Levine was privy to information that, in the hands of someone with plenty of capital, could be used to make hundreds of millions of dollars, virtually without risk.

The ethics of this situation are not in dispute. When Boesky was buying shares on the basis of the information Levine gave him, he knew that the shares would rise in price. The shareholders who sold to him did not know that, and hence sold the shares at less than they could have obtained for them later, if they had not sold. If Drexel's client was someone who wished to take a company over, then that client would have to pay more for the company if the news of the intended takeover leaked out, since Boesky's purchases would push up the price of the shares. The added cost might mean that the bid to take over the target company would fail; or it might mean that, though the bid succeeded, after the takeover more of the company's assets would be sold off, to pay for the increased borrowings needed to buy the company at the higher price. Since Drexel, and hence Levine, had obtained the information of the intended takeover in confidence from their clients, for them to disclose it to others who could profit from it, to the disadvantage of their clients, was clearly contrary to all accepted professional ethical standards. Boesky has never suggested that he dissents from these standards, or believed that his circumstances justified an exception to them. Boesky also knew that trading in inside information was illegal. Nevertheless, in 1985 he went so far as to formalize the arrangement he had with Levine, agreeing to pay him 5 percent of the profits he made from purchasing shares about which Levine had given him information.

Why did Boesky do it? Why would anyone who has $150 million, a respected position in society, and – as is evident from the dedication to his book – values at least the appearance of an ethical life that benefits the community as a whole, risk his reputation, his wealth, and his freedom by doing something that is obviously neither legal or ethical? Granted, Boesky stood to make very large sums of money from his arrangement with Levine. The Securities and Exchange Commission was later to describe several transactions in which Boesky had used information obtained from Levine; his profits on these deals were estimated at $50 million. Given the previous track record of the Securities and Exchange Commission, Boesky could well have thought that his illegal insider trading was likely to go undetected and unprosecuted. So it was reasonable enough for Boesky to believe that the use of inside information would bring him a lot of money with little chance of exposure. Does that mean that it was a wise thing for him to do? In these circumstances, where does wisdom lie? In choosing to enrich himself further, in a manner that he could not justify ethically, Boesky was making a choice between fundamentally different ways of living. I shall call this type of choice an 'ultimate choice'. When ethics and self-interest seem to be in conflict, we face an ultimate choice. How are we to choose?

Most of the choices we make in our everyday lives are restricted choices, in that they are made from within a given framework or set of values. Given that I want to keep reasonably fit, I sensibly choose to go for a walk rather than slouch on the sofa with a can of beer, watching the football on television. Since you want to do something to help preserve rainforests, you join a coalition to raise public awareness of the continuing destruction of the forests. Another person wants a well-paid and interesting career, so she studies law. In each of these choices, the fundamental values are already assumed, and the choice is a matter of the best means of achieving what is valued. In ultimate choices, however, the fundamental values themselves come to the fore. We are no longer choosing within a framework that assumes that we want only to maximize our own interests, nor within a framework that takes it for granted that we are going to do whatever we consider to be best, ethically speaking. Instead, we are choosing between different possible ways of living: the way of living in which self-interest is paramount, or that in which ethics is paramount, or perhaps some trade-off between the two. (I take ethics and self-interest as the two rival viewpoints because they are, in my view, the two strongest contenders. Other possibilities include, for example, living by the rules of etiquette, or living in accordance with one's own aesthetic standards, treating one's life as a work of art; but these possibilities are not the subject of this book.)

Ultimate choices take courage. In making restricted choices, our fundamental values form a foundation on which we can stand when we choose. To make an ultimate choice we must put in question the foundations of our lives. In the fifties, French philosophers like Jean-Paul Sartre saw this kind of choice as an expression of our ultimate freedom. We are free to choose what we are to be, because we have no essential nature, that is, no given purpose outside ourselves. Unlike, say, an apple tree that has come into existence as a result of someone else's plan, we simply exist, and the rest is up to us. (Hence the name given to this group of thinkers: existentialists.) Sometimes this leads to a sense that we are standing before a moral void. We feel vertigo, and want to get out of that situation as quickly as possible. So we avoid the ultimate choice by carrying on as we were doing before. That seems the simplest and safest thing to do. But we do not really avoid making the ultimate choice in that way. We make it by default, and it may not be safe at all. Perhaps Ivan Boesky continued to do what would make him richer because to do anything else would have involved questioning the foundations of most of his life. He acted as if his essential nature was to make money. But of course it was not: he could have chosen living ethically ahead of money-making.

Even if we are ready to face an ultimate choice, however, it is not easy to know how to make it. In more restricted choice situations we know how to get expert advice. There are financial consultants and educational counsellors and health care advisers, all ready to tell you about what is the best for your own interests. Many people will be eager to offer you their opinions about what would be the right thing to do, too. But who is the expert here? Suppose that you have the opportunity to sell your car, which you know is about to need major repairs, to a stranger who is too innocent to have the car checked properly. He is pleased with the car's appearance, and a deal is about to be struck, when he casually asks if the car has any problems. If you say, just as casually, 'No, nothing that I know of', the stranger will buy the car, paying you at least $1,000 more than you would get from anyone who knew the truth. He will never be able to prove that you were lying. You are convinced that it would be wrong to lie to him, but another $1,000 would make your life more comfortable for the next few months. In this situation you don't see any need to ask anyone for advice about what is in your best interest; nor do you need to ask what it would be right to do. So can you still ask *what to do?*

Of course you can. Some would say that if you know that it would be wrong to lie about your car, that is the end of the matter; but this is wishful thinking. If we are honest with ourselves, we will admit that, at least sometimes, where self-interest and ethics clash, we choose self-interest, and this is not just a case of being weak-willed or irrational. We are genuinely unsure what it is rational to do, because when the clash is so fundamental, reason seems to have no way of resolving it.

We all face ultimate choices, and with equal intensity, whether our opportunities are to gain, by unethical means, $50 or $50 million. The state of the world in the late twentieth century means that even if we are never tempted at all by unethical ways of making money, we have to decide to what extent we shall live for ourselves, and to what extent for others. There are people who are hungry, malnourished, lacking shelter, or basic health care: and there are voluntary organizations that raise money to help these people. True, the problem is so big that one individual cannot make much impact on it; and no doubt some of the money will be swallowed up in administration, or will get stolen, or for some other reason will not reach the people who need it most. Despite these inevitable problems, the discrepancy between the wealth of the developed world and the poverty of the poorest people in developing countries is so great that if only a small fraction of what you give reaches the people who need it, that fraction will make a far greater difference to the people it reaches than the full amount you give could make to your own life. That you as an individual cannot make an impact on the entire problem seems scarcely relevant, since you can make an impact on the lives of particular families. So will you get involved with one of these organizations? Will you yourself give, not just spare change when a tin is rattled under your nose, but substantial amounts that will reduce your ability to live a luxurious lifestyle?

Some consumer products damage the ozone layer, contribute to the greenhouse effect, destroy rainforests, or pollute our rivers and lakes. Others are tested by being put, in concentrated form, into the eyes of conscious rabbits, held immobilized in rows of restraining devices like medieval stocks. There are alternatives to products that are environmentally damaging, or tested in such cruel ways. To find the alternatives can, however, be time-consuming, and a nuisance. Will you take the trouble to find them?

We face ethical choices constantly in our personal relationships. We have opportunities to use people and discard them, or to remain loyal to them. We can stand up for what we believe, or make ourselves popular by going along with what the group does. Though the morality of personal relationships is difficult to generalize about because every situation is different, here too we often know what the right thing to do is, but are uncertain about what to do.

There are, no doubt, some people who go through life without considering the ethics of what they are doing. Some of these people are just indifferent to others; some are downright vicious. Yet genuine indifference to ethics of any sort is rare. Mark 'Chopper' Read, one of Australia's nastiest criminals, recently published (from prison) an horrific autobiography, replete with nauseating details of beatings and forms of torture he inflicted on his enemies before killing them. Through all his relish for violence, however, the author shows evident anxiety to assure his readers that his victims were all in some way members of the criminal class who deserved what they got. He wants his readers to be clear that he has nothing but contempt for an Australian mass murderer – now one of Read's fellow-prisoners – who opened up on passersby with an automatic rifle.[4] The psychological need for ethical justification, no matter how weak that justification may be, is remarkably pervasive.

We should each ask ourselves: what place does ethics have in my daily life? In thinking about this question, ask yourself: what do I think of as a good life, in the fullest sense of that term? This is an ultimate question. To ask it is to ask: what kind of a life do I truly admire, and what kind of life do I hope to be able to look back on, when I am older and reflect on how I have lived? Will it be enough to say: 'It was fun'? Will I even be able to say truthfully that it *was* fun? Whatever your position or status, you can ask what – within the limits of what is possible for you – you want to achieve with your life.

The Ring of Gyges

Two and a half thousand years ago, at the dawn of Western philosophical thinking, Socrates had the reputation of being the wisest man in Greece. One day Glaucon, a well-to-do young Athenian, challenged him to answer a question about how we are to live. The challenge is a key element of Plato's *Republic*, one of the foundational works in the history of Western philosophy. It is also a classic formulation of an ultimate choice.

According to Plato, Glaucon begins by retelling the story of a shepherd who served the reigning king of Lydia. The shepherd was out with his flock one day when there was a storm and a chasm opened up in the ground. He went down into the chasm and there found a golden ring, which he put on his finger. A few days later, when sitting with some other shepherds, he happened to fiddle with the ring, and to his amazement discovered that when he turned the ring a certain way, he became invisible to his companions. Once he had made this discovery, he arranged to be one of the messengers sent by the shepherds to the king to report on the state of the flocks. Arriving at the palace, he promptly used the ring to seduce the queen, plotted with her against the king, killed him, and so obtained the crown.

Glaucon takes this story as encapsulating a common view of ethics and human nature. The implication of the story is that anyone who had such a ring would abandon all ethical standards – and what is more, would be quite rational to do so:

> . . . no one, it is thought, would be of such adamantine nature as to abide in justice and have the strength to abstain from theft, and to keep his hands from the goods of others, when it would be in his power to steal anything he wished from the very marketplace with impunity, to enter men's houses and have

intercourse with whom he would, to kill or to set free whomsoever he pleased; in short, to walk among men as a god . . . if any man who possessed this power we have described should nevertheless refuse to do anything unjust or to rob his fellows, all who knew of his conduct would think him the most miserable and foolish of men, though they would praise him to each other's faces, their fear of suffering injustice extorting that deceit from them.[5]

Glaucon then challenges Socrates to show that this common opinion of ethics is mistaken. Convince us, he and the other participants in the discussion say to Socrates, that there are sound reasons for doing what is right – not just reasons like the fear of getting caught, but reasons that would apply even if we knew we would not be found out. Show us that a wise person who found the ring would, unlike the shepherd, continue to do what is right.

That, at any rate, is how Plato described the scene. According to Plato, Socrates convinced Glaucon and the other Athenians present that, whatever profit injustice may seem to bring, only those who act rightly are really happy. Unfortunately, few modern readers are persuaded by the long and complicated account that Socrates gives of the links between acting rightly, having a proper harmony between the elements of one's nature, and being happy. It all seems too theoretical, too contrived, and the dialogue becomes one-sided. There are obvious objections that we would like to see put to Socrates, but after the initial presentation of the challenge, Glaucon's critical faculties seem to have deserted him, and he meekly accepts every argument Socrates puts to him.

Ivan Boesky had, in the information he received from Dennis Levine, a kind of magic ring; something that could make him as close to a king as one can get in the republican, wealth-oriented United States. As it turned out, the ring had a flaw: Boesky was not invisible when he wanted to be. But was that Boesky's only mistake, the only reason why he should not have obtained and used Levine's information? The challenge that Boesky's opportunity poses to us is a modern-day version of the challenge that Glaucon put to Socrates. Can we give a better answer?

One 'answer' that is really no answer at all is to ignore the challenge. Many people do. They live and die unreflectively, without ever having asked themselves what their goals are, and why they are doing what they do. If you are totally satisfied with the life you are now living, and quite sure that it is the life you want to lead, there is no need to read further. What is to come may only unsettle you. Until you have put to yourselves the questions that Socrates faced, however, you have not *chosen* how you live.

'What in the hell are we doing this for?'

Today the question of how we are to live confronts us more sharply than ever. We have emerged from the eighties – the decade that has become known as 'The Decade of Greed' – but not yet determined the nature of the nineties. Boesky himself helped to define the eighties by giving a commencement address at the School of Business Administration at the University of California, Berkeley, in which he told his audience: 'Greed is all right ... greed is healthy. You can be greedy and still feel good about yourself'.[6] Twenty years after the Free Speech Movement had made the campus the centre of radical thought in America, Berkeley business students applauded this praise of greed. They were looking forward to earning money, lots of it, and soon. What was happening was, as Michael Lewis put it in his popular *Liar's Poker*, 'a rare and amazing glitch in the fairly predictable history of getting and spending'. Smart bond traders like Lewis were earning a million dollars a year in salary and bonuses before they turned twenty-five. 'Never before', Lewis could truthfully assert, 'have so many unskilled 25-year-olds made so much in so little time as we did this decade in New York and London'.[7] Yet even that was peanuts compared to the sums made by the older heavyweights: corporate raiders like Carl Icahn, T. Boone Pickens, or Henry Kravis, developers such as Donald Trump, the junk bond financier Michael Milken, or Wall Street chiefs like Salomon Brothers' John Gutfreund.

In the hothouse, money-directed United States of the eighties, these people were heroes, written up in magazines, talked about endlessly. Yet at the end, many were wondering what it was all for. Donald Trump confessed:

It's a rare person who can achieve a major goal in life and not almost immediately start feeling sad, empty, and a little lost. If you look at the record – which in this case means newspapers, magazines, and TV news – you'll see that an awful lot of people who achieve success, from Elvis Presley to Ivan Boesky, lose their direction or their ethics.

Actually, I don't have to look at anyone else's life to know that's true. I'm as susceptible to that pitfall as anyone else . . . [8]

During the eighties Peter Lynch worked fourteen-hour days and built the Fidelity Magellan mutual fund into a $13 billion giant among funds. But at the age of forty-six, when most executives are still aiming higher, Lynch startled his colleagues by quitting. Why? Because he had asked himself: 'What in the hell are we doing this for?' And in answering that question, he was moved by the thought that 'I don't know anyone who wished on his deathbed that he had spent more time at the office'.[9]

Symptomatic of the changing view was Oliver Stone's movie *Wall Street*, starring Michael Douglas as a convincingly unpleasant Gordon Gekko, a financial wheeler-dealer whose manner of operation resembles that of Boesky, with some elements of a corporate raider like Carl Icahn thrown in for good measure. Bud Fox, the ambitious young stockbroker played by Charlie Sheen, is for a time taken in by the prospect of making it big, but when Gekko attempts his usual takeover and asset-stripping procedure on the airline for which Fox's father works as a mechanic, an angry Fox asks:

Tell me, Gordon, when does it all end, huh? How many yachts can you water-ski behind? How much is enough?[10]

That question suggested something that the philosophers had always known, and the rich of the eighties were re-discovering: affluence has no limits. More people were beginning to wonder 'what in the hell are we doing this for?' Like Lynch, they were making decisions about the rest of their lives, instead of just continuing in the course that seemed to have been set for them by economic and social expectations. They were beginning to live their lives with a purpose.

The recession that followed the boom has helped make people think again about the world they would like to see emerge when the economy picks up again. Though some may want to reinflate the balloons and resume the party, for many people that idea just reminds them of the still-lingering hangover. In any case, in the nineties, the intimidating shadow of Japan would dampen any celebrations in which those from other nations might be tempted to indulge. George Bush's 1992 visit to Tokyo was an extraordinary event. Here was the president of what still is, in military terms, indisputably the mightiest power on earth, begging the Prime Minister of Japan for trade concessions so that United States manufacturers could survive in the face of Japanese standards of excellence that had made Honda the number one selling car in the United States. Bush's visit made Westerners wonder, once more, what it was that made Japanese society so cohesive, harmonious, orderly, and successful. A spate of books about Japan sought to analyze the nature of the Japanese difference. Do the Japanese know more about how to live well together than we do? Japan's success is another reason for the West's self-doubt.

The end of history or the beginning of secular ethics?

The failure of the ideals of the West in the eighties is the short-term, immediate reason why the question: 'How are we to live?' confronts us with more force than usual at this particular moment. There is also, however, a more momentous, longer term picture that invests the question with peculiar sharpness, perhaps even with world-historical significance. Communism, according to Marx, should have been 'the genuine resolution of the antagonism between man and nature and between man and man; the true resolution of the conflict between . . . individual and species'.[11] In other words, Marx would have answered Glaucon's question by saying that it could have no satisfactory answer unless we change the nature of society. As long as we are living in a society in which economic production is geared to satisfy the interests of a particular class, there is bound to be a conflict between individual self-interest and the interests of society as a whole. In that situation, the shepherd would be acting quite rationally if he used the magic ring to take what he pleased and kill whom he wished to kill. Once the means of production are organized in the common interests of all, however, Marx would say that human nature, which is not fixed but socially conditioned, would change with it. Greed and envy are not engrained forever in the character of human beings. Citizens of the new society, based on common ownership, would find their own happiness in working for the good of all.

For many critics of Marx it was clear from the start that this was a dream; but with the collapse of communist societies in Eastern Europe and the former Soviet Union, the utopian nature of Marxist thought has become apparent to all. For the first time, we are living in a world that has only one dominant social model for developed societies. The hope of resolving the conflict between individual self-interest and the good of all by building an alternative to the free market economy is now a self-confessed failure. Only a brave few cling to the socialist ideal, rejecting the distortions Lenin and Stalin wrought, and claiming that it has never had a proper trial. It seems that the individualist view of self-interest is the only one that is still viable.

So strongly does the liberal democratic free enterprise model impose itself on our vision of the possibilities that Francis Fukuyama, a former deputy director of policy planning at the US State Department, has been given a respectful, and from some quarters even enthusiastic, hearing for a bold, surprisingly well-defended, but in the end scarcely plausible idea. Fukuyama has revived Hegel's conception of history as a process with a direction and an End. History has an End, according to Hegel and Fukuyama, not so much in the sense of coming to a full stop, but rather in the sense of a final goal or destination. In *The End of History and the Last Man*, Fukuyama argues that this end is, precisely, the universal acceptance of the liberal, democratic, free enterprise form of society.[12] Yet just when this model has taken so strong a hold on the minds of those who consider themselves politically realistic, we are gradually becoming aware that we are nearing the end of an epoch. Like Daniel Bell, who predicted 'the End of Ideology' shortly before the rise of the

New Left and the resurgence of radical ideologies in the sixties,[13] Fukuyama may have predicted the permanence of the liberal free enterprise system just when it is about to face its gravest crisis.

There are two intriguing and very different counterweights to Fukuyama's vision of 'the End of History'. One is summed up in the title of a book by Bill McKibben: our era is witness to, McKibben says, not the End of History, but rather *The End of Nature*. Living in the Adirondack Mountains of New York State, McKibben is sharply aware of the fact that for the first time in the history of our species, there is no longer a natural world, unaffected by human beings.[14] Not in the Adirondacks, nor in the rainforests of the Amazon, not even on the Antarctic ice-cap, can one get away from the effects of human civilization. We have depleted the ozone layer that shields our planet from solar radiation. We have added to the amount of carbon dioxide in the atmosphere. Thus the growth of plants, the chemical composition of the rain, and the very forces that form the clouds, are, in part, our doing.

Throughout human history, we have been able freely to use the oceans and the atmosphere as a vast sink for our wastes. The liberal democratic free enterprise society that Fukuyama proposes as the ultimate outcome of all history is built on the idea that we can keep doing this forever. In contrast, responsible scientific opinion now tells us that we are passengers on a runaway train that is heading rapidly towards an abyss. We *cannot* continue with business as usual. We shall either change voluntarily, or the climate of our planet will change, and take entire nations with it. Nor are the changes minor ones. They involve the basic values and ethical outlook that underlie the free enterprise societies of the late twentieth century. Perhaps the liberal democratic free enterprise society will survive this challenge, and adapt to cope with it; but if it does, it will be a significantly different form of liberal democratic free enterprise society, and the people living in it will need to have very different values and ways of living. So the pressure to re-examine the ethical basis of our lives is upon us in a way that it has never been before.

The other intriguing line of thought to place against the idea that history has reached its end was put forward several years ago by

Derek Parfit, an Oxford philosopher unknown outside academic circles but esteemed by his colleagues for seeing further into some of the most difficult problems of ethical theory than anyone else had done before. At the conclusion of his major work, *Reasons and Persons*, after 450 pages of detailed, intricate argument, Parfit permits himself a glance at the broader question of whether there can be progress in ethics. Against the claim that everything there is to say in ethics has already been said, he argues that until quite recently the study of ethics has very largely been carried out within a religious framework. The number of non-religious people who have made ethics their life work is remarkably small. (Parfit mentions among these few Buddha, Confucius, the eighteenth century Scottish philosopher David Hume, and the late Victorian utilitarian philosopher, Henry Sidgwick.) For much of the twentieth century, when for the first time many professional moral philosophers were atheists, it was unfashionable for philosophers to grapple with questions about what we ought to do. Instead, they studied the meanings of the moral terms and argued over whether ethics is subjective or objective. Thus it is only since about 1960 that many people have systematically studied non-religious ethics; as a result, it is, Parfit says, 'the youngest and the least advanced' of the sciences. So Parfit ends his book on a hopeful note:

> The Earth will remain inhabitable for at least another billion years. Civilization began only a few thousand years ago. If we do not destroy mankind, these few thousand years may be only a tiny fraction of the whole of civilized human history. . . Belief in God, or in many gods, prevented the free development of moral reasoning. Disbelief in god, openly admitted by a majority, is a very recent event, not yet completed. Because this event is so recent, Non-religious Ethics is at a very early stage. We cannot yet predict whether, as in Mathematics, we will all reach agreement. Since we cannot know how Ethics will develop, it is not irrational to have high hopes.[15]

If Parfit is right, and the development of non-religious ethical thinking is still in its infancy, it is clearly premature to say that history has reached its final destination. We are only now breaking with a past in which religion and ethics have been closely identified. It is too early to tell what changes may lie ahead, once we have a better understanding of the nature of ethics, but they are likely to be profound.

Because people who are not religious have tended to extend their scepticism about religion to ethics as well, they have yielded the field of ethics to the religious right. This has allowed the right to pre-empt 'morality' for crusades against abortion and homosexuality. Yet those who regard the interests of women as overriding the merely potential interests of the fetus are taking their stand on a morally impregnable position;[16] and the moral case for acceptance of sexual relationships between consenting adults that do not harm others is even more clear-cut. It is time to reclaim the moral high ground from the pretenders who occupied it when it was left vacant by progressives who instead placed their faith in Marxist dreams of a transformed society in which all dilemmas would be resolved. The crucial moral questions of our day are not about homosexuality or abortion. Instead moralists should be asking: what are the obligations of all of us in the affluent world when people are slowly starving in Somalia? What is to be done about the racist hatred that prevents people living together in Bosnia, in Azerbaijan, and in Los Angeles? Are we entitled to continue to confine billions of non-human animals in factory farms, treating them as mere things to serve the pleasures of our palate? And how can we change our behaviour so as to preserve the ecological system on which the entire planet depends?

The more enlightened Christian readers have themselves now recognized that their Church's preoccupation with sex has been a mistake: Dr George Carey, Archbishop of Canterbury, has admitted that the church has been guilty of 'being caught up with the idea that sexual sins were "more significant" than other sins' and has said that instead we should think more in terms of global problems such as world poverty. In saying this, the Archbishop was belatedly preaching what philosophers doing applied ethics have been saying since the seventies.[17] Once it is generally understood that ethics has no necessary connection with the sexually-obsessed morality of conservative Christianity, a humane and positive ethic could be the basis for a renewal of our social, political and ecological life.

The dominant political and economic model today allows, indeed encourages, citizens to make the pursuit of their own interests (understood largely in terms of material wealth) the chief goal of their lives. We rarely reflect, either collectively or as individuals, on whether this dominant conception is a wise one. Does it truly offer the best lives for us all? Should each one of us, in deciding how to live, assume that wealth is the thing to aim at? What is the place of ethics in such decisions? We must not make the error of assuming that the failure of past utopian ideals means that values should not play a central role in our lives. I share Parfit's view that in the advancement of ethics lies the possibility of a new and more hopeful turn in world history; but it must be an advancement not only in ethical theory, but also in ethical practice.

We need a new force for change. Changing the way in which we see the role of ethics in our lives may seem like something that changes individual lives, but leaves the larger society and the world of politics untouched. That appearance misleads. The early years of the nineties have made it clear that the promotion of greed by proponents of the free market has failed even to achieve the narrow economic goal of creating a thriving economy. In broader social and environmental terms, too, this policy has been a disaster. It is time to try the only alternative left to us. If enough individuals disavow a narrowly materialist idea of self-interest, it may be possible to rebuild trust and to work together for larger, more important goals. Politicians would then learn that they can dare to espouse policies that do more than promise greater material prosperity to every voter. (In New Zealand, after a decade in which the major parties have agreed on lowering income tax rates and cutting government spending, the newly formed Alliance Party has promised that, if elected, it will *raise* taxes – on the grounds that a good state system of health care, social security and education is worth paying for. Opinion polls suggest that the Alliance is doing well enough to pose a threat to the major parties.)

A better life is open to us – in every sense of the term, *except* the sense made dominant by a consumer society that promotes acquisition as the standard of what is good. Once we get rid of that dominant conception of the good life, we can again bring to the centre of the stage questions about the preservation of the planet's ecology, and about global justice. Only then can we hope to see a renewal of the will to deal with the root causes of poverty, crime, and the short-term destruction of our planet's resources. A politics based on ethics could be radical, in the original sense of the term: that is, it could change things from the roots.

Ethics and self-interest

More personal doubts about ethics remain. To live ethically, we assume, will be hard work, uncomfortable, self-sacrificing and generally unrewarding. We see ethics as at odds with self-interest: we assume that those who make fortunes from insider trading ignore ethics, but are successfully following self-interest (as long as they don't get caught). We do the same ourselves when we take a job that pays more than another, even though it means that we are helping to manufacture or promote a product that does no good at all, or actually makes people sick. On the other hand, those who pass up opportunities to rise in their career because of ethical 'scruples' about the nature of the work, or who give away their wealth to good causes, are thought to be sacrificing their own interests in order to obey the dictates of ethics. Worse still, we may regard them as suckers, missing out on all the fun they could be having, while others take advantage of their futile generosity.

This current orthodoxy about self-interest and ethics paints a picture of ethics as something external to us, even as hostile to our own interests. We picture ourselves as constantly torn between the drive to advance our self-interest, and the fear of being caught doing something that others will condemn, and for which we will be punished. This picture has been entrenched in many of the most influential ways of thinking in our culture. It is to be found in traditional religious ideas that promise reward or threaten punishment for good and bad behaviour, but put this reward or punishment in another realm and so make it external to life in this world. It is to be found, too, in the idea that human beings are situated at the mid-point between heaven and earth, sharing in the spiritual realm of the angels, but trapped also by our brutish bodily nature in this world of the beasts. The German philosopher Immanuel Kant picked up the same idea when he portrayed us as moral beings only in so far as we subordinate our natural physical desires to the commands of universal reason that we perceive through our capacity for reason. It is easy to see a link between this idea and Freud's vision of our lives as rent by the conflict between id and super-ego.

The same assumption of conflict between ethics and self-interest lies at the root of much modern economics. It is propagated in popular presentations of sociobiology applied to human nature. Books like Robert J. Ringer's *Looking Out for # 1*, which was on the *New York Times* bestseller list for an entire year and is still selling steadily, tell millions of readers that to put the happiness of anyone else ahead of your own is 'to pervert the laws of Nature'.[18] Television, both in its programs and its commercials, conveys materialist images of success that lack ethical content. As Todd Gitlin wrote in his study of American television, *Inside Prime Time:*

> . . . prime time gives us people preoccupied with personal ambition. If not utterly consumed by ambition and the fear of ending up as losers, these characters take both the ambition and the fear for granted. If not surrounded by middle-class arrays of consumer goods, they themselves are glamorous incarnations of desire. The happiness they long for is private, not public; they make few demands on society as a whole, and even when troubled they seem content with the existing institutional order. Personal ambition and consumerism are the driving forces in their lives. The sumptuous and brightly lit settings of most series amount to advertisements for a consumption-centred version of the good life, and this doesn't even take into consideration the incessant commercials, which convey the idea that human aspirations for liberty, pleasure, accomplishment, and status can be fulfilled in the realm of consumption.[19]

The message is coming over strongly, but something is wrong. Today the assertion that life is meaningless no longer comes from existentialist philosophers who treat it as a shocking discovery; it comes from bored adolescents, for whom it is a truism. Perhaps it is the central place of self-interest, and the way in which we conceive of our own interest, that is to blame here. The pursuit of self-interest, as standardly conceived, is a life without any meaning beyond our own pleasure or individual satisfaction. Such a life is often a self-defeating enterprise. The ancients knew of the 'paradox of hedonism', according to which the more explicitly we pursue our desire for pleasure, the more elusive we will find its satisfaction. There is no reason to believe that human nature has changed so dramatically as to render this ancient wisdom inapplicable.

The questions are ancient but the modern inquirer is not limited to the ancient answers. Though the study of ethics may not progress in the dramatic fashion of physics or genetics, much has been learned in the past century. Progress not only in philosophy, but also in the sciences, has contributed to our understanding of ethics. Evolutionary theory helps us to answer ancient questions about the limits of altruism. 'Rational choice theory' – that is, the theory of what it is to choose rationally in complex situations involving uncertainties – has highlighted a problem not discussed by ancient thinkers, called 'the Prisoner's Dilemma'. The modern discussion of this problem suggests that when each of two or more people, acting quite rationally, deliberately, and with the best possible information, independently pursue their own interests, they may both end up worse off than they would have been if they had acted in a less rationally self-interested manner. Exploring this problem reveals ways in which human nature may have evolved to be capable of more than narrow self-interest. Modern feminist thought, too, has forced us to reflect on whether previous thinking about ethics has been limited because it has been dominated by a male perspective on the world. The same may be true of our conception of self-interest. The prisoner's dilemma, the paradox of hedonism, and feminist influences in ethical thinking are some of the threads to be drawn together later in this book, in order to develop a new and broader conception of self-interest.

Here, ethics returns to complete our picture. An ethical life is one in which we identify ourselves with other, and larger, goals, thereby giving meaning to our lives. The view that the ethical life and the life of enlightened self-interest are one and the same is an ancient one, now often scorned by those too cynical to believe in any such harmony. Cynicism about ethical idealism is an understandable reaction to much modern history – to, for example, the tragic way in which the idealistic goals of Marx and his followers were twisted by the Russian communist leaders until they led, first, to the Stalinist terror, and then to the utterly corrupt dictatorship of the Brezhnev era. With such examples before us, it is no wonder that cynicism is more fashionable than hope for a better world. But we may be able to learn from history. The ancient view was that an ethically good life is also a good life for the person leading it. Never has it been so urgent that the reasons for accepting this older view should be widely understood. To do so we must question the view of self-interest that has dominated Western society for a long time. Then, if there is a viable alternative to this view, the ultimate choice may have a rational solution after all.

CHAPTER 2

'*What's in it for me?*'

The standard Western view of self-interest has led us to not one, but two distinct contemporary crises. The first, which I shall outline in this chapter, is a crisis of Western society as a whole, epitomized by recent developments in the United States. The second is a crisis that threatens the biosphere of our planet, on which all life depends. That is the topic of the next chapter. Taken together, these two crises give rise to a compelling and potentially tragic irony about our present conception of self-interest: if we continue to conceive of our own interests in materialist terms, then the collective impact each of us has in pursuing our individual self-interest will ensure the failure of all our attempts to advance those interests.

A failing social experiment

America stands as a beacon, showing where a society based on individual self-interest is heading. There was a time, in the development of this society, that gave such scope to the individual, when the Statue of Liberty aptly summed up what the society meant to the rest of the world; but in the early nineties, the symbol of America became the smoke rising from the fires of the Los Angeles riots.

Crime in America is the most vivid indication of the direction that a society of self-seeking individuals can take. A survey of New York City residents carried out in 1990 asked: 'How frequently do you worry about crime?' Only 13 percent could answer 'rarely or never'; fully 60 percent said that they worried about crime all the time, or often. No wonder: in that year they opened their papers to read of such crimes as the stabbing to death of 22-year-old Brian Watkins, on a subway platform in midtown Manhattan. Watkins was on his way to dinner, part of a family group that included three men, when attacked by a gang of eight youths. According to *Time*, the gang was seeking money to finance 'an evening of frolicking at Roseland, a nearby dance hall'.[1] But such selfish, callous killings occur regularly in New York. Guns are now the leading cause of death among teenagers in the United States. In March 1992, the *New York Times* reported that in the first half of the school year there had been fifty-six shootings in and around the city's schools: sixteen pupils, two parents and one policeman had been shot, six of the children fatally. Twenty-one New York high schools were using metal-detectors to check students for weapons as they came to school.[2]

New York is not a special case. Its homicide rate is below that of eight other American cities. In virtually every major American city the possibility of crime has poisoned everyday life. In 1973, after growing up in Australia and spending four years in Oxford, I arrived in New York to begin a visiting position in the Department of Philosophy at New York University. As I walked in the front door of the university's main building on Washington Square, I was greeted by a shocking sight: university security guards with guns swinging on their hips. By the end of the year, I was taking for granted the presence of lethal weapons in a university setting. I learned to walk around, not through, Washington Square Park as I returned to my Bleecker Street apartment after teaching a late class. If I was uptown after dark, I knew that it was better to return by the West 4th Street subway stop and walk through the busy streets of Greenwich Village than to use the Lexington Avenue line, which would let me off closer to home, but in territory too far east in the Village to be safe. Such maps of 'no-go' areas are now part of the education of every American city dweller. Something as natural as an evening stroll in the local park has become, depending on the neighbourhood, either risky or downright mad. On lower-floor windows, one looks out through bars; the prison is on the outside. Those who can afford it live in apartment buildings with 24-hour security staff controlling who goes in and out. Children are brought up to carry 'mugging money' with them, because muggers are more likely to turn nasty if they get nothing. *Time* reports: 'Nursery-school teachers in some of the city's tougher neighbourhoods train children barely old enough to talk to hit the floor at the sound of gunshots'.[3]

Los Angeles has its own characteristic form of anonymous killing: freeway shootings. Beginning in 1987, individuals or gangs parked on freeway bridges and shot at cars passing below. Others would take pot shots at cars as they passed on the road. The message went out from Los Angeles police: don't look into the eyes of the driver of the car alongside you.[4]

Less threatening crime is almost ignored, but it too carries a message. Every day 155,000 subway riders jump the turnstiles. In a year, this fare evasion costs the city at least $65 million that could have been used to improve public transport.[5] It also sets a very public example of scorn for the idea that those who benefit from a public utility should play their part in supporting it. But why not ride for free, if you can get away with it? Isn't everyone else doing it? So wouldn't you be stupid to behave differently? One American interviewed for *Habits of the Heart*, an influential study of American values in the mid-eighties put it this way:

> Everybody wants to be on top and get their own way. It's like in a relationship . . . I mean, I don't want to be the only one who suffers. I don't want to be the only sucker. I don't want to be the fall guy for people who are not doing their part.[6]

In the United States today the social fabric of society has decayed to the point at which there are grounds for fearing that it has passed the point of no return. The problem is that people who begin with the attitude of not wanting to be the only sucker are likely to treat each new encounter with suspicion, and the more who hold this attitude, the more difficult it is to make co-operative efforts work for the common good (as we shall see in more detail in Chapter 6). There are no precedents for halting the decay of a society as populous, as egoistic, and as heavily armed with lethal weapons as the United States is today; so no-one working for change can be confident of reversing the current drift towards social anarchy. At the same time, the alternative is so appalling to contemplate that it would be crazy not to try, as long as there is a chance of success.

The situation is not helped when the society's leaders themselves are busy making sure that they are not going to be suckers working for the common good while others line their own pockets. In 1991 dozens of members of the United States Congress, including the Speaker, the House Democratic Party leader and the House Republican Party whip were shown to have been overdrawing their bank accounts at the House Bank. The overdrawals were often for substantial sums, and incurred no interest or penalty. The cost of this interest-free money was being borne by the taxpayer. A poll showed that 83 percent of American adults believed that legislators who overdrew their bank accounts did so not by mistake but 'because they knew they could get away with it'.[7]

These revelations about the United States Congress caused a stir, but they were modest stuff compared to the attitudes and practices of state legislators revealed in an investigation in Arizona. Transcripts of police undercover videotapes show the legislators being extraordinarily candid about their attitudes to life and ethics. Senator Carolyn Walker explained: 'I like the good life, and I'm trying to position myself so that I can live the good life and have more money'. As she reached across to accept a bribe of $25,000, she added, 'We all have our prices'. State Representative Bobby Raymond was blunter still: 'There is not an issue in this world that I give a (expletive) about. My favorite line is, "What's in it for me?"'[8]

Others who seem to care only about what they can get for themselves include the chief executive officers of many of America's largest corporations, who paid themselves enormous increases while their corporations were losing money and firing employees. In 1990, for example, the stock price of ITT corporation fell 18 percent; yet in that year Rand Araskog, ITT's chairman, president and chief executive officer received a pay rise of 103 percent, taking his annual earnings to $11 million. Joseph Nocera, a writer for *GQ*, went to ITT's annual meeting in order to hear Araskog respond to questions about his pay. According to Nocera, Araskog 'seemed to be saying that so long as he was in the position to be able to grab this kind of money, he was going to grab it, and he didn't much care what anyone else thought about it'.[9] That attitude must be common in the corporate ethos. Although IBM shareholders gained less than 1 percent compounded annual return over the six years to 1990, the salary of IBM's head, John Akers, went up 400 percent in the same period, growing to $8 million in 1990. Even these earnings are dwarfed by those of Steven Ross and N. J. Nicholas, co-chief executives of Time-Warner, Inc., who took home a combined total of $99.6 million in 1990, a year in which Time-Warner reported a loss. United States chief executives are paid at least eighty-five times as much as the average American worker – up from a 1975 average ratio of 35:1, which itself was higher than comparable ratios for Japanese (16:1) or German (21:1) chiefs. Some recent estimates suggest that the ratio in the United States is still leaning further in favour of the chief executive, and has risen as high as 160 times the pay of a worker.[10]

Trade union leaders may be the natural opponents of corporate chiefs, but they are clearly capable of learning from the enemy. Gus Bevona, head of the New York building service union, earned $412,000 in 1989, while most of his union members were earning less than $25,000.[11] In February 1992, while municipal employees were being laid off by New York City, the municipal workers union chose to hold its budget meeting in the Bahamas, booking more than 100 rooms and luxury suites at a resort hotel, and picking up all the expenses for union officials attending the meeting.[12]

Even the universities were getting greedy. In 1991 a probe by a congressional sub-committee headed by John Dingell showed that Stanford, Harvard, MIT, Rutgers and many other universities had charged to federal research funds – and thus to taxpayers – millions of dollars worth of goods that had nothing to do with research. Dingell asked: 'I challenge you to tell me how fruitwood commodes, chauffeurs for the university president's wife, housing for dead university officials, retreats in Lake Tahoe and flowers for the president's house are supportive of science'. No-one answered Dingell's challenge. Further investigation showed that Harvard Medical School charged the Federal Government, as 'research costs', $1,800 for a reception for a retiring dean. The University of Texas Medical Center in Dallas spent $2,095 of public funds for ten engraved decanters; Washington University in St Louis charged for a sculpture that had already been paid for by private donations; and the University of Pittsburgh received the cost of trips to Ireland and Florida by the wife of the President of the University.[13]

The Reagan–Bush era ended with a final demonstration that cynicism about ethics and justice extended right to the top. Less than a month from the end of his term of office, President Bush granted pardons to six officials of the Reagan administration for their role in the Iran-Contra affair. Those pardoned included Caspar Weinberger, a former defence secretary. The pardons saved Bush himself from being called as a witness in any of the trials; they also demonstrated that the president put his own interests above justice being done, and being seen to be done.[14]

Greed at the top is one side of a society that appears to be losing any sense of a common good. The other side is easy to see in any American city. Early one morning in Washington, DC, I came across a group of people lying on pieces of cardboard on top of a grating, trying to warm themselves from the air that was rising out of the subway. Looking through the trees, I could discern the familiar shape of the White House. The homeless and the President of the United States of America were neighbours. It wasn't a political protest. It was just somewhere to sleep. Homelessness has become part of American life, and is increasing also in countries like Britain that have far better social support services. After photographing homeless people for the book *A Day in the Life of America*, Italian photographer Letizia Battaglia said: 'I have never experienced such a sense of sadness. Above were the Manhattan skyscrapers and down below the desperation. I have never seen such misery, even in Palermo'.[15]

Beggars, too, were once something that Americans could talk about on their return from trips to India. Now it is hard to walk down a New York street without being accosted, either in a friendly manner or with a touch of aggression, by a street beggar. The dramatic increase in the number of homeless people and beggars has many causes: rising rents, unemployment, drug and alcohol abuse, the decline of family support networks, and the Reagan administration's hard-hearted changes to welfare laws and cuts in funding for housing. If we are interested in the nature of a social system, however, it is the acceptance of the homeless that tells us more than its causes. When the numbers of people living on the streets began to rise dramatically during the Reagan years the first reaction was one of shock, and the demand that something be done. But the shock soon ebbed. As *Time* put it, 'After years of running hurdles over bodies in train stations, of being hustled by panhandlers on the street, many urban dwellers moved past pity to contempt, and are no longer scalded by the suffering they see'.[16]

The visible presence of the homeless is now just another facet of American life. Though there have been many local initiatives to do something about it, there has been no major national effort to tackle the problem. By the end of the Reagan years the federal government was spending $8 billion a year on housing, as compared with $32 billion at the end of the Carter administration, when homelessness was far less widespread. During these same years, however, income tax rates were falling. By then, even the very richest members of society – those earning a taxable income of more than $200,000 a year – were paying federal income tax at a rate of only 24 percent. Had they been taxed at 1979 rates, an extra $82 billion would have been raised – far more than was saved by cutting the housing budget. A society that prefers to cut tax rates on the very rich rather than to help the poor and homeless has ceased to be a community in any real sense of the term.

The loss of community

A major factor in the narrowing of the individual outlook is the reduced sense of community that results from the fact that so many Americans come from somewhere else and will probably move on to somewhere else again in a few years. In the name of economic efficiency, corporations move their managerial staff around as it suits them, and to refuse an invitation to move is to risk being considered not to be serious about one's career. The authors of *Habits of the Heart* noted that the people they interviewed often seemed to forget about what they had received from their parents, and were equally uneasy about being connected to their adult children. They point out that while for the Japanese 'leaving home' is a term that is used only for the rare event of going into a monastic life and abandoning all ties of ordinary existence, for Americans leaving home is expected and childhood is seen as a preparation for it. This seems to be a long-standing tendency in American society, for it was noted already by Tocqueville, who wrote that the American cultural heritage makes 'men forget their ancestors... clouds their view of their descendants and isolates them from their contemporaries'.[17]

Frances Fitzgerald interviewed residents of Sun City, a Florida retirement community, and found that they saw dependence on children as a weakness. Living together with one's children was, as one Sun City resident said, not for them: 'Other people – Negroes and Cubans – all live together, but we've reached the point where we don't have to do it'. Another, comparing the benefits of living near his children in a northern state to life in Florida, said, 'Do you want to sacrifice five months of good weather for three days – Thanksgiving, Christmas, and Easter?', thus giving eloquent testimony to the dwindling significance of family bonds in American society, in or out of retirement villages.[18]

In a remarkable work that compares many different societies around the world, Raoul Naroll, a pioneer of cross-cultural anthropology who taught at the State University of New York, Buffalo, has emphasized the importance of what he calls 'moralnets' – that is, family and community connections that tie people together and provide an ethical background to what each individual does. Moralnets support individuals in their ethical choices, making it easier for them to choose what the moralnet regards as the right thing to do. According to Naroll, strong moralnets are built by deep social ties, emotional warmth between members of the community, social and economic support or 'insurance' for those who fall on hard times, and various common emblems, ceremonies, traditions, myths and ideologies that bind the society together. An association of isolated individuals bound together only by acquisitive self-interest is not likely to have a strong moralnet. Of course, strong moralnets are compatible with all sorts of appallingly unethical conduct, especially against those outside the net. So a strong moralnet is not enough to guarantee a good society. At the same time, when moralnets are weak, Naroll argues, there is more crime, drug and alcohol abuse, suicide, domestic violence and mental illness.[19] It is a frightening thought that we may be witnessing, in the United States today, the first large-scale society in which the moralnets have become too weak to support ethical ways of living.

In 1887 Ferdinand Tonnies, a German sociologist, published a work called *Gemeinschaft und Gesellschaft*, in which he distinguished between two conceptions of society. A *Gemeinschaft* – a term usually rendered in English as 'community' – is a traditional group bound by a strong communal sense. It is an organic community, in the sense that the members identify with the larger whole, and can scarcely conceive of themselves as having a meaningful life apart from it. A *Gesellschaft*, on the other hand, is an association of individuals. They see themselves as independent beings who could live easily enough outside the association. Society is therefore regarded as a human creation, perhaps the result of some kind of social contract, and individuals may opt to join or leave as they see fit.

Tonnies's distinction between community and association derives in part from the work of one of the greatest of the German philosophers, Georg Wilhelm Friedrich Hegel. Hegel believed that in ancient Greece individuals did not see themselves as having interests separate from those of their community. They could conceive of their own good only as part of the good of membership in a successful community. This communal conception of self-interest existed, according to Hegel, because the Greeks had not yet become aware of the possibilities of individual freedom and individual self-consciousness. Socrates was, in Hegel's view, the pivotal figure in making Athenians think critically about what they had taken for granted. Hence he was rightly regarded by the conservatives as a dangerous subversive: once the Socratic questions had been raised, they could not be answered within the accepted framework of ancient Greek society.

Socrates represents the spirit of self-conscious thought that is necessarily destructive of a society based on custom. From this point, the course of Western history led away from customary society and toward more reflective awareness of oneself as an individual. Yet in Hegel's philosophy this movement, which came to full fruition after the Protestant reformation and the rise of the market economy, also brought with it the problem with which this book is concerned: without the bonds of custom and community, what reason does the individual have for acting ethically?

The first and in some ways still the most striking answer to this question was given by Thomas Hobbes. Hobbes published his greatest work, *Leviathan*, in 1651, in the aftermath of the English Civil War and the overthrow of the Stuart monarchs who had claimed to rule by Divine Right. Reflecting the breakdown of traditional authority, Hobbes began from the assumption that all mankind has one basic desire: 'a perpetual and restless desire of power after power, that ceaseth only in death'.[20] For this reason, in the natural condition of mankind all human beings would live in a state of war: 'where every man is Enemy to every man . . . And the life of man, solitary, poor, nasty, brutish, and short'.[21] This posed an immediate problem: from such uncompromisingly self-directed beings, living in such an appalling situation, how can a society ever arise, or once it arises, survive? Hobbes's answer was as blunt as his view of human nature: society arises only by the application of superior force. Society exists because it is in the interests of us all to have peace, and peace can prevail only if we set up a sovereign with unlimited authority and sufficient power to punish those who breach the peace.

Perhaps no society has ever been so pure an association of individuals as that pictured by Hobbes. Most societies have been, and still are, organic communities rather than associations of free individuals. If we apply Tonnies's distinction to the modern world, the organic community survives to a significant degree in Asia, Africa, the Middle East and Latin America. According to one estimate, perhaps 70 percent of the world's population live in societies in which loyalty to the family or tribe overrides personal goals.[22]

In contrast, Western society has been tending, at least since the

Protestant Reformation, away from community and towards a looser association of individuals. Hobbes's authoritarian theory of society as a social contract was followed by that of John Locke. Locke was more optimistic in his view of human nature than Hobbes, and hence favoured a more limited form of government in which individual citizens retained rights against the government; but he still saw society very much as a loose and indeed optional association of individuals.

Locke's conception of society strongly influenced the American revolutionaries and the authors of the American constitution. Tocqueville, in the 1830s, found America already strikingly a nation of individuals, and while he admired the self-reliance and independence of its citizens, he feared where this might lead: 'Each man is forever thrown back on himself alone, and there is danger that he may be shut up in the solitude of his own heart'.[23] Individualism triumphed over the traditional idea of community in the Protestant countries of Northern Europe, including Britain and its offshoots in North America, Australia and New Zealand. In late twentieth century America, however, individualism has been pushed to a new extreme. Social scientists have developed scales for placing societies on a continuum between individualism and collectivism: by these tests, the United States comes out as the most individualistic of all societies.[24] It is a society in which everyone 'does their own thing' or 'goes for it' where 'it' means 'whatever I want'. In many large American cities there simply is no community, in Tonnies's sense of the term.

In the view of Robert Bellah, a Berkeley sociologist and principal author of *Habits of the Heart*, though America has long been individualist, modern American society is more one-sidedly so than ever before:

> In earlier days the individualism in America was one that also honored community values. Today we have an ideology of individualism that simply encourages people to maximize personal advantage. This leads to a consumer politics in which 'What's in it for me?' is all that matters, while considerations of the common good are increasingly irrelevant.[25]

It is ironic that as the despised communist regimes of Eastern Europe and the Soviet Union were collapsing and reformers were hastily ushering in the forces of the free market, Western sociologists and philosophers were reviving theories of the importance of community in politics and ethical life. Karl Marx's criticisms of capitalism have held up far better than his scanty positive proposals for a better form of society. *The Communist Manifesto* is a powerful attack on the idea of society as a free association of individuals. Marx and his co-author Friedrich Engels were certainly no friends of traditional or feudal forms of society; they nevertheless wrote with a mixture of anger and awe of the way in which such societies had been destroyed by the rise of a society based on money:

> The bourgeoisie, wherever it has got the upper hand, has put an end to all feudal, patriarchal, idyllic relations. It has pitilessly torn asunder the motley feudal ties that bound man to his 'natural superiors', and has left remaining no other nexus between man and man than naked self-interest, than callous 'cash payment'.

Capitalism had thus ruthlessly created a society of free individuals; but this was not a free society. On the contrary, it was a society out of control:

> Modern bourgeois society with its relations of production, of exchange and of property, a society that has conjured up such gigantic means of production and of exchange, is like the sorcerer, who is no longer able to control the powers of the nether world which he has called up by his spells.[26]

Among these 'powers of the nether world', Marx thought, was the proletariat, the great class of propertyless labourers who are, for the bourgeoisie, merely another commodity, to be bought when their labour power is needed, and thrown on the scrap heap at a time of recession. Marx was convinced that, in creating the proletariat, the capitalist system had produced the seeds of its own destruction.

About this, Marx was simply wrong. The contradictions of

capitalism did not relentlessly intensify; capitalism improved the lot of most of its workers, and, in the most advanced capitalist nations, enlisted a substantial part of the working classes on its side. In contrast, those who successfully carried out revolutions in Marx's name found themselves unable to create a society that satisfied the needs of the majority, and remained in power only as long as they were prepared to use force to suppress opposition. Thus capitalism survived, and now, at the end of the twentieth century, appears to have triumphed. Yet there is something valid in Marx's vision of capitalism as a society that has created forces it cannot control. We see this once again in the recession that followed the boom years of the eighties. Economic confidence declines for reasons no-one quite grasps, commodity prices fall, and there are millions of people who want jobs, but for whose energies and skills the capitalist system has no use.

Marx was right to suggest that the free market society, by breaking traditional ties, reducing every bond to the cash nexus and unleashing the forces of individual self-interest, has conjured up a genie that it cannot control. The genie has brought us a society in which politics is dominated by economics. At every election the great issues of the day are economic. We are told that we cannot stop development that is environmentally damaging because our nation must compete economically with its overseas competitors. Proposals for better health care, welfare or housing for the poor are wrecked on the reefs of the desire for lower taxes to provide more incentives for investment. To turn away from greater and greater material prosperity has become unthinkable. Our political leaders assume that to do so would be to commit electoral suicide.

Now GATT – the General Agreement on Tariffs and Trade, the Holy Scripture of global economic rationalism – extends this dominance of economics around the entire globe. The lords of GATT tell the nations of the European Community that they must expose their peasant farmers to competition from the mega-farms of North America and Australia – competition that would surely wipe them out, and change irreversibly the landscape of Western Europe. When the European Patent Office hesitates over the ethical question of whether a living animal can be patented, the United States argues at GATT negotiations that to refuse to accept the patenting of animals is an illegal restraint of trade that prevents American inventors from reaping their due rewards. (The United States was acting to protect potential profits from the work of US scientists who had patented such animals as the 'onco-mouse', an unfortunate creature genetically engineered to develop tumours that scientists can study.[27]) In another triumph of economics over ethics, however, the United States found itself attacked by a similar argument. Invoking its Marine Mammal Protection Act, the United States banned Mexican tuna on the grounds that the Mexican fishing fleet, using methods now abandoned by the US fleet, needlessly kills 50,000 dolphins each year. Mexico appealed to GATT, claiming that the ban was an unfair trade barrier – and won![28]

The genie released by our encouragement of naked self-interest has eroded our sense of belonging to a community. Every individual pursues the ethos of 'looking out for number one'. We regard others as potential sources of profit, and we expect others to see us in the same way. The assumption is that you had better look after yourself because the other party will take advantage of you whenever possible – and the assumption becomes a self-fulfilling prophecy, because there is no point in being co-operative towards those who will not sacrifice their own short-term gain for long-term mutual benefits. But an association of isolated individuals bound not by a sense of place, nor by extensive family connections, nor by loyalty to an employer, but only by the fleeting ties of self-interest, cannot be a good society. Such a society will fail even if it professes that its role is only to allow each individual citizen 'life, liberty and the pursuit of happiness'. It will fail to allow this, not only for the poor, but even for the rich. As Robert Bellah and his colleagues write in *Habits of the Heart*: 'One cannot live a rich private life in a state of siege, mistrusting all strangers and turning one's home into an armed camp'.[29] In ethics and the formation of a community there are virtuous spirals and vicious spirals. If Aristotle was right to say that we become virtuous by practising virtue then we need societies in which people are enouraged to begin to act virtuously. In major cities whose populations are embued with the individualist ethos of material self-interest, the green shoots of mutual trust or a virtuous disposition struggle to survive, let alone grow and flourish. Bizarre as it may seem, we shall see in Chapter 6 that enemy soldiers facing each other from the trenches of World War I had a better basis for practising reciprocity than do the anonymous members of modern cities. We are in the process of creating societies that are mere aggregations of mutually hostile individuals, teetering on the brink of Hobbes's war of all against all. Wherever the sovereign cannot bring enough force to bear, the war could break out, and the individuals are more lethally armed than Hobbes could ever have imagined. Unless we begin now on the difficult task of restoring a sense of commitment to something other than oneself, that is the future we face.

I wrote the preceding paragraph early in April, 1992, and wondered if readers would consider it an exaggeration. But at the end of that month, television viewers around the world saw it confirmed all too vividly in the Los Angeles riots sparked by the acquittal of policemen videotaped in the act of beating Rodney King. While the acquittal undoubtedly caused justified outrage, the riots soon took on a life of their own. A key element was that the riots made it possible to take consumer goods without paying for them. Everyone was doing it, and the police could not be everywhere at once. In addition to the police, at the time of the riots, there were 3,500 private security firms in Los Angeles, employing 50,000 guards, but even that was not enough.[30] One journalist painted this picture:

> The five-mile length of Western Avenue up to Hollywood Boulevard was a looter's alley of a bizarre modern kind. Like all the other Los Angeles commuters, the looters came by car, parking on the pavements with doors and boots open, as shoes, clothes, television sets, compact disc players, and bottles were tossed inside.
>
> The parking lots of the big shopping malls look like so many bankruptcy sales. Looters stacked supermarket trolleys with their takings and wheeled them to their cars. Beds and sofas were piled precariously on to trucks and driven triumphantly away. There was a traffic jam to get in to loot the giant FedCo discount store on La Cienaga, and at one Sears store, a helicopter

television crew filmed looters arriving in a yellow cab . . . On Sunset Boulevard on Thursday evening I watched children with mobile phones co-ordinate the movements of their gangs with the arrival of police and fire trucks, warning looters when police were on their way.[31]

Richard Schickel correctly made the link between the looting and the nation's passion for acquisition: 'Modern America's great guiding principle, shop till you drop, was in process of revision; steal till you kneel was more like it'.[32] But Andrew Stephen of the London *Observer* made a more important connection:

> It is no coincidence . . . that it all happened in the city that most epitomises the burgeoning growth, under Presidents Reagan and Bush, of a powerless underclass – a Rich v Poor polarisation in a city where the world's most obscene conspicuous consumption of wealth exists so closely alongside Third World-type ghettoes.[33]

Nothing could have shown more clearly how in a society that elevates acquisitive selfishness into its chief virtue, the Hobbesian war of all against all lurks just beneath the surface.

CHAPTER 3

Using up the world

Jean-Jacques Rousseau or Adam Smith?

When Dennis Levine helped tie up the Revlon takeover deal, he celebrated by buying a Ferrari Testarossa. He may have found it enjoyable to drive, but essentially he was spending $125,000 on a symbol of success. Donald Trump, with greater means at his disposal, bought a $30 million yacht that he himself describes as 'a trophy'. Those with lesser incomes must do the best they can. The car industry relies on people changing over their cars at frequent intervals that, in most cases, have little to do with whether the car is still a safe and reliable means of getting from one place to another. When the 1991 recession hit and people began holding on to their cars a little longer, the American automobile industry went billions of dollars into the red.

The same attitude is evident in many areas of consumption. At one social level, one cannot be seen in the same clothes one wore to the last society gathering; lower down, it is a matter of not wearing something that was fashionable two or three years ago. Alongside stories of famines in Africa or the destruction of rainforests, and without the slightest sign of awareness of any incongruity, glossy colour magazines feature advertisements for new cars, high-fashion clothes, furniture and ocean cruises. Newspapers carry stories of Indian villagers forced to sell their kidneys to clear their debts while the same papers sprout supplements that promote gourmet eating and drinking, or tell readers how to redecorate their homes. Such supplements make economic sense for the newspapers, since their readers are a ready market for advertisers. But we should stop and ask: in what direction are we – collectively – going?

If any single person pointed the direction in which the free enterprise economy was to march, that person was Adam Smith, and the pointer was his extraordinarily influential work, *The Wealth of Nations*, published in 1776. Smith argued that in a market economy, we can each become wealthy only by being more efficient than our competitors at satisfying the wants of our customers or clients – a thought epitomized in his famous sentence: 'It is not from the benevolence of the butcher that we expect our dinner but from his regard to his own self-interest'. To serve our own interests, we will strive to produce goods that are cheaper or better than those already available. If we succeed, the market will reward us with wealth; if we fail, the market will put us out of business. Thus, wrote Smith, the desires of countless individuals for their private interests are drawn together, as if by a hidden hand, to work for the public interest. The collective outcome of the individual desire for wealth is a prosperous nation, which benefits not only the wealthy, but also 'the very meanest person in a civilised country'. On this last point, Smith waxed lyrical:

> the accommodation of an European prince does not always so much exceed that of an industrious and frugal peasant, as the accommodation of the latter exceeds that of many an African king, the absolute master of the lives and liberties of ten thousand naked savages.[1]

This became a standard justification for the inequality that results from the pursuit of wealth under a free enterprise system. Even the poorest, we are told, have no grounds for complaint, because they are better off than they would have been if we had remained in a pre-industrial society. They are better off, in fact, than a king in Africa![2]

Twenty years before he published *The Wealth of Nations*, Smith wrote a critique of a recent work that was then causing something of a sensation among intellectuals on the Continent: Jean-Jacques Rousseau's *Discourse on Inequality*. Rousseau's essay, which compared modern civilization unfavourably with the life of the 'noble savage', was an attack on everything that Smith was later to champion. In Rousseau's vision of the original state of human beings, the earth was left to 'its natural fertility' and was covered with 'immense forests whose trees were never mutilated by the axe'. These conditions provided 'on every side both sustenance and shelter for every species of animal'. As for the noble savage himself:

> I see him satisfying his hunger at the first oak, and slaking his thirst at the first brook; finding his bed at the foot of the tree which afforded him a repast; and with that, all his wants supplied.[3]

For taking us out of this idyllic state, Rousseau blamed the institution of private property, which allowed us to accumulate more than we needed, and so made us compare what we had with what others had, and desire to surpass them in wealth. This multiplication of our wants he saw as the source not only of inequality, but also of hatred, civil strife, slavery, crime, war, deceit, and all the other evils of modern life.

Adam Smith, however, took a very different view of the desire to accumulate possessions. Both in his critique of Rousseau and in a larger work, *Theory of the Moral Sentiments* (which he was then delivering as lectures at the University of Glasgow), he defended the multiplication of wants and the desire to accumulate possessions. It was, he thought, our desire to accumulate more and more that led our ancestors to develop the arts and sciences in ways which:

> have entirely changed the whole face of the globe, have turned the rude forests of nature into agreeable and fertile plains, and made the trackless and barren ocean a new fund of subsistence ... The rich ... are led by an invisible hand to make nearly the same distribution of the necessities of life, which would have

been made, had the earth been divided into equal portions among all its inhabitants, and thus without intending it, without knowing it, advance the interest of society, and afford means to the multiplication of the species.

A modern reader cannot help being struck by the difference in the attitudes of Rousseau and Smith to the forests and nature generally. Since the world has followed Smith, rather than Rousseau, the continuing destruction of our forests is not surprising. But now it is time to stop and ask: why are we *still* following Smith rather than Rousseau? It is significant that Smith did not defend the desire to accumulate possessions on the grounds that accumulation is the way to happiness. On the contrary, this belief was, he thought, a 'deception'. Regarding the grand houses and possessions for which we strive, Smith says:

> If we consider the real satisfaction which all these things are capable of affording . . . it will always appear in the highest degree contemptible and trifling. But we rarely view it in this abstract and philosophical light.

Instead, when we think about 'the pleasures of wealth and greatness', they strike us 'as something grand and beautiful and noble, of which the attainment is well worth all the toil and anxiety which we are so apt to bestow upon it'. Now comes the punchline of all this: although we are deceived when we imagine that wealth will bring us real satisfaction, the deception is a fortunate one, because 'it is this deception which rouses and keeps in continual motion the industry of mankind'.[4] Thus the father of modern economics and the greatest orginal advocate of the free enterprise society admitted that this form of society sprung from the pursuit of vain desires that, even if we could satisfy them, would not bring us any real satisfaction!

It is true that all this economic development conformed to the Biblical notion that it is good for our species to 'Be fruitful, and multiply, and replenish the earth, and subdue it, and have dominion over the fish of the sea and over the fowl of the air, and over every living thing that moveth upon the earth'.[5] Today, however, the desirability of any further 'multiplication of the species' is highly dubious, and there are few who would advocate turning more forests into 'agreeable plains'. We need to challenge the view of nature that lies behind Adam Smith's economics.

Living on our inheritance

As a generation, we have inherited the accumulated resources of our planet: fertile soils, forests, oil, coal and minerals like iron and bauxite. We began the twentieth century with a relatively clean and stable natural global environment. On this basis we have built an economy that produces, for the upper- and middle-class citizens of developed nations, an unprecedented standard of luxury, supplemented by an extraordinary range of gadgets. The global economy now produces as much in seventeen days as the economy of our grandparents, around the turn of the century, produced in a year.[6] We assume that this expansion can go on without limit, but the economy we have built depends on using up our inheritance. Since the middle of the century the world has doubled its per capita use of energy, steel, copper and wood. Consumption of meat has doubled in the same period and car ownership has quadrupled. And these are items that were already being used in large quantities in 1950; the increase for relatively new materials, like plastic and aluminium, is higher still. Since 1940, Americans alone have used up as large a share of the earth's mineral resources as did everyone before them put together.[7]

I read once of a corporate manager whose division was the slackest in the entire corporation. Productivity was appalling, and it seemed inevitable that the division was running at a loss. Yet, year after year, the accounts showed that the division had produced a respectable profit. The secret was that a previous division manager had bought a large area of land for possible future expansion. Encroaching suburbs had made the land very valuable, and the division manager was now selling a sizable chunk each year for a very healthy profit. His immediate superior was aware of how the trick of finishing the year in the black was done, but had no interest in putting a stop to it, because the profitable results improved the appearance of the overall performance in the several divisions for which he was responsible. We are playing the same trick in our national accounts. We are eating up capital, rather than living on what we produce. The faster we chop down our forests, sell off our minerals and use up the fertility of our soils, the more our Gross National Product grows. In our stupidity, we take this to be a sign of our prosperity, rather than a sign of the speed at which we are using up our capital. From the food we produce to the exhaust we emit from our cars, the pattern is the same. We take what we want from the earth, and leave behind toxic chemical dumps, polluted streams, oil slicks on the oceans, and nuclear wastes that will be deadly for tens of thousands of years. The economy is a sub-system of the biosphere, and it is rapidly running up against the limits of the larger system.

Many of the costs of economic growth have been familiar since the factories of the industrial revolution began belching their fumes across England, and a once-green area of the West Midlands became so despoiled and covered in industrial grime that it is still known as the Black Country. Only now, however, are we realizing that our most precious finite resource is the atmosphere itself. We think of the nineteenth century as a period of dirty industries polluting the atmosphere, but since 1950, the concentration of carbon dioxide in the atmosphere has climbed by more than it did in the previous two centuries. The result is likely to be the end of climate stability, with the immediate effect being to make the planet warmer than it has been at any time in human history.[8] Acid rain, another outcome of atmospheric pollution, is destroying ancient forests in Europe and North America. The use of gases that destroy the ozone layer is a third atmospheric problem that has already, according to the United States Environmental Protection Authority, ensured that there will be an additional 200,000 deaths from skin cancer in the US alone over the next fifty years.[9]

Consider food, something really basic to life that we do not normally associate with consumerism. The United States began the century with some of the richest, deepest soils in the world. Now the farming methods it uses are responsible for the loss of about seven billion tonnes of topsoil each year – Iowa, for example, has lost over half its topsoil in less than a century. In dry areas these methods are using up underground water supplies like the Ogallala Aquifer that underlies the cattle country from Western Texas to Nebraska – an irreplaceable resource that has taken millions of years to accumulate. Finally and most significantly, these farming methods are also energy intensive, relying on fossil fuels for machinery and for the production of chemical fertilizers. Traditionally, agriculture was a way of using the fertility of the soil and the energy provided by sunlight to increase the amount of energy available to us. Corn grown by small farmers in Mexico, for example, produces 83 calories of energy for every calorie of fossil fuel energy used. Beef produced in an American feedlot reverses the equation: it uses 33 calories of fossil fuel energy for every calorie of food energy it produces. We have developed a pattern of agriculture that relies on using up stored energy instead of capturing solar energy.

Nor is any of this being done in response to any crisis of hunger or malnutrition. It is the appetite for huge quantities of meat – especially beef – that is primarily responsible. Although red meat consumption has declined in recent years in the United States and some other developed nations, it remains at levels that are, historically speaking, far above those of most other human cultures. The Western image of the good life is one in which there is a slab of steak on every plate and a chicken in every foil bag. To produce this, we have invented an entirely new form of farming in which pigs, chickens and veal calves never see sunlight or walk in the fields, and cattle spend much of their lives packed into feedlots, eating grain instead of grazing on the grass for which their stomachs are suited. The animals have ceased to be regarded as our fellow sentient beings; instead they are treated as machines for converting cheap grain into high-priced flesh.[10] But I have discussed the ethics of our treatment of animals elsewhere; here my concern is the inefficiency of intensive animal raising.

We are using our best soils to grow grain and soybeans in order to feed them to cattle, pigs and chickens, whose carcasses will return only a small fraction of the food value to the humans who eat them. When we raise cattle in feedlots, for example, only 11 percent of the grain goes to produce the beef itself, with the remainder being burned off as energy, excreted, or absorbed into parts of the body that are not eaten. Cattle in feedlots produce less than 50 kilograms of protein from the consumption of over 790 kilograms of plant protein.[11] The huge appetite for beef in industrialized nations is a form of conspicuous consumption that drives us to demand more and more land and resources. In the affluent nations, each citizen is responsible for the consumption of nearly 1 tonne of grain every year; in India, the comparable figure is no more than a quarter of a tonne. The difference is accounted for not by our eating more bread or pasta (we physically could not eat that much grain in this way) but by the pile of grain hidden behind every steak, every slice of ham, and every leg of chicken we consume.

Because we equate the good life with meat on the table, there are now three times as many domestic animals on this planet as there are human beings. The weight of the world's 1.28 billion cattle is greater than that of the entire human population. In the last thirty years more than 25 percent of the forests of Central America have been cut down so that cattle can graze where the forest once stood. In Brazil the bulldozers are still pushing on, clearing the Amazon jungle so that cattle can graze for a few years. More than 40 million hectares have gone already, an area larger than the whole of Japan.[12] Once the soil has lost its fertility the cattle ranchers will move on, but the forest will not return. When the forests are cleared billions of tonnes of carbon dioxide are released into the atmosphere, enhancing the greenhouse effect.

The destruction of the rainforests is not the only way in which the huge population of animals being raised for food contributes to warming the greenhouse. Cattle fart large quantities of methane, the most potent of all the greenhouse gases. The world's cattle are thought to produce about 20 percent of the methane released into the atmosphere, and methane traps twenty-five times as much heat from the sun as carbon dioxide. Chemical fertilizers used to grow crops to feed the animals we eat produce nitrous oxide, another greenhouse gas. The heavy use of fossil fuels also contributes to the greenhouse effect. By eating so many animals and animal products we are helping to heat up our planet. The local effects of this are difficult to predict, but some areas that now support large populations would be stricken by droughts, while others get more rain. What is predictable is that sea levels – which have already risen by between 10 and 20 centimetres over the past century – will rise further as polar ice melts. The Intergovernmental Panel on Climate Change has estimated a 44-centimetre rise by 2070.[13] This means that entire island nations like Tuvalu, Vanuatu, the Marshall Islands, and the Maldives, could disappear. It has been reported that the government of the Maldives has already had to evacuate four islands. A report on the Marshall Islands produced by the United States National Oceanic and Atmospheric Administration concludes that within a generation, 'many parts of the islands may be unsafe to live on'.[14] That is serious enough, but the loss of human life could be greater still in densely populated low-lying delta areas like the Nile Delta and the delta region of Bengal. The latter, which makes up 80 percent of Bangladesh, is already prone to violent storms and floods. In these two regions alone, the selfishness of the rich is, by its effect on rising sea levels, putting the land and lives of 46 million people at risk.[15] In addition, we can expect the loss of entire ecological systems, and the species of animals and plants that are restricted to them, because such systems will be unable to adapt to the rapidity of artificially induced climatic change.

How an overflowing sink makes Adam Smith obsolete

Our economy is simply not sustainable. This is true even if we focus only on the developed countries. But we cannot limit our focus in this way. Jeremy Leggatt, science director of Greenpeace in Britain, has warned that China's plans to increase its coal burning sixfold in the next forty years could mean that China will be emitting three times as much of the world's greenhouse gases as the United States does today. These fears led to the signing of the Climate Change Convention at the Earth Summit meeting held in Rio de Janeiro in 1992. But all the Climate Change Convention does is encourage – not require – nations to hold their greenhouse gas emissions at 1990 levels by the year 2000. The Intergovernmental Panel on Climate Change has said that in order to stabilize carbon dioxide levels in the atmosphere, emissions need to be cut by 60 percent.[16]

Moreover there is a fundamental ethical flaw in dealing with the problem by taking present levels of emissions as the benchmark, either for holding emissions steady or for cutting them. The average American is responsible for the burning of between 4 and 5 tonnes of carbon per year; the average Indian and Chinese contribute roughly one-tenth of this amount. How can the citizens of rich nations tell China to stop, when even if China's ambitious plans succeed, each Chinese citizen would still be adding less carbon dioxide to the atmosphere than the citizens of most rich countries do today?

No wonder that Third World economists are starting to see Western concern about the environmental effects of Third World economic development as a new form of colonialism. Anil Agarwal of the Centre for Science and the Environment in New Delhi has put the case forcefully:

> India and China today account for more than one-third of the world's population. The question to be asked is whether we are consuming one-third of the world's resources or contributing one-third of the muck and dirt in the atmosphere and the oceans. If not, then surely these nations should be lauded for keeping the world in balance because of their parsimonious consumption despite the Western rape and pillage of the world's resources.

Agarwal suggests that we see our planet's facility for dealing with waste as a very large but finite global sink. The use of this sink should be shared out equally between the people of the world. Every individual on the planet might be regarded as having an entitlement to dump, say, half a tonne of carbon down the sink. On that basis, Americans are now using more than six times their fair share, while most Indians and Chinese are using less than their entitlement. The greediest users of the sink are the people of the United States, Canada, Australia, Germany, and the bloc that made up the former Soviet Union.[17]

Adam Smith denied that the rich deprive the poor of their share of the world's wealth. In another part of the passage cited earlier in this chapter, he wrote:

The rich only select from the heap what is most precious and agreeable. They consume little more than the poor, and in spite of their natural selfishness and rapacity, though they mean only their own conveniency, though the sole end which they propose from the labours of all the thousands whom they employ, be the gratification of their own vain and insatiable desires, they divide with the poor the produce of all their improvements.[18]

Smith then refers to the 'invisible hand' which brings about a distribution of the necessaries of life that is 'nearly the same' as it would have been if the world had been divided up equally among all its inhabitants. I doubt that this was true even in Smith's day; but if we move to the present time, and consider 'the rich' to include all the developed nations, then it is clear that Smith's argument has ceased to apply.

Smith never dreamt that the capacity of the atmosphere to absorb pollutants might be a finite resource. So while he knew that the rich could be selfish and rapacious, he did not imagine that they could take six times their share of the global atmospheric sink. Far from dividing with the poor the produce of all their improvements with the poor, the rich are presently on course to drown tens of millions of poor people who have the misfortune to live in low-lying coastal areas, and to starve untold millions more, as climate changes make the lands on which they depend increasingly arid. These consequences remain probable even if the rich abide by the Climate Change Convention and hold emissions at 1990 levels. Should such disasters miraculously be avoided, it will still be true that unless the rich drastically reduce their greenhouse gas emissions, they are effectively depriving the poor of the opportunity to develop along the lines that the rich themselves have taken; for if the poor were to behave as the rich do, the global emissions would rise dramatically, and the global sink would certainly overflow.

When are we well off?

Economic growth has become a sacred icon of the modern world. The desirability of continued expansion of the economy was subjected to sustained criticism from the environmental movement of the late sixties and early seventies, but the criticism was soon brushed off by the politicians, business leaders and trade unionists for whom the ideology of growth was the answer to all problems.[19] The earlier proponents of limits to growth did their computer models crudely. They were too ready to extrapolate present trends into the future. As a result they predicted that we would soon start running out of resources. By making our use of energy and other resources more efficient, we have succeeded in postponing the day when we must make tougher decisions. Controlling population growth is another key to limiting the damage we do to the global ecosystem, and hence to postponing the day when irreversible damage becomes apparent to all; but even that will not be sufficient. Sandra Postel and Christopher Flavin, researchers at the Worldwatch Institute in Washington, DC, have in mind economic growth when they write:

> If growth continues along the lines of recent decades, it is only a matter of time before global systems collapse under the pressure . . . Continuing growth in material consumption – the number of cars and air conditioners, the amount of paper used, and the like – will eventually overwhelm gains from efficiency, causing total resource use (and all the corresponding environmental damage) to rise . . . This aspect of the transition from growth to sustainability is thus far more difficult, as it goes to the heart of people's consumption patterns.[20]

Lester Brown, President of the Worldwatch Institute, has written:

> Movement toward a lasting society cannot occur without a transformation of individual priorities and values . . . Because of the strain on resources it creates, materialism simply cannot survive the transition to a sustainable world.[21]

According to a Brazilian study, if fossil fuel is used efficiently and we make greater use of renewable resources, we might be able to provide everyone in the world with modest but comfortable homes, refrigeration for food, access to public transport, and occasional limited use of a car; but we will never be able to provide everyone with the more profligate lifestyle of, say, Americans today. As Alan Durning puts it: 'In the end, the ability of the earth to support billions of human beings depends on whether we continue to equate consumption with fulfillment'.[22]

The problem is that our conception of the good life depends on constantly rising levels of consumption. When the celebrated Harvard economist J.K. Galbraith published *The Affluent Society* in 1958, no-one disputed the accuracy of its title as a description of the United States; nor did they disagree with the picture presented in the book of a land that had reached heights of affluence undreamt of by earlier generations. Yet America has since become, in terms of material goods, considerably more affluent than it had been twenty-five years earlier. By the early eighties, Americans owned five times as many air-conditioners per head, four times as many clothes dryers and seven times as many dishwashers.[23] In 1960, only 1 percent of American homes had colour television; by 1987, this had risen to 93 percent. Microwaves and video cassette recorders entered American homes in the seventies and eighties, and within a decade were to be found in nearly two-thirds of all homes.[24] Despite this dramatic increase in material goods, people felt neither more affluent nor happier. The University of Chicago's National Opinion Research Center has for many years been asking Americans how happy they are. The proportion describing themselves as 'very happy' has hovered around one-third since the 1950s.[25] Why has it not risen with material levels of affluence? Essentially, because though the society was still becoming more affluent, the rate at which it was doing so had slowed:

> In judging how well off we are economically . . . we assimilate new input to our 'adaptation level'. For many Americans, having one or several color television sets, two or more cars, a home in which there are more rooms than people . . . these and other features of their lives are experienced as the 'neutral point'. They do not excite us or arouse much feeling. Only a *departure* from that level is really noticed. Some pleasure may be afforded by our background level of material comfort, but unless we look

elsewhere than the accumulation of goods for the main sources of pleasure and excitement in our lives, we are bound to be on a treadmill – one which, we are increasingly recognizing, can damage our health and shorten our lives.[26]

Contemporary academic psychologists have explored this feature of human psychology, and found that it holds quite generally:

> The phenomenon of adaptation (or habituation) to maintained states is a fundamental biological regularity, which is observed at all levels of functioning . . . At all these levels, the maintenance of a state and the frequent repetition of a stimulus event are associated with a decreasing response to that stimulus . . . Adaptation has two general consequences for subjective experience. The first is that exposure to repeated stimulation tends to produce a neutral subjective state, or null state . . . The second consequence of adaptation is that contrast is the primary determinant of experience.[27]

Adaptation works at a quite simple physiological level, as well as at a psychological level. If we look for a time at a theatre stage bathed in red light, a neutral mixture of red-green will appear green to us, although it would appear colourless to someone who walks into the theatre without any prior adaptation. In a similar way, people who have won lotteries are, after a little while, no happier than other people who have not won lotteries. There are limits to adaptation. Even a long time after their accident, paraplegics are not as happy as others.[28] In general, though, no matter what level of comfort, luxury or pleasurable stimulus we achieve, it will soon cease to bring us pleasure that is any more intense than we had before.

The message is that, once we have satisfied our basic needs, there is no level of material comfort at which we are likely to find significantly greater long-term fulfillment than any other level. A 1992 *Time* cover story entitled 'Why the Gloom?' confirms that our judgments of how well off we are are relative to that to which we have become accustomed. From 1959 to 1973 American incomes grew, in real terms, by 2.7 percent per year; from 1973 to 1991, they grew by only 0.3 percent per year. This is still an increase: there has been no falling back below the levels of the early seventies, although there may have been a retreat from the debt-financed investment and consumer binge of the eighties. Yet when asked whether Americans today can enjoy the same standard of living as recent generations, two thirds of those who gave a clear answer said no. *Time* quotes a leading economist, Allen Sinai, as saying: 'The 1973 period marked the beginning of the decline of the American standard of living'. Whatever the psychological perceptions may be, it is clear that the figures do not bear this out, unless American economists have become so growth-orientated that they view a fall in the rate of growth as itself constituting a decline.[29]

If we judge our success at least in part by the rate at which our living standard is improving, we also judge it by comparing it with our neighbours, friends and colleagues. Here too, the increasing affluence of society as a whole brings no increase in the average sense of well-being, because as our collection of material goods increases, so does that of our neighbours. Whether people compare themselves with their own wealth the year before, or with what their neighbours have, it is clear that for most people, most of the time, the pursuit of material affluence cannot bring happiness. That may be why the glaring disparities of wealth between Nigerians and West Germans, or between Filipinos and Japanese, do not give rise to any differences in how people from these nations rate their level of happiness. R. A. Easterlin, of the University of Pennsylvania, has carried out a comparative international study of the link between wealth and happiness. His conclusion is that there is very little relationship between the two: 'Economic growth does not raise a society to some ultimate state of plenty. Rather, the growth process itself engenders ever-growing wants that lead it ever onward'.[30]

If the world continues to pursue material affluence on the Western model, it will therefore risk environmental disaster while failing to make us happier, even if economic growth is achieved. To say this is not to be against economic growth. There is potential for environmentally sustainable growth. Often ways of doing things that are environmentally friendly are also more labour-intensive than alternatives that consume more fossil fuels or cause more pollution. The Worldwatch Institute has estimated that generating 1,000 gigawatt-hours of electricity per year requires 100 workers in a nuclear power plant, 116 in a coal-fired plant, 248 in a solar thermal plant, and 542 on a wind farm.[31] Those figures partially explain, of course, why the nuclear and coal plants produce electricity that, in straight dollar terms, is cheaper than the more environmentally friendly alternatives; but the cost to our global ecosystem is not included in the dollar figures. The same is true of a comparison between an industry based on the use of a natural resource, such as a forest or a bauxite deposit, and one based on recycling paper or aluminium cans. The use of the natural resource may be cheaper, but it uses up an irreplaceable resource; recycling will be more labour intensive and therefore costlier, but it is sustainable.

To move towards a sustainable economy would cause unemployment in some industries, but on balance it would create jobs, not reduce them. Nevertheless, in strictly material terms, it has to be assumed that we would be worse off. Consuming irreplaceable resources is a quick and easy way of enriching ourselves; and pouring our wastes down the global sink is cheaper than the ecologically sustainable alternatives. If we cut back on these ways of enriching ourselves, the economic loss must be felt somewhere. Products now made by consuming irreplaceable resources or polluting the environment will become more expensive, and so we will be able to afford fewer of them. That may include cars, consumer goods, the use of energy for air-conditioning, heating and transport, and even food, like feedlot beef and intensively farmed pork and poultry, produced by methods that are extravagant uses of energy, soil and water.

If we retain our narrow view of our own self-interest, particularly the conception that has been moulded by the development of consumerism since World War II, we will see the reduction in material affluence as nothing but a setback. Even if we recognize that the reduction is inevitable and that the present economy cannot be sustained, we will consider it a regrettable necessity, desirable in the interests of the world as a whole, but bad in its impact on our own lives. But if we have a broader view of self-interest we will welcome the change, not just for the good of the global environment, but also for ourselves. Walking, riding bicycles and using public transport may use fewer resources than sitting in slow-moving traffic in one's own air-conditioned car, but does the lower use of resources lead to less overall satisfaction for those who walk, cycle or take the train? This is just one way in which the size of a nation's Gross National Product is no guide to the level of welfare of the population.

This is one reason why we need to change our conception of self-interest; but there is another, which goes deeper. For centuries Western society has sought satisfaction from the holy grail of material abundance. The search has been exciting, and we have discovered many things that were well worth finding, but in so far as our goal was ever a sensible one, we reached it long ago. Unfortunately we have forgotten that there could be any other goals at all. What is there to live for, other than to be richer than others, and richer than we were before? Many who are outstandingly successful in terms of the materialistic conception of success find that the rewards for which they have worked so hard lose their appeal once they have been achieved. Adam Smith would not have been at all surprised. The search for happiness through material wealth is based on a deception. Considered just from the standpoint of our own real interests the case for changing our conception of the good life is very strong. Now we can also see, moreover, that this conception has to be changed for quite different reasons. It was constructed and became entrenched during a period when no-one thought of limits to material wealth or consumption. As the idea of unlimited growth has become untenable, so too has our conception of the good life. So what should our goals be? The pressing ecological need to change our economy offers us the best opportunity for centuries to reflect on this question, and to find out what it really is to live well.

CHAPTER 4

How we came to be living this way

A perverse instinct

In America in the eighties, the ethos of money-making reached a new historical high point, both in the amounts of money that were made in a very short time, and in the openness with which the goal of money-making was pursued. Such a society does not develop from nothing in a decade. Its foundations had been carefully laid over centuries. If we are to understand what went wrong in the eighties, and what the broader lessons of that decade are for the pursuit of the good life, we need to be aware of these foundations. The ideas that grew to dominate life in the United States have now spread to influence, to a greater or lesser degree, all of the developed world. They beckon onwards what we call the 'developing' world as well.

The most celebrated essay on the origins of the capitalist mind – and still one of the most illuminating – is Max Weber's *The Protestant Ethic and the Spirit of Capitalism*, first published in 1904. Weber, a German sociologist, had read widely about Western and Eastern religious, ethical and economic life, ancient as well as modern. He found something unique about the spirit of capitalism. Not that it was unusually greedy – on the contrary, wrote Weber, 'the greed of the Chinese Mandarin, the old Roman aristocrat, or the modern peasant, can stand up to any comparison'.[1] What is distinctive about capitalism is the idea of acquisition for its own sake as an *ethically sanctioned* way of life. Before the modern era, money and possessions were valued only for what one could do with them. At a minimum level money and possessions meant that one could afford food, shelter and clothing; at a level of greater abundance, money and possessions signified a grand estate, servants, lavish entertainment, travel, perhaps also the ability to attract lovers or gain political power. In the capitalist era money is valued for its own sake, not just for what it can buy. At the higher levels of income, the natural order of things goes into reverse: instead of money being valued for the things it buys, things become valuable for the amount of money they cost. Van Gogh's *Irises* would have been much less interesting to the wealthy Australian Alan Bond if he could have bought it for half a million dollars. The fact that he had to pay nearly a hundred times that figure made *Irises* the most expensive painting in the world, and owning the most expensive painting in the world was what Bond, who knows very little about art, wanted when he was at the height of his success. (Now, being bankrupt, Bond might settle for less.) For capitalist man, the sole purpose of one's life's work is, in Weber's words, 'to sink into the grave weighed down with a great material load of money and goods'. We do not acquire goods in order to live, instead we live in order to acquire goods. Ivan Boesky had a T-shirt on which was printed: 'He who owns the most when he dies, wins'. That neatly sums up the attitude that Weber has in mind. In a pre-capitalist society, Weber says, to get this the wrong way round, making acquisition for its own sake the goal, would be unworthy and contemptible, 'the product of a perverse instinct'.[2]

What changes did the development of capitalism make in our values and goals, in our conception of what it is to make a success of our lives? To appreciate the differences capitalism has made to our attitude to acquisition and money-making we need to go back to the roots of Western ideas.

Aristotle on the art of making money

The origins of Western ways of thinking are to be found in two places: in ancient Greece, and in the Judeo-Christian tradition. If we turn first to Greece, we find a vigorous philosophical debate about the real nature of the good life; but none of the leading philosophers taking part in this debate see success in terms of the acquisition of money or material goods. When Plato, in *The Republic*, sketched an ideal community, he made it consist of three classes, in which only the lowest class – the farmers and artisans – would work for profit and accumulate property. The rulers and guardians were not even to own their own homes, but were to live communally. Free of the corrupting effect of money, they would be better able to rule wisely and justly. This utopian proposal bore no relationship to Athenian civic life. The philosophy of Aristotle was more in tune with human beings as they were in his times, and still are today. Under Plato's idea of common ownership, Aristotle objected, people will not share equally in the work that needs to be done. Those who work hard will resent others who 'labour little and receive or consume much'.[3] He also recognised the pleasures of ownership, and considered them legitimate, for 'the love of self is a feeling implanted by nature and not given in vain, although selfishness is rightly censured; this, however, is not the mere love of self, but the love of self in excess, like the miser's love of money . . .'[4]

Consistently with this distinction between legitimate love of self and selfishness, Aristotle distinguished 'the natural art of acquisition' from an excessive desire for money. The natural art of acquisition is a form of 'household management', that is, providing the household with the means for life. To this Aristotle fixes no definite limit, but implies that we can develop a sense of what is proper for the needs of the household. Money-making can be a means to the end of providing the household with what it needs, but because it is only a means to an end, it is limited by the nature of the end itself.

With this proper form of money-making Aristotle contrasts a different kind of behaviour:

> . . . some persons are led to believe that making money is the object of household management, and the whole idea of their lives

is that they ought either to increase their money without limit, or at any rate not to lose it . . . some men turn every quality or art into a means of making money; this they conceive to be the end, and to the promotion of the end all things must contribute.[5]

Such people, Aristotle says, have mistaken the means for the end. They believe that money is wealth. To show that this cannot be correct, Aristotle points to the fable of King Midas, who greedily wished that everything he touched should turn to gold, and starved when food turned to gold in his mouth. How can something be wealth, Aristotle asks rhetorically, if you can have it in superabundance, and yet perish from hunger?

For Aristotle, to acquire goods to meet one's needs is natural, and thus 'the art of making money out of fruits and animals is always natural'; but to acquire money for its own sake is unnatural and erroneous. Trading as a business or means of making money Aristotle thought to be unnatural, and 'justly censured' because it is 'a mode by which men gain from one another'. Another way of putting this would be to say: when we grow crops or raise animals we make our gain from nature, adding to the store of goods available for human beings; whereas when we buy a product and resell it for more than we paid for it, we have not added to the value of the product. We make our gain from others, who are prepared to buy our goods at more than we paid for them.

Aristotle added that the most hated sort of trade is earning money from lending money, for this

> makes a gain out of money itself, and not from the natural use of it. For money was intended to be used in exchange, but not to increase at interest . . . Wherefore of all modes of making money this is the most unnatural.[6]

This idea came to be known as Aristotle's doctrine of the sterility of money. For animals and plants to increase is natural, and for us to make use of this is also natural. But money is sterile, and to make money from its increase is unnatural.

Can a merchant be pleasing to God?

When we turn to the other major source of Western ideas, the Jewish and Christian tradition, we find that the ancient Hebrew scriptures also condemn charging interest on loans, but they put forward, in this respect as in many others, a tribal ethic, suited to a small group of people living amidst other groups. Thus in *Deuteronomy* we read:

> Thou shalt not lend money upon usury to thy brother; usury of money, usury of victuals, usury of anything that is lent upon usury: unto a stranger thou mayest lend upon usury; but unto thy brother thou shalt not lend upon usury.[7]

When, much later, Christianity arose among the Jewish people, it proposed a universal ethic. Everyone knows that Jesus urged us to love our enemies; less well known today is the fact that he also told us to stop charging them interest:

> But love ye your enemies, and do good, and lend, hoping for nothing again; and your reward shall be great, and ye shall be the children of the Highest.[8]

This injunction against seeking interest from anyone is consistent with Jesus's attitude to money-making in general, most famously illustrated by his casting out of the temple of Jerusalem not only the money-changers but 'all of them that sold and bought in the temple'. In doing so he said to those he was evicting that the temple should be a house of prayer 'but ye have made it a den of thieves'.[9] Did he mean that to profit from trade is a form of theft?

Jesus's attitude to earthly riches is equally well-known, thanks to his response to the rich man who asked him what he had to do in order to inherit eternal life. Although the man had, from his youth, observed all the commandments, Jesus told him that this was not enough: 'One thing thou lackest: go thy way, sell whatsoever thou hast, and give to the poor, and thou shalt have treasure in heaven'. And when the disciples were astonished at this, he said to them:

'Children, how hard is it for them that trust in riches to enter into the kingdom of God! It is easier for a camel to go through the eye of a needle, than for a rich man to enter into the kingdom of God'.[10]

In keeping with these teachings, the early Christian communities appear to have held what little property they had in common. The teachings of the Church Fathers were consistent with this. The giving of alms to the poor was not a matter of mercy, but of justice, for the earth was seen as belonging to all people, and no-one had a right to more than he or she needed.[12] The fact that the apostle Matthew, who had been a money-changer, did not return to his former trade after the resurrection of Jesus, whereas Peter the fisherman did, was noticed by Gregory, who in a memorable passage said that just as there are menial tasks that soil the body, like cleaning sewers, so there are others that stain the soul, and money-changing is one of them.[12]

Not surprisingly, then, the Christian tradition was unfriendly to money-making. In the fifth century, Pope Leo the Great wrote to the bishop of Narbonne that it is difficult to avoid sin in the course of buying and selling; this statement was quoted over and over again, and became part of canon law, the law of the Church. So did another oft-quoted dictum: 'Seldom or never can a man who is a merchant be pleasing to God'. In the early twelfth century Honorius of Autun wrote a theological dialogue in which a disciple asks the master about the prospects of salvation for those living in various ways. When asked about the chances for merchants, the master says that they have only a slight chance of being saved, because virtually everything they have they get by fraud, lies and selfish desire for gain. Those who till the soil, on the other hand, have a much better chance of being saved, because they live simply and feed the people of God by the sweat of their brows.[13]

As commerce developed in Christian Europe, the sin of usury received repeated condemnation. In introducing his scholarly study of the debate over usury in the Catholic Church, John Noonan points out that from our present perspective

> . . . we find it impossible to imagine that usury could once have been defined as 'profit on a loan', that the vice of usury could

have implicated every part of Western society, and that concern with his culpability of it could have plagued every European businessman and landowner.[14]

Yet so it was, for at least five centuries. In 1139 the Lateran Council condemned usury – by which it meant charging interest on money lent, no matter how moderate the rate might be – as 'ignominious'. Forty years later another Lateran Council decided that usurers were to be excommunicated, denied Christian burial, and their gifts or offerings refused. By this time the definition of usury had been broadened to include charging a higher price to those who bought on credit than to those who paid cash. The Council of Vienne in 1311 extended excommunication to anyone who authorized or protected usury, including princes who protected usurers (many princes were prepared to pay interest if they needed money to wage a war, and they would then protect the money-lenders). The prohibition on usury also gave a fatal impetus to anti-semitism: because Christians could not be money-lenders, this became a Jewish role; and the hatred felt for usury fuelled existing prejudices against the already despised 'killers of Christ'.

Some of the grounds for the condemnation of usury make an intriguing contrast with our present ways of thinking. One medieval theologian, Thomas of Chobham, found usury objectionable because 'the usurer wants to make a profit without any work at all and even while sleeping, which is against the teaching of the Lord: "You will earn your bread by the sweat of your brow."' Moreover, Thomas added, the usurer sells nothing that actually belongs to himself: he sells only time, which belongs to God. This made the usurer a robber, and indeed usury was often classified as a form of robbery or theft. But it was also frequently compared with prostitution, another occupation that was both well-known and shameful. Thomas found the comparison unfair to the prostitute: she at least worked for her money, even if the work was ignominious. As if all this was not enough, another text points out that while the peasant lets his cattle rest on Sundays, the usurer does not let his money, which is his cattle, respect the day of rest.

Tales of the wretched deaths of usurers were among the most popular themes for preachers during this period.[15] So was what happened to the usurers beyond the grave. Bernard of Siena wrote this portrayal of the usurer on the Day of Judgment:

> All the saints and all the angels of paradise then cry out against him, saying, 'To hell, to hell, to hell'. Also the heavens with their stars cry out, saying, 'To the fire, to the fire, to the fire'. The planets also clamour: 'To the depths, to the depths, to the depths'.[16]

Usury was linked with avarice. For the first Christian millenium, on most of the innumerable occasions on which some religious teacher thought it desirable to warn the faithful against falling into vice, it was pride, the vice of the aristocracy, that headed the list of vices. As commerce increased, however, the emphasis shifted. Avarice, the vice of the bourgeoisie, joined pride at the head of the lists. In 1043 Peter Damian stated unequivocally that avarice is the root of all evil, and advised the monk seeking to live a Christian life that 'Christ and money do not go well together'. John of Salisbury wrote that there is no vice worse than avarice, and Bernard said simply that an avaricious man 'is like hell'.

Sculptors and painters, reflecting this current of opinion, personified avarice in their works and delighted in showing its punishment. Avarice was often a small crouching figure, mouth open, clutching moneybags; but it could also be a fat monster stooped down by the weight of a bag of money around the neck. In a sculpted relief on a church near Parma, such a figure is shown being punished. In addition to the money bag around the neck, a devil presses down the weight of a treasure chest that avarice carries on his back; for good measure, another devil yanks out his teeth with pincers. The porch of the monastic church of Moissac portrays the story told in Luke's gospel, of Lazarus and the rich man. At the top, the rich man is enjoying a sumptuous banquet while Lazarus, poor and sick, lies on the ground outside. The rich man's dogs lick his sores. But later Lazarus is nestled in the bosom of Abraham, while the rich man, now dead, is tormented by demons.[17]

Not only usury and avarice, but money itself came into bad odour

– quite literally. A priest in Brittany was accused not only of stealing coins from his own collection money, but of smearing excrement on a cross. The bizarre second charge can only have arisen from some symbolic association between money and shit. That this association existed is confirmed by the practice, evident around the end of the thirteenth century, of illustrating manuscripts in the margins with pictures of humans (and also apes) defecating coins.[18]

The Judeo-Christian tradition received an infusion of new ideas in the thirteenth century, when the medieval scholastics rediscovered Aristotle. For many centuries, only his writings on logic had been known in Europe; now his *Ethics* and his *Politics*, preserved by Arabic scholars, were read, discussed, and incorporated in treatises on a wide range of ethical and social questions. Thomas Aquinas made it his life's work to blend the views of Aristotle – whom he referred to simply as 'The Philosopher', as if there were no other philosopher worth discussing – with Christian teachings. In the area of economics, that was not difficult to do. When the scholastics read Aristotle they found that his view of the central issue of charging interest on loans was entirely in keeping with the prevailing view of the Church on usury. Aquinas also readily accepted Aristotle's view of the limits to natural, rational and justifiable acquisition. This led him to a view that is strikingly at odds with the generally accepted view of Aquinas as a staunch pillar of the prevailing order in a highly conservative Church. For Aquinas holds that there are some things that we may acquire to satisfy our needs, and other things that, if we acquire and retain them, are surplus. In discussing the duty of giving alms he explains this concept as follows:

> On the part of the giver, it must be noted that he should give of his surplus, according to Luke xi.41: 'That which remaineth, give alms' . . . since it is not possible for one individual to relieve the needs of all, we are not bound to relieve all who are in need, but only those who could not be succored if we did not succor them. For in such cases the words of Ambrose apply, 'Feed him that dies of hunger: if thou hast not fed him, thou hast slain him'.[19]

This is a radical doctrine; but there is more to come. Aquinas also poses the question: 'Whether it is lawful to steal through stress of need?' In answering, he draws from the natural law view of property an implication that is downright revolutionary:

> . . . whatever certain people have in superabundance is due, by natural law, to the purpose of succoring the poor. For this reason Ambrose says, and his words are embodied in the *Decretals*: 'It is the hungry man's bread that you withhold, the naked man's cloak that you store away, the money that you bury in the earth is the price of the poor man's ransom and freedom'.
>
> Since, however, there are many who are in need, while it is impossible for all to be succored by means of the same thing, each one is entrusted with the stewardship of his own things, so that out of them he may come to the aid of those who are in need. Nevertheless, if the need be so manifest and urgent that it is evident that the present need must be remedied by whatever means be at hand (for instance when a person is in some imminent danger and there is no other possible remedy), then it is lawful for a man to succor his own need by means of another's property, by taking it either openly or secretly; nor is this, properly speaking, theft or robbery . . . In a case of a like need a man may also take secretly another's property in order to succor his neighbor in need.[20]

Property, in other words, has its limits. The institution of private property has a purpose, and if some own so much that they exceed the purpose of the institution, what they have in excess is a surplus for those who do not have enough.[21] There is no just title to retain surplus wealth when others are in dire need. Those in danger of starvation, or those who are coming to their aid, are entitled to take from those with surplus wealth. Since the Christian use of the term 'neighbour' knows no geographical boundaries, we may take from the wealthy to help those suffering from famine anywhere in the world. To do so is neither theft nor robbery, because I am taking something that belongs, by natural law, to those in need rather than to those who already have more than enough.

So from ancient Greece through the earliest Christian times until the end of the middle ages – in other words, for more than three quarters of the history of Western civilization – money-making in general was often under a stigma, and the use of money to make more money was particularly severely condemned. Yet the use of money to make more money is essential to capitalism, the form of economy that has dominated the Western world for the past two centuries at least, and is now without serious rival anywhere in the world. With the growth and eventual triumph of capitalism has come a very different attitude to money and acquisition.

Luther's calling and Calvin's grace

The increasing influence of the commercial class in medieval Europe put the traditional Christian view of money-making under increasing pressure; but it was the coming of the Protestant religion that blew the old view apart. Martin Luther saw the priesthood as corrupt, self-serving, and a barrier between the believer and God. This led him to reject the division of the Christian community into two castes, the priests (including by this term everyone in holy orders from the Pope down to the lowliest monk or nun) and the ordinary lay believers. Buttressing this division in Catholic Christianity was the notion that those in holy orders had a 'calling', while the rest of us, thanks to Adam's sin, had to labour. In place of this view Luther said that each of us has a 'calling', merchants and peasants no less than religious leaders, and to succeed in our calling is a religious duty. Accordingly, it was necessary to abandon completely the old idea that to be a merchant is inherently discreditable and makes it difficult to be saved. No doubt abandoning this view also served the Protestant rebels very well. To resist the power of the established Church, they needed the support of the rising middle class, whose wealth and economic power were at that time in inverse proportion to the esteem they were granted by the Church.

Of all the leaders of the Reformation, John Calvin went furthest in revising the traditional religious attitudes to the business classes. A distinctive (and repugnant) element of his theology is the doctrine of predestination according to which salvation cannot be earned by good deeds or even by a morally faultless life, but must be bestowed by divine grace – the 'amazing grace' of the song that is so popular with American congregations. For anyone who took the prospect of hellfire seriously, doubts about whether one did or did not have grace were a source of deep and enduring anxiety. This is the background for the most salient fact about Calvin's view of wealth: he saw worldly success as a mark of grace. Calvinists, then, reversed the previous Christian view: wealth, far from imperilling one's chances of salvation, was a sign of salvation, and the more wealth one had, the more unmistakable the sign.

Nor did Calvinists need to fear that in using money to make money, they were violating natural law. Sweeping aside the writings of scores of saints, popes and scholastics, Calvin ridiculed Aristotle's doctrine that money is intended to be merely a means of exchange, and that it is therefore unnatural to use it in order to earn more money. A child can see, Calvin tells us, that money locked in a box is sterile. But those who borrow money do not do so in order to leave it idle. For example, if money buys a field, then money bears more money. Merchants borrow to increase their stock of goods, and for them money can, quite properly, be as fruitful as any other kind of goods. On this, of course, Calvin was quite right. The decline of the feudal economy, the rise of the towns, the greater freedom of craft workers and merchants to buy and sell where they chose, all contributed to a more complex economy in which money, in the form of capital, was an essential tool for earning one's livelihood. So it was entirely reasonable to suggest that the doctrine prohibiting usury should be modified to take account of the growing use of money as capital.

Equally convincing was Calvin's scornful dismissal of the casuistry of the scholastics, who had by his time developed many exceptions to the rule against usury. The ingenuity of these commercial devices remained without parallel until the rise of tax-minimizing accounting methods in the modern era. The exceptions to the laws against usury effectively allowed bankers to profit from lending money while pretending that they were doing something quite different. This, Calvin pointed out, is a trick that will not deceive God. But is usury truly sinful? Calvin went back to the Golden Rule: usury is sinful only if it hurts one's neighbour. And when does usury hurt one's neighbour? One should not, Calvin preached, expect a parson to know all the details of business. Let each believer's conscience be his guide.[22] Perhaps Calvin was here a little naive about the nature of business and the efficacy of conscience, untutored by any specific principles, when it is up against the drive for profit; or possibly he was primarily interested in gaining the support of the business community for his teachings. In practice, as far as charging interest was concerned, 'Let each believer's conscience be his guide' meant: anything goes.

Luther's idea of an earthly calling and Calvin's view of worldly wealth spread rapidly in Protestant nations, and nowhere more rapidly than in England, under Queen Elizabeth I and her successors. During the late sixteenth century and the first half of the seventeenth century, many English clergymen published works in which they assured their readers 'that one served God by laboring ceaselessly in an earthly calling'.[23] When, in this period of intellectual and religious ferment the Pilgrim Fathers and other Puritan settlers left England for the New World, they took Protestant, and especially Calvinist, doctrines with them.

Andre Siegfried, a French observer of American life, has noted the striking contrast between the Catholic and Calvinist ways of thinking about worldly wealth, and the impact of the latter on attitudes to wealth:

Calvin . . . united religion and daily life for the first time since the days of the ancients, for, according to his creed, the better the faithful performed their daily task, the more they worked for the glory of God. Though the Catholic Church has always allied itself to riches, it has never held up wealth as a symbol of godliness, believing that the poor man can retain his nobility of soul, and possibly be even nearer to God. The Puritan on the contrary regards his wealth as an honour, and when he hoards up his profits, he says smugly that Providence has been kind. In his eyes and in the eyes of his neighbours, his riches become the visible sign of divine approbation, and in the end he cannot tell when he is acting from a sense of duty, and when from self-interest. In fact he has no wish to make any distinction, for he is accustomed to regard as a duty everything that is most useful to his own advancement. As a result of this more or less deliberate lack of psychological penetration, he does not even rise to the level of a hypocrite.[24]

The religious and the secular converge

Since the Puritans in America had a new community to build, they embraced with great enthusiasm the idea that work is a divine calling and wealth a mark of grace. Cotton Mather, the most influential of the New England preachers, told his congregation that a Christian should 'glorify God by doing of good for others and getting of good for himself'.[25] William Penn, the founder of Quaker Pennsylvania, taught that wealth is a visible sign that one is living 'in the Light'.[26] Of course, for both Mather and Penn, this worldly calling was only one side of life; it had to be balanced with a proper spiritual life in order to please God. It was, however, the blessing of the life of acquisition that left the more lasting mark on American society. For this perhaps Benjamin Franklin bears some responsibility.

Although Franklin habitually signed himself 'Benjamin Franklin, Printer', today his name stands for many things: writer, philosopher, scientist, revolutionary, statesman, and member of the American Constitutional Convention. To many of his eighteenth century contemporaries, however, Franklin was best known as a self-made man, 'the supreme symbol of the poor boy who made good' and as the publisher of an almanac that purported to be the work of a farmer of modest means known as Poor Richard.[27] In his autobiography, Franklin tells us that, in order to make the almanac more entertaining and useful, he 'filled all the little spaces that occurred between the remarkable days in the calendar with proverbial sentences, chiefly such as inculcated industry and frugality . . .' The almanac became an annual bestseller, bringing both fame and fortune to the young Franklin. In 1757 Franklin marked the twenty-fifth anniversary of the first almanac by weaving many of the maxims together and publishing them in the form of a speech by a man he named Father Abraham, under the title *The Way to Wealth*. If the almanac had sold well, the speech was a smash hit, being reprinted at least 145 times in seven different languages before the end of the eighteenth century. Moreover, this popularity endured: in the nineteenth century Nathaniel Hawthorne called the now-deceased Franklin 'the counsellor and household friend of almost every family in America'; and towards the end of that century one scholar calculated that *The Way to Wealth* had been printed and translated more often than any other work by an American.[28]

Included in *The Way to Wealth* were such aphorisms as:

Plough deep, while sluggards sleep

A fat kitchen makes a lean Will

Fools make Feasts, and wise Men eat them

Get what you can, and what you get hold
'Tis the Stone that will turn all your Lead into Gold.

This attitude to thrift, to hard work, and to the importance of acquiring and keeping wealth is also represented in another of Franklin's writings, his *Advice to a Young Tradesman*. Max Weber quotes at length from this work, which he regards as displaying the spirit of capitalism 'in almost classical purity'. What follows is not the entire passage Weber quotes, but enough to give the flavour:

Remember that *time* is money. He that can earn ten shillings a day by his labour, and goes abroad, or sits idle, one half of that day, though he spends but sixpence during his diversion or idleness, ought not to reckon *that* the only expense; he has really spent, or rather thrown away, five shillings besides . . .

In short, the Way to Wealth, if you desire it, is as plain as the Way to Market. It depends chiefly on two Words, INDUSTRY and FRUGALITY; i.e. Waste neither Time nor Money, but make the best Use of both. He that gets all he can honestly, and saves all he gets (necessary Expenses excepted) will certainly become RICH . . .

Weber thought that an attitude like Franklin's would have been considered, both in ancient times and in the middle ages, 'the lowest form of avarice'.[29] He accuses Franklin of putting forward the view that we should live in order to acquire more. This accurately characterizes the passage Weber quotes, but it is unfair to Franklin, who was neither Father Abraham nor Poor Richard. The real Franklin founded or helped to found Philadelphia's first college and first hospital as well as the American Philosophical Society and many other public projects.[30] He retired from business at the age of forty-two, when he reckoned that the 'sufficient tho' moderate Fortune' he had acquired was enough to provide him with 'Leisure during the rest of my Life, for Philosophical Studies and Amusements'. Thus he showed in the most definite way possible that he was not interested in acquisition for its own sake. (He also showed himself far wiser than his counterparts in the 1980s, men like Boesky, Trump and Milken, who acquired fortunes that were more than 'sufficient' but could conceive of nothing more interesting to do than make still more money.) Franklin was actively involved in the play of ideas and politics of his time, at both a theoretical and a practical level. But this was not the message that he left to the great bulk of his contemporaries. Franklin's significance in the development of modern American ways of thinking about money-making lies in the impetus he gave to a secular version of the Puritan idea of a calling. In his popular writings, industry and frugality were recommended, not as a way of honouring God and doing His will, but as the way to become rich.

On both religious and secular grounds, nineteenth century America felt justified in fostering the view that attaining wealth is the proper goal of life. Peter Baida, author of the aptly titled *Poor Richard's Legacy*, has seen America's early fixation on wealth as the result of the break from Europe's rigid class structures: 'The idea that all men were created equal, and that all could be free to rise as high as their own efforts could lift them, stirred everyone it touched in the young nation. For white males, at least, no country in the world raised fewer barriers to success, and none came closer to realizing the ideal of equal opportunity'.[31]

The secular goal of the pursuit of wealth popularized by Franklin was given an economic justification by Adam Smith, as we saw in the last chapter. American religious leaders continued to show that they were no less supportive of the money ethic than anyone else. In 1836 the Reverend Thomas P. Hunt published a book entitled *The Book of Wealth; in Which It Is Proved from the Bible that It Is the Duty of Every Man to Become Rich*. In *Hunt's Merchants' Magazine*, in 1854, one writer argued that the Original Sin was a failure to attend to business: 'Adam was created and placed in the Garden of Eden for business purposes; it would have been better for the race if he had attended closely to the occupation for which he was made'. And Thomas Parker, a Boston Unitarian clergyman, suggested canonizing the businessman as 'a moral educator, a church of Christ gone into business . . . Build him a shrine in Bank and Church, in the Market and the Exchange . . . No Saint stands higher than this Saint of Trade'. McGuffey's Readers, probably read by at least half the school children of America during most of the nineteenth century, 'assured them that making money was a moral duty sanctioned by divine decree'.[32]

By the beginning of the twentieth century, John D. Rockefeller, Jr. was justifying the size of the business he was about to inherit from his father in terms more suited to the modern scientific age:

> The growth of a large business is merely a survival of the fittest . . . The American Beauty rose can be produced in the splendor and fragrance which bring cheer to its beholder only by sacrificing the early buds which grow around it. This is not an evil tendency in business. It is merely the working out of a law of nature and a law of God.[33]

Behind such thoughts lies Social Darwinism, the philosophical outlook associated with the English philosopher and social scientist Herbert Spencer. Darwin himself firmly disavowed any attempt to see a moral direction in the course of evolution, but Spencer developed a conception of social ethics that was modelled on evolution. The struggle for survival was, in his view, the chief cause of social progress. Hence it should be allowed to continue with an absolute minimum of state interference. Great wealth was a reward for taking great risks, or great pains, and without it society would stagnate.

Spencer's philosophy was extraordinarily popular in America. One admirer, F. A. P. Barnard, described Spencer as 'not only the profoundest thinker of our time, but the most capacious and most powerful intellect of all time'.[34] Such praise is so absurdly disproportionate to Spencer's merits as a philosopher that it can only be explained by the superb fit between Spencer's evolutionary ideas and the mood of America. At the time, the United States Supreme Court was using the Fourteenth Amendment – the amendment forbidding any state to 'deprive any person of life, liberty, or property, without due process of law' – to strike down attempts to regulate industry. Spencer appeared to provide a philosophical justification for opposing state interference with free enterprise, market forces, and the evolutionary struggle for survival. So often was Spencer invoked in this context that Mr Justice Holmes, one of the greatest of the Supreme Court judges, and himself an admirer of Spencer, was finally moved to his famous protest, in the midst of a legal judgment, that 'the fourteenth Amendment does not enact Mr Herbert Spencer's *Social Statics*'.[35]

Spencer also attracted the enthusiastic support of one of America's greatest industrialists: Andrew Carnegie. Carnegie was an unusual mixture: the son of a poor Scottish immigrant, he founded Carnegie Steel and became one of the world's richest men. He saw it as his duty to give away, during his own lifetime and for the public good, much of what he earned, and advocated steeply progressive scales of death duties for the rich who did not do likewise. He nevertheless described himself, in his *Autobiography*, as a disciple of Spencer, and under Spencer's influence wrote an essay that became known as his 'Gospel of Wealth', in which he lauded free competition: 'while the law may be sometimes hard for the individual, it is best for the race, because it insures the survival of the fittest in every department'. Like Adam Smith – though with more intermediate steps – he argued that the existence of the rich was good for the poor:

> The poor enjoy what the rich could not before afford . . . The laborer has now more comforts than the farmer had a few generations ago. The farmer has more luxuries than the landlord had, and is more richly clad and better housed. The landlord has books and pictures rarer, and appointments more artistic, than the King could then obtain . . . We must accept and

welcome, therefore . . . the concentration of business, industrial and commercial, in the hands of the few . . . they must accumulate wealth . . . Individualism, Private Property, the Law of Accumulation of Wealth, and the Law of Competition [are] the highest results of human experience . . . the best and most valuable of all that humanity has yet accomplished. [36]

Observers of America over a long period noted the importance placed on getting money as a distinctive feature of American culture. It was already evident in 1835 when Alexis de Tocqueville published *Democracy in America*, in which he observed: 'I know of no country, indeed, where the love of money has taken a stronger hold on the affections of men . . .' and elsewhere in the same work he noted that 'The love of wealth is therefore to be traced as either a principal or accessory motive, at the bottom of all that the Americans do . . .'[37] In a book on American culture published in 1855 the German writer Ferdinand Kurnberger made fun of Benjamin Franklin's popular homilies. They represented, Kurnberger thought, a philosophy that makes 'tallow out of cattle and money out of men'.[38] In 1864 Thomas Nicholls wrote: 'Nowhere is money sought so eagerly; nowhere is it so much valued . . . The real work of America is to make money for the sake of making it. It is an end, and not a means'.[39] After extensive travels in the United States in the first quarter of the twentieth century, the Frenchman Andre Siegfried found America 'a materialistic society, organized to produce things rather than people, with output set up as a god . . . In the light of the American contrast we see that material pursuits have not entirely absorbed the soul of Europe . . .'[40] Later the English political scientist Harold Laski asserted: 'in no previous civilization has the business man enjoyed either the power or the prestige that he possesses in the United States . . . The great businessman in the United States has an aristocratic status comparable to that of the landowner or the soldier or the priest in pre-capitalist Europe'.[41]

The English historian, R. H. Tawney, found a name for that type of society of which America had become the paradigm example:

Such societies may be called Acquisitive Societies because their whole tendency and interest and preoccupation is to promote the acquisition of wealth. The appeal of this conception must be powerful, for it has laid the whole modern world under its spell . . . The secret of its triumph is obvious. It is an invitation to men to use the powers with which they have been endowed by nature or society, by skill or good fortune, without enquiring whether there is any principle by which their exercise should be limited . . . it offers unlimited scope for the acquisition of riches, and therefore gives free play to one of the most powerful of human instincts.

America was, by the beginning of the twentieth century, clearly cast in this mould. Nowhere else in the world was the free market so clearly triumphant. Nowhere else had socialist or other left-wing ideas had so little effect. In Europe, and even in other countries of Anglo-Saxon descent like Australia, political parties of the left were either forming their first governments, or were at least strong enough to be a serious political threat to the conservative governing parties; but in the United States, the tag 'socialist' continued to be a term of abuse, and if taken seriously, a path to political suicide. When Friedrich Engels surveyed the American labour movement in 1887, he could find only one political party that he regarded as truly socialist. It was founded by German immigrants, and called the Socialist Labor Party; but the extent to which it was part of American life can best be gauged by the fact that Engels thought it necessary to recommend that if this party was to grow in numbers and influence, its members 'must, above all things, learn English'.[42]

The consumer society

This set of both religious and secular ideas about the importance of wealth formed the foundations for our modern conception of the Good Life. That conception took its present form in the United States in the 1950s. The productive capacity of United States industry had expanded to meet the needs of the victorious struggle against Nazism and Japanese imperialism; now the slack was taken up – in part – by the production of consumer goods. But there is no point in producing consumer goods unless people will buy them; and so people had to be persuaded that these goods were what they really wanted. Vance Packard's *The Hidden Persuaders* described the situation:

> By the mid-fifties American goods producers were achieving a fabulous output, and the output with automation promised to keep getting more fabulous. Since 1940, gross national product had soared more than 400 per cent; and man-hour productivity was doubling about every quarter century.
>
> One way of viewing this rich, full life the people were achieving was the glowing one that everyone could enjoy an ever-higher standard of living. That view was thoroughly publicized. But there was another way of viewing it: that we must consume more and more, whether we want to or not, for the good of our economy.[43]

The sections of Packard's book that really caused a stir were those in which he described how the then-booming advertising industry had begun to employ psychologists to study the hidden motivations that led consumers to purchase. Once these motivations had been found, the image of a product would be designed accordingly. So advertising began to play on our desires for status, our fears of falling behind our neighbours, and our worries about our body odour.

Consider the American car industry during the fifties. Each year's new model was bigger than the one before. All through the fifties and well into the sixties, American cars remained absurdly large, they were dangerous, they guzzled fuel as if it could never run out, they polluted the air, they were unreliable, and they handled poorly; yet they sold wonderfully well. Skilful advertising encouraged the idea that there was something shameful about driving a car more than two or three years old. After all, this year's car was longer, or lower, or it had sprouted fins. Customers who bought new cars were buying status rather than improved transportation.

Only when a crusading young lawyer called Ralph Nader began his relentless pursuit of General Motors over the ill-fated Corvair, which had an alarming tendency to flip over when going around bends, did safety become an issue. (Even then, Nader might never have got anywhere, had General Motors not made the fatal mistake of employing an attractive young woman to seduce him so as to get some dirt that could be used against him; a tactic that, when it was revealed, did not make the company look good.) Only when the oil-producing nations cut off America's supply, in 1973, did fuel efficiency begin to matter. Only when the Japanese began selling large numbers of more reliable, better handling cars, did American manufacturers begin to concern themselves with those qualities. Even then, of course, status did not cease to be a factor in buying a car; it just became a tiny bit more subtle.

A withered greening

During the sixties, first the civil rights movement, then the opposition to the war in Vietnam, and finally the entire counterculture movement, made many young Americans ask questions about the kind of society in which they were living. Soon they were also asking questions about the future life that American society held out for them – and finding radically new answers. Charles Reich, a professor of law at Yale University, wrote a book at the end of the sixties called *The Greening of America*. It began with a prediction:

> There is a revolution coming . . . It will not require violence to succeed, and it cannot be successfully resisted by violence. It is now spreading with amazing rapidity, and already our laws, institutions and social structure are changing in consequence . . . This is the revolution of the new generation. Their protest and rebellion, their culture, clothes, music, drugs, ways of thought and liberated life-style are not a passing fad or a form of dissent and refusal, nor are they in any sense irrational. The whole emerging pattern, from ideals to campus demonstrations to beads and bell-bottoms to the Woodstock festival, makes sense and is part of a consistent philosophy. It is both necessary and inevitable, and in time it will include not only youth, but all people in America.[44]

Reich didn't explain how bell-bottoms were part of a consistent philosophy. Nor was he a success as a prophet. He wrote his book just as the counterculture of the sixties was peaking. For a few months the book was a hit, selling more than a million copies. Everyone was talking about it. Then the vogue was interrupted by reality. By the time *The Greening of America* had reached the book-shops, the peace and love of Woodstock had already turned into the murderous violence of the rock festival at Altamont. When Richard Nixon won the 1972 presidential election by a landslide over the peace candidate George McGovern, the opening passage of *The Greening of America* was beginning to look like a joke in very poor taste. Unable to change the world, disillusioned radicals came to believe that they needed to change themselves first.

It was, in a way, a logical progression. Peter Weiss's much-acclaimed play (and later film) *Marat/Sade* had put the logic behind it into the mouth of the Marquis de Sade. De Sade told the French Revolutionary leader Jean-Paul Marat where he had gone wrong:

> Marat
> These cells of the inner self
> Are worse than the deepest stone dungeon
> And as long as they are locked
> All your Revolution remains . . .
> Only a prison mutiny
> To be put down
> By corrupted fellow-prisoners.[45]

So the revolutionaries turned inwards. In 1972 Michael Rossman, who had been with 'the Movement' since the Free Speech Movement at the University of California, Berkeley, wrote:

> Forecast for the next five years: Consciousness will be the coun-try's quickest-flourishing growth industry. A kaleidoscope of mutant flowers will appear on every block. Too many people will take to the easy lotus, giving up the task of integrating what we have begun.[46]

A few months later one of the most dramatic of conversions showed that Rossman had not exaggerated. Rennie Davis was a leading, indeed near-legendary, anti-war activist and Movement organizer. He was one of the Chicago Eight, a group put on trial for their role in the anti-war protests at the 1968 Democratic Party convention. In 1973 Davis announced that he had received Knowledge from the fifteen-year-old guru Maharaj Ji, the 'Perfect Master' whose chubby, smiling image suddenly was everywhere, and whose devotees seemed to be in a permanent state of bliss. Two months after his conversion, Davis spoke in Berkeley's Pauley Ballroom, where over the previous decade so many debates had taken place on the vital issues of Free Speech on the Berkeley campus, the war in Vietnam, and strategies for pursuing radical politics. Davis told the meeting that the Perfect Master was going to bring perfection on earth right now, in three years – to America this year, then to China (where Chairman Mao, it was said, may already have received Knowledge from Maharaj Ji), and after that to the entire world.[47] Rossman explains it as a flight from the painful reality of the disintegration of the Movement after the shock of the killing of student protesters at Kent State University:

> . . . by the time of Kent State, whatever organizational focus the Movement once had had fallen apart and the loose common myth that guided the investment of our energies in political change was dissolving . . . Yoga, encounter groups, life in the country, Dianetics, free schools, McGovernism, Jesus – a multitude of devotional ideologies appeared to sap the energies of political expression, lulling weary activists and hypnotizing the young with blissful panaceas, away from dealing with an increasingly problematic social reality.[48]

Jerry Rubin, a former leader of the zany radical group known as Yippies, carried the trend to an extreme:

> In five years from 1971 to 1975 I directly experienced est, gestalt therapy, bioenergetics, rolfing, massage, jogging, health foods, tai chi, Esalen, hypnotism, modern dance, meditation, Silva Mind Control, Arica, acupuncture, sex therapy, Reichian

therapy, and More House – a smorgasbord course in New Consciousness.[49]

The Movement had now become the 'human potential movement'. The flood of people attempting to create a better society was sucked up into the sands of millions of individual attempts to create a better self.

In the end, even Rubin tired of it. Early in the eighties, to the delight of all those who had lacked his commitment in the first place, Rubin started work on Wall Street. It seemed to be the end of a cycle that had begun more than two decades previously: 'From Freedom Train to Gravy Train', one story was headed; or 'From "J'accuse" to Jacuzzi' as another writer put it.[50] In going to Wall Street, of all places, Rubin showed himself, again, to be sensitive to the swings of fashion. For Wall Street was about to become the symbol of the eighties. Greed was about to reassert itself, and become good.

The Reagan years: 'Enrich thyself'

Here is Kitty Kelley's description of Ronald Reagan's inauguration celebrations:

> Hordes of Ronald Reagan's wealthy supporters . . . displayed what was to become the hallmark of the Reagan era: bright, shiny, new, noisy wealth that is most often seen in long limousines, rustling furs, ornate gowns and jewels the size of cow pats. Their celebration continued during the four days and 103 parties of the inaugural.[51]

After the parties came the china. Although the White House contained 10,000 pieces of china when the Reagans moved in, Nancy Reagan decided to order 220 new place settings of seven different styles of plate each, plus finger bowls, ramekins and more, with a 24-carat gold seal in the middle of each plate. The acquisition of $209,508 worth of china for the White House might not have attracted much attention, had the First Lady not announced it on the day that her husband released his administration's decision that, as a cost-saving measure, ketchup would be counted as a vegetable in the federally subsidized school lunch program.[52]

Time, usually no great enemy of the rich, described the Reagan Administration as one 'whose clarion call is: "Enrich thyself"', and noted that Reagan made it clear that he regarded money as the measure of achievement. Accordingly, he preferred the company of the wealthy. Among these was the multimillionaire businessman Justin Dart, a member of Reagan's 'kitchen cabinet'. Strictly speaking, it is Dart, rather than Ivan Boesky, who deserves the credit for kicking off the 'greed is good' theme that typified the eighties. Said Dart, in a 1982 interview in the *Los Angeles Times*: 'Greed is involved in everything we do. I find no fault with that'.[53]

This was also the decade in which Christianity completed its long journey from a religion that despised material wealth to one that cherished it. L. Ron Hubbard, the founder of the Church of Scientology, once wrote that the quickest way to make a million in America is to start a new religion.[54] But refurbishing an old one seemed to do just as well. Jerry Falwell, then pastor of the Thomas Road Baptist Church in Lynchburg, Virginia, and president of the pro-Reagan Moral Majority, wrote a pamphlet on the Christian foundations of capitalism, in which he reiterated the Calvinist theme that money is a sign of God's grace. Perhaps for that reason, Falwell paid himself an annual salary of $100,000, in addition to the money he earned from perhaps a dozen speaking engagements a year at $5,000 each.[55] Falwell was, however, a man of modest tastes by the standards of some of his rivals. In 1987, *Time* investigated the finances of the most successful American television evangelists of the decade.[56] It found that the Louisiana preacher Jimmy Swaggart ran a ministry that was like a family business, with seventeen members of his family on the payroll. Jimmy and his wife borrowed $2 million from the ministry to build three luxurious homes, and drove two Lincoln Town Cars. Robert Schuller, who broadcast his *Hour of Power* every week from the $20 million Crystal Cathedral in Garden Grove, California, was paid $86,000 plus a tax-exempt housing allowance of $43,500; eight members of his family were on the payroll of Robert Schuller Ministries. Oral Roberts, another popular 'televangelist' had the use of two houses worth $2.9 million, and owned another worth over half a million. But if money was a sign of God's grace, Jim Bakker was, until adultery with a secretary led to his downfall, the most bountifully blessed of them all. According to the Internal Revenue Service, Bakker earned $638,112 in 1983; he owned six luxurious homes and had bathroom taps plated with gold.

The astonishing part of all this is that the more these purportedly Christian evangelists flaunted their wealth, the more Americans flocked to them. That, more than anything, indicates how far the American love affair with wealth and with wealthy celebrities had gone. Nor was this positive attitude to wealthy religious leaders limited to Christians. Bhagwan Shree Rajneesh, the Indian guru whose followers were known as the Orange People after the colourful robes they wore, showed that religious leaders who drew on the traditions of the East could easily adapt to the America of the eighties. Rajneesh collected Rolls-Royces the way children collect Matchbox cars. In 1983, he had twenty-one; by December 1985, when Rajneesh had been deported and his property was being sold to pay off debts, there were ninety-three of them.[57]

Every aspect of culture joined in the chorus in praise of the pursuit of wealth. Madonna sang that she was just a 'material girl' and Cyndi Lauper had a hit with 'Money Changes Everything'. If there was any satirical intent in either of these pop songs, it surely escaped many of those who danced to them. Even New York's Metropolitan Museum of Art became more innovative in raising money, sending a letter to corporations suggesting that art can be profitable:

> Learn how you can provide creative and cost-effective answers to your marketing objectives by identifying your corporate names with Vincent Van Gogh . . . Canaletto . . . Fragonard, Rembrandt or Goya . . .[58]

In the same year, the museum let it be known that it was for hire. For a fee of $30,000, one could throw a party in the Great Hall, or even in the lofty space surrounding the Temple of Dendur, which the Egyptian Government had shipped to America as a way of saying thanks to the American people for their assistance in saving Abu Simbel from the waters of the Aswan Dam. Parties there became so common that one gossip columnist took to referring to the museum as 'Club Met'. The wedding of Laura Steinberg, daughter of financier Saul Steinberg, and Jonathan Tisch, son of Laurence Tisch, chief executive of CBS, was celebrated in the museum, which had been festooned with 50,000 French roses, gold-dipped magnolia leaves, a hand-painted dance floor, and a ten-feet-high wedding cake. The night's festivities cost $3 million.[59]

For those who had ethical qualms about such expenditure while welfare programs were being cut, the wealthy supporters of Ronald Reagan had their answer in George Gilder's much-acclaimed *Wealth and Poverty*. Gilder lauds the wealthy while arguing that welfare harms the poor. 'In order to succeed', Gilder wrote, 'the poor need most of all the spur of their poverty'.[60] In his preface, Gilder thanks David and Peggy Rockefeller for their generosity and faith in his work. In the body of his book, he repays their generosity by hailing the wealthy as the 'greatest benefactors' of society. In an updated version of Adam Smith's 'the humblest peasant lives better than a King in Africa' argument, Gilder and other supporters of 'Reaganomics' asserted that the wealth made by the super-rich in the eighties was bound to benefit the whole of society, and trickle down even to the poor. Not until Reagan had gone and the decade was over did detailed economic statistics explode this assumption. Using figures released by the Congressional Budget Office, Paul Krugman, an economist at the Massachusetts Institute of Technology, calculated that 60 percent of the growth in the average after-tax income of all American families between 1977 and 1989 went to the richest 1 percent of families. (These families had an average annual income of at least $310,000 a year, for a household of four.) Another 34 percent went to families whose incomes were in the top 20 percent, leaving only 6 percent of the total growth in income to be divided between the remaining 80 percent of the population. Krugman's calculations were challenged. Critics noted that tax rates had been lowered during the Reagan years; therefore, they said, the rich may have become more honest in reporting their income. That is possible, of course, but it hardly seems likely to account for more than a small portion of the increase, because the figures show that corporate salaries to chief executives – which cannot be concealed from the tax authorities – soared during the decade. Even among the critics, there is general agreement that the top 1 percent had done better during the 1980s than the rest of the nation, and that by the end of the decade, the 2.5 million Americans at the top of the income scale were taking in as much each year as the 100 million Americans at the bottom. This was not true of the beginning of the decade.[61]

The eighties were to be the decade in which greed overcame its unfortunate bad odour, and was openly rehabilitated as a civic virtue that made everyone better off. It didn't turn out like that. By the early nineties, the giants of Wall Street – men like Ivan Boesky and Michael Milken – had been sent to gaol. Donald Trump was selling off his assets and negotiating with his creditors to stay afloat. Alan Bond was bankrupt, *Irises* long sold. And then it became clear that the wealth of the rich remained concentrated among the rich, after all. Suddenly greed did not look so good. But the alternative ideals of Aristotle or the pre-reformation Church were now buried deep under centuries of teachings that tied the good life closely with wealth and acquisition. From where could an alternative ideal of the good life emerge?

CHAPTER 5

Is selfishness in our genes?

The biological case for selfishness

A true 'it fell off the back of a truck' story occurred some years ago
in the United States when a man of limited means found a sack of
money that had fallen from a Brinks truck. He returned the money
to Brinks, who had not yet even discovered the loss. The media
made him a hero – but he received scores of letters and phonecalls
telling him that he was a fool, and should look out for himself in the
future.[1]

This story illustrates how far our society has gone towards the
twin assumptions that 'looking out for number one' is the only sensible thing to do, and getting more money is the way to do it. If we
accept these assumptions, we are not making the ultimate choice
about how we are to live. Our culture makes it for us. It limits the
range of possible ways of living that seem to be worth taking
seriously.

The story also suggests one reason why some people hesitate to
do what they know to be right, if they can get more money, or
something else they want, by doing what they know to be wrong.
Absurd as it may sound, they don't want to do what is right because
they think that by doing so they will look bad in the eyes of their

friends. Their worry is not, of course, about looking morally bad, but about looking stupid. Behind this response lies the idea that ethics is some kind of fraud. Since, according to this line of thinking, everyone – or almost everyone – *does* put herself or himself first, and this includes those who keep preaching to us about ethics and self-sacrifice, you'd have to be a fool not to do the same.

In an earlier book called *The Expanding Circle*, I discussed the view that no-one ever acts ethically. There I suggested that every blood donor who gives blood to strangers without any reward beyond an indifferent cup of tea and a biscuit redeems human nature from the denigration of its cynical critics. For this simple claim I was severely taken to task by Richard Alexander, professor of evolutionary biology at the University of Michigan, and one of the leading biologists writing about morality. According to Alexander, I had been led astray by my 'commonsense' assumption that people who give blood do so in order to help others. This appeal to commonsense, Alexander sternly informed his readers, fails to take into account 'well established biological facts and theories' and ignores 'the probability that what one thinks is the reason behind one's act may not convey its real significance'.[2]

Is there really something in our biological nature that compels us to be selfish? Is this the biological equivalent of Original Sin? When eminent biologists say that established biological facts show the impossibility of genuine altruism, are they right? How serious is the threat from established biological theories to our commonsense belief in the possibility of living unselfishly? This and the following two chapters of this book examine the constraints our biological nature really does – or does not – impose on our ultimate choice.

Here, in popular form, is the gist of the biological argument that leads many to think that selfishness is inevitable:

> Modern human beings are the outcome of a long and unceasing evolutionary struggle. In that struggle some individuals succeed in feeding themselves and surviving long enough to reproduce. Others do not. Those who succeed pass their genes on to the next generation; the genes of those who lose are extinguished from the population. Egoists who act first and foremost in their

own interests stand a better chance of winning than altruists, who put helping others to win ahead of maximizing their own chances of winning. Since traits like selfishness are at least in part determined by our genes, this means that the number of egoists will grow and the number of altruists will shrink. In the long run – and evolution has already had a very long run indeed – there will be no true altruists at all.

This is not a quotation; it is a distillation of a strand of thought that can be found in many books and popular articles, as well as in general conversation and letters to the editors of newspapers. It has scientific supporters like Richard Alexander. Edward O. Wilson, founding father of the field of sociobiology (which studies the biological basis of social behaviour in humans and other animals), has also denied the possibility of pure altruism. Confronted with the example of Mother Teresa's lifelong dedication to the sick and dying street people of Calcutta, he pointed out that she is a Christian, and therefore presumably believes that she will receive her reward in heaven.[3] Another sociobiologist, Pierre van den Berghe, has said flatly: 'We are programmed to care only about ourselves and our relatives'.[4] Garrett Hardin, an American professor with a background in the biological sciences, has gone even further, suggesting that social institutions and public policies should be based on 'an unwavering adherence to the Cardinal Rule: *Never ask a person to act against his own self-interest*'.[5]

It is, of course, true that humans have evolved from other animals. We are apes. We share 98.6 percent of our genes with chimpanzees. Genetically, we are closer to chimpanzees than chimpanzees are to orang-utans. Human beings and chimpanzees evolved from a common ancestor by a process of natural selection, sometimes called 'the survival of the fittest'. But if this phrase conjures up images of 'nature red in tooth and claw', those images should be put aside. The 'fittest' simply means, in evolutionary theory, those who are best equipped to have offspring who will themselves survive and reproduce. Together with other apes, and primates more generally, humans are social mammals. Social mammals live in groups, and care for their young. That is how they manage, not always but often, to leave descendants when they die.

Among the social mammals, it is relatively easy to find examples of animal behaviour that are anything but selfish. Perhaps the most famous – because it has sometimes been directed at humans – is the way in which dolphins help injured members of their group to survive. Dolphins need to come to the surface of the water to breathe. If a dolphin is so badly wounded that it cannot swim to the surface by itself, other dolphins will group themselves around their wounded companion, pushing it upward to the air. If necessary, they will do this for many hours. Social animals also share. Wolves and wild dogs bring meat back to members of the pack who were not in on the kill. Chimpanzees lead each other to trees that have ripe fruit. When a whole group of chimpanzees is at a good tree, they make a loud booming noise that attracts other chimpanzees up to a kilometre away. Social animals warn each other of danger. When hawks fly overhead, blackbirds and thrushes give warning calls, helping other members of the flock to escape, but perhaps at some risk of attracting the hawk to themselves. An even more remarkable case is that of Thomson's gazelle, a small species of antelope that is hunted by packs of African wild dogs. When a gazelle notices a dog pack, it bounds away in a curious stiff-legged gait known as 'stotting'. This appears to be a warning signal; every other gazelle immediately flees. But stotting is a slower gait than normal running, so the stotting gazelle gives up some precious ground in order to warn others of the danger.[6]

When animals do fight with other members of their species, they will often appear to obey rules, much like the ethical rules of combat adopted by medieval knights. When one wolf gets the better of another, the beaten wolf makes a submissive gesture, exposing the soft underside of its neck to the fangs of the victor. Instead of taking the opportunity to rip out the jugular veins of his or her foe, the conquering wolf trots off, content with the symbolic victory.[7] From a purely selfish point of view, such noble conduct seems foolish. Why let the beaten enemy live to fight another day? Could the answer lie in something larger than the interests of the victorious wolf?

In short, it is a mistake to view nature as a life and death struggle in which those who worry only about their own food, safety and sexual satisfaction are bound to eliminate the others. This is not what biology and evolutionary theory tell us. The landscape we must traverse in order to survive and pass on our genes is much more complex than that represented in the crude sketch given above; or to put it another way, there is more to life, and more to passing on our genes, than eating and copulating. In this chapter, I shall give three reasons why we are not biologically determined to think and act in the narrowly selfish way that the popular view suggests; a fourth, more complex reason, receives separate treatment in Chapter 7, and I put forward a more speculative fifth reason in the final chapter.

Caring for our children

Dimity Reed is an architect and writer who lives in Melbourne, not far from where I live. She is also the mother of Josh. At nineteen, Josh became seriously ill. The diagnosis was kidney failure. He went on dialysis, but over the next three years, his health gradually deteriorated. He was on a waiting list for a transplant; so, however, were many others whose condition was just as bad or worse. After Josh graduated from university his uncertain health caused him to miss out on a job he wanted. Dimity had read somewhere that parents may be able to donate kidneys to a child. She suggested the possibility to Josh's doctor. He told her that while she could live in good health with one remaining kidney, if something were to happen to it, she could die. She replied: 'We're a family of optimists'. That was three years ago. Dimity and Josh now have one healthy kidney each.[8]

Renuka Natarajan lives in the village of Villivakam, near Madras, in India. Renuka is a mother who, like Dimity Reed, has given up her kidney to help her child. But Renuka's child did not have kidney disease. She and her husband had no work. They had debts, and they were worried that, without a dowry, their daughter would be unable to marry. Renuka's husband saw an advertisement in the local newspapers offering about $1,500 for a kidney. That was the equivalent of about eight year's wages for an Indian villager. Renuka sold the kidney, paid off some debts, and set aside some money for her daughter's dowry. But her operation did not go well. She was in pain afterwards, and had to spend some of the money she had been paid on further medical treatment.[9]

These two stories come from worlds that are far apart, culturally, economically and geographically; but they reveal the same readiness of a mother to make a significant sacrifice for a child. There is nothing in such stories to surprise any evolutionary biologist. We do not pass on our genes simply by spreading our seeds and leaving the resulting offspring to fend for themselves as best they can. Having children is only the first step. If our genes are to survive, our children must themselves live long enough to have their own children, who must in turn have children, and so on. Immediately, therefore, we can see that we must care for one very significant group of other beings: our children. Not every parent would undergo a major operation and give up a kidney for a child, but the fact that some do indicates the extent to which caring for our children can lead us to act unselfishly, for the good of another person.

That people often put the interests of their children ahead of their own interests is something we take for granted. We notice it only in extreme cases, like those of Dimity and Renuka, or in the opposite cases, when parents abandon or neglect their children. The love of parents for their children is so basic to human nature that when people occasionally behave in aberrant ways that show neglect or lack of concern for their children, we fail to comprehend how a mother or father can lack something that is so natural to us. We will be satisfied only if we can find an explanation as to why they are missing something that the rest of us take for granted – and the explanation is itself often in terms of a deprived childhood, thus testifying once again to the importance we place on family life for both the parents and the children. We are (and were, even in more puritanical times) more ready to pardon mothers who resort to prostitution to feed their children, than mothers who neglect or abandon them.

Around the turn of the century, Edward Westermarck gathered all the information he could find on the ethical systems of different societies into a bulky two-volume work called *The Origin and Development of the Moral Ideas*. In this he points out that a mother's duty to look after her children has seemed so obvious that most anthropological accounts scarcely bother to mention it. What of a father's duty to look after his children? Although Westermarck says that the duty of a married man to support and protect his family is as widely recognized as that of a mother to care for her children, he does not say that the father's duty is taken for granted, as he does in the case of a mother's duty to her children. Evolutionary theory gives grounds for believing that mothers might generally be more prepared to make sacrifices for their children than fathers. First, mothers can be sure that the children for whom they care are indeed their genetic children; fathers often cannot. Second, barring multiple births, or the application of modern reproductive technology of the kind now used with prize cows, women are limited in the number of children they can have to an absolute maximum of one every nine months between the ages of approximately thirteen and forty-five (or possibly just a few more, since she may have some twins or other multiple births). There is no obvious physical limit to the number of children a man can have. Thus men might leave more descendants if they spread their seed widely and give no support to their offspring. Some of the mothers could succeed in rearing the children alone or with the support of other males. (I am not, of course, suggesting that males consciously pursue this strategy in order to have more children; only that this pattern of behaviour, among males, could be passed on to future generations of male descendants.)

On the other hand, a woman who abandoned her children without caring for them would be much less likely to have descendants with a similar pattern of behaviour. In addition to women's inability to produce as many children as a male, more of her children would die, because, until very recently, infants needed to be breast-fed to survive. The biological facts of pregnancy mean that a woman necessarily has a larger investment of time and energy in each child than the father of the child need have.

Nevertheless, that fathers do care for their children is undeniable. David Gilmore, a comparative anthropologist, studied a wide range of societies in order to discover if there are any universal traits which are regarded as 'manly'. He found that having children, and providing for and protecting one's family, are universally respected in a man.[10] In general, then, we can speak of parental care, and not only maternal care.

The readiness of parents to put the interests of their children ahead of their own interests is a striking counter-example to the general thesis that people are selfish. When parents comfort a crying baby, they are not doing it because they are thinking of the time, twenty or thirty years ahead, when the child may be able to support them in their old age. They are responding directly from their love for the baby and their empathy with the picture of misery that a crying baby presents – especially when it is *your* crying baby. To provide comforts for their children, parents go without things that they need. If necessary, to see that their children are well-fed, well-clothed and well-educated, parents go without the holiday they would like to take or the new car they would like to drive. 'I always wanted the best for you', they say in explanation to their children, and it is usually true. In many countries, prudent people take out life insurance so that their families will have some money if they should die. Paying an annual premium means that they have less money to spend now than they would otherwise have. There is nothing odd about that – except that they are not being 'prudent' for themselves at all. This very common precaution makes sense only on the assumption that we care for the welfare of at least one other being.

To be effective parents we must be able to understand what our children need, and we must want to give them what they need. I may have just eaten a large meal; the thought of eating more makes me ill; but if I find that my child is hungry, I will try to get some more food. This is the first step beyond egoism. The nineteenth century British philosopher John Stuart Mill described the family as 'a school of sympathy, tenderness and loving forgetfulness of self'.[11] The full story is not quite so simple, but the importance of sympathy, tenderness and loving forgetfulness of self in the family is, in one sense, exactly what biological theories tell us to expect. Biologists, however, will only classify an action as altruistic or unselfish if it reduces one's 'reproductive fitness' – that is, one's prospects of leaving descendants. Hence they often fail to acknowledge that what happens between parents and children is a step beyond egoism at all.

Caring for our kin

It is easy to understand that:

(a) evolution is a matter of passing on our genes to the next generation; and

(b) one way of passing on our genes is to have children, and do our best to ensure that our children survive.

It is not so obvious that there are other ways of acting that will also increase the survival of our genes in the next generation – in particular, that:

(c) we can increase the number of our genes that exist in the next generation by doing our best to ensure the survival of brothers, sisters, nieces, nephews and other relatives who share many of their genes with us.

One reason why some people do not see this is that the genes that survive when our relatives pass on their genes are genes *like* ours, that is they are other sets of genes similar to ours, rather than *our* genes. But then, the genes that we pass on through our own sperm or eggs are also just one set of genes that are like the genes from which we ourselves developed. If we think of genes as sets of instructions, like software programs, rather than as the physical forms in which these sets of instructions are written down, we should be able to see that it makes no difference to the survival of my genes whether the genes pass through my body, or through the body of another who carries similar genes.

Of course, passing on genes is not like copying software on a computer, because computers make exact copies, while heterosexual reproduction mixes in new genes and leaves out old ones. That is why we are all different. The relevance of this fact is nicely put by a story about J. B. S. Haldane, a noted British biologist who died in 1964. In a casual conversation over a drink, someone asked Haldane whether, as an evolutionary biologist, he could ever lay down his life for his brother. After a quick calculation he replied that he would lay down his life for two brothers or sisters, four nephews or nieces, or eight first cousins.

The basis for this peculiarly measured form of heroism is the degree of relationship between us and our kin, or, to be more specific, the percentage of our genes that we share with them. My sisters and brothers will, on average, have 50 percent of my genes, since, like me, they have half of my mother's and half of my father's genes. (The figure is an average one. Depending on how the genetic lottery falls out, brothers and sisters could have all or none of their genes in common – but given the very large number of genes involved, either extreme is wildly improbable.) I share 25 percent of my genes with my nieces and nephews, and 12.5 percent with my first cousins. Haldane's witty response reflects these ratios; the exchange of his life for eight of his first cousins would not result in any loss of his genes from the population. So saving the lives of my kin will, to a degree that corresponds to the closeness of the genetic relationship, increase the chances of genes like mine surviving.

Here we can find a genetic basis for an extension of altruism beyond our own children. In the evolutionary struggle for 'survival of the fittest', a gene or group of genes that increases the likelihood that I will save the lives of my close kin, if I have the opportunity to do so, will make my genotype (the total set of genes that I carry in my body) more 'fit' to survive than my genotype would be if it lacked that gene or group of genes. So a genetic tendency for helping one's kin is likely to spread through the population. Of course – as Haldane well knew – we are not really interested in spreading our genes, as such. That is why his calculations amuse us. But that in no way refutes the suggestion that we are motivated to protect and help our kin, to a degree that varies roughly in proportion to the degree of kinship. We should never fall into the trap of thinking that a biological explanation of why we do what we do can only be valid if we are conscious of, and motivated by, the biological significance of our actions. Just as our desire for sex arises immediately from the love or sexual attraction we feel for our sexual partners and not from any wish to have children with them, so we may help our kin because we love and care for them, not because we want our genes to spread. But in both cases the feelings that motivate our actions have spread because genes that lead us to act in this way are more likely to leave copies of themselves in the next generation than genes that do not lead us to act in this way.

Human ethical systems map the biology of kinship with remarkable accuracy. In *The Methods of Ethics* Henry Sidgwick set out the duty of benevolence, as it was generally understood in Victorian England. He begins the list by saying:

> We should all agree that each of us is bound to show kindness to his parents and spouse and children, and to other kinsmen in a less degree; and to those who have rendered services to him, and any others whom he may have admitted to his intimacy and called friends; and to neighbours and to fellow-countrymen more than others . . .

That the first duties of benevolence are to our kin is not peculiar to Sidgwick's culture. In his *Origin and Development of the Moral Ideas*, Westermarck gives an account of the duties that are accepted by every society, or virtually every society. It closely follows Sidgwick's list of the degrees of the duty of benevolence. It places duties to parents alongside those to children and wives; then comes the duty to help a brother or sister. Duties to aid more distant relatives vary more widely between societies, but they are still prominent. More modern anthropological accounts agree on the absolute centrality of kinship in ethical, social and political life. As Marshall Sahlins, a leading anthropologist and no friend of the sociobiological view of society has said: 'Kinship is the dominant structure of many of the peoples anthropologists have studied, the prevailing code not only in the domestic sphere but generally of economic, political and ritual action'.

Though its precise form varies, the family seems an inescapable part of our lives. It satisfies desires for closeness and intimacy that are impossible to satisfy in any other way. A network of family and kin can also be a powerful aid to survival. Donald Grayson, an anthropologist at the University of Washington, Seattle, studied the survival of members of one of the most famous tragedies of the nineteenth century pioneers of the American West, the ill-fated Donner party. In 1847 George and Jakob Donner led a party of eighty-seven overlanders across Utah and Nevada, heading for California via a little-known route through the mountains. Delayed by trivial problems in setting out, the party was then trapped by heavy October snowfalls in the midst of the Sierra Nevada mountains. Most of the group passed the winter in the mountains, eating all their provisions, then their draught animals, and their pets, and finally, those of their party who had died. (Suspicion surrounds the cause of death of some of those who were eaten.) When rescue came with the melting of the snows in April, there were forty-seven survivors. Grayson found that the survivors tended to be members of large kinship groups. All the women in the party were members of such groups, and 70 percent of the women survived. Among men the survival rate was only 43 percent, and those who lived had an average of 4.6 relatives in the party, compared with 2.1 for those who died. Of the fifteen males with no relatives at all, only two survived. In these extreme conditions, large groups shared food and water and provided care for weaker members of the group; they also provided emotional support and, Grayson speculates, helped to sustain the will to live.[12]

While virtually all human societies place the ethical obligation to look after one's own children ahead of obligations to strangers, some philosophers and social reformers have challenged the ethical propriety of our attachment to the family. They have seen the family as a means of passing on inherited advantage, and as a bastion of conservative ideas of all kinds. The family is, therefore, a barrier to the creation of a more egalitarian society. Plato was one of the family's early critics; in the *Republic* he proposes that among the Guardians who will rule the community, family units should be replaced by communal marriage. In this way the Guardians would be 'all of one opinion about what is near and dear to them', and so would work collectively for the common good.[13]

Plato was unable to translate his proposal into reality. The Jewish form of socialism that led to the establishment of the *kibbutzim*, or collective settlements, that now exist in Israel, had the opportunity to put its opposition to the family into practice. Believing that deep attachment to spouse and children would interfere with loyalty to the kibbutz as a whole, the early pioneers of the movement brought up all children communally, in a separate house from their parents. Eating and entertainment were communal activities. Parents were not supposed to show more affection towards, or spend more time with, their own children than other children of the kibbutz. Childen were encouraged to call their parents by their first names, rather than 'father' or 'mother'. For a time these communal ways of living were seen as a model of voluntary socialism, and to some extent they still are. Yet, as far as the family is concerned, the kibbutz has succeeded only in demonstrating the strength and resilience of family ties. Gradually the kibbutz has had to accommodate itself to the demands of parents to spend more time with their children. In modern Israeli kibbutzim, children may sleep and eat from time to time in their parents' unit rather than in the children's house; and they have resumed calling their parents 'father' and 'mother'.[14]

This theme of the attempted suppression and resurgence of the family has been replayed many times: in idealistic religious communities in nineteenth century America, after the Russian revolution of 1917, among the hippy communes and 'intentional societies' that grew out of the alternative movement of the sixties and seventies. That the family always survives does not in itself prove that the family is an ethically desirable institution, but it does call into question the wisdom of any plans for social reform that do not take the strength of the family into account. Moreover, while parents' preferences for their own children undeniably do support continuing inequalities of wealth and educational advantage, the idea that parents have a duty to look after the needs of their children has a solid ethical basis. For if parents do not look after their own children, who will? A modern state could allocate children to professional child-minders, but financial incentives are no substitute for a mother's or father's care and affection. In the absence of any alternative likely to work better, there is a lot to be said for encouraging parents to take responsibility for the welfare of their own children.

Thus in the case of parental care for children, ethics and biology are, at least to a degree, in harmony. But only to a degree. As with almost every desire, a parent's wish to see a child do well can be pushed too far. Wanda Holloway, a mother living in a small town in Texas, wanted her thirteen-year-old daughter Shanna to be elected to the seventh grade position on the local football cheerleading team. But another girl, Amber Heath, won the election. The following year, Shanna and Amber were again rivals for the coveted position. This time Wanda Holloway decided to give her daughter an advantage. She contacted a man she knew had a criminal record, and asked him how much she would have to pay him to murder both Amber Heath and her mother. Fortunately, the convicted criminal was still capable of being shocked. He told the police, no-one was murdered, and Wanda Holloway received a sentence of fifteen years in gaol. In an interview, the police officer to whom the scheme was reported made an interesting comment. Saying that in his seventeen years as an undercover officer he had never seen a murder-for-hire scheme with such a frivolous motive, he added: 'In ten years time, what difference would it make if she was a cheerleader? It wasn't like this was over a Rhodes scholarship'. Was the officer suggesting that he could well have understood a mother commissioning a murder to ensure that her daughter got a Rhodes scholarship?[15]

What of obligations between other kin: of children to their parents, for example, or between brothers and sisters, or cousins? The obligation of grown-up children to support their parents is perhaps a special case. It does not fit so neatly within evolutionary theory, since the parents of adult children are usually past the period at which they are likely to have further offspring. Perhaps for that reason it is also less universally accepted, especially when families are no longer living together. Where it is recognized, it seems in part an obligation of kinship, and in part one of gratitude. No doubt reasons for encouraging gratitude, which I will discuss in Chapter 6, spill over into our thinking about the obligations of children to support their parents. Obligations to help siblings and more distant kin, on the other hand, seem to be proportionately weaker variants of the obligations of parents to support their children. They rely on similar natural ties of affection, and, from a broad social perspective, can be defended as a system of insurance against hardship that is secured by natural ties rather than an impersonal bureaucracy.

Caring for our group

One popular view of evolution is that it favours the development of characteristics that are 'for the good of the species'. Since this approach seems to offer a very simple way of explaining why we are not all selfish, readers may wonder why I have been labouring so mightily over something that can be explained so much more easily. It is important to see why this explanation will not work.

The flaw in this explanation for the evolution of morality has nothing to do with morality in particular. It is a defect in all attempts to explain something as having evolved because it is 'for the good of the species'. Here is an illustration. As part of a BBC series on endangered animals, Douglas Adams, author of *The Hitchhiker's Guide to the Galaxy*, travelled with Mark Carwardine, a zoologist, to New Zealand to look for one of the rarest species on the planet, a ground-dwelling parrot called the kakapo. The birds used to have no predators; now introduced animals like stoats and cats have run wild, and the kakapo is believed to be extinct on the main islands. The New Zealand Department of Conservation has established colonies on two small islands, and is hoping that the kakapo will multiply there. But one conservation officer tells Adams and Carwardine:

> It's so difficult getting the blighters to breed. In the past they bred very slowly because there was nothing else to keep their population stable. If an animal population rises so fast that it outgrows the capacity of its habitat to feed and sustain it, then it plunges right back down again, then back up, back down, and so on. If a population fluctuates too wildly, it doesn't take much of a disaster to tip the species over the edge into extinction. So all the kakapo's peculiar mating habits are just a survival technique as much as anything else.[16]

The conservation officer has offered an 'altruistic' explanation for the low breeding rate of the kakapo. He does not, presumably, think that individual kakapos breed slowly because they are conscious of the need to do so for the good of the species, but he does try to explain their slow breeding by saying that, in the absence of predators, this worked for the good of the species as a whole. This sounds plausible, but the plausibility evaporates once we think about how this trait of slow breeding might survive in a population. Suppose that, in a population of kakapos who breed very slowly, a random mutation leads one kakapo to breed a little more rapidly, and to pass this characteristic of more rapid breeding on to her offspring. Would her offspring become more, or less, common in the overall population? Obviously, if there are no costs to the individual birds from their more rapid breeding, they would become more frequent, and tend to replace the slower breeding birds. So now, as the conservation officer says, the population expands more rapidly and outgrows the capacity of its habitat, and there is a population crash. What happens then? Do only more slowly-breeding birds survive? What would lead to that result? In the absence of any selection mechanism that can lead to this result, the cycle will just be repeated. It is hard to see how slower breeding could evolve within the species to stop that result, since the slower breeding birds will always be at a disadvantage compared to the faster breeding ones. J. Maynard Smith, an evolutionary theorist, introduced the term 'evolutionarily stable strategy' to refer to an inherited behavioural policy which, if adopted by most members of a population, cannot be bettered by any other such inherited behavioural policy. In other words, the pressures of evolution will penalize those members of the population who depart from the evolutionarily stable strategy. Clearly, in the situation of the kakapo as described by the Conservation officer, slow breeding is not an evolutionarily stable strategy; slow breeders will be displaced by rapid breeders. Maybe this will mean that, in the long run, the population will go through boom and bust cycles, and eventually, in one of them, will crash to the point of extinction. But if that is what happens, then it just happens, and there is neither an evolutionary mechanism, nor a hidden Protector of Endangered Species, that can stop it happening.[17]

Sadly, then, it seems unlikely that many of us come into the world with any inherited tendency to sacrifice our own interests, or those of our kin, for the good of all human beings. Though there are many exceptions, David Hume was not too far off the mark when he observed that 'there is no such passion in human minds as the love of mankind, merely as such, independent of personal qualities, of services, or of relation to ourself'.[18] In other words, most of us lack a general feeling of benevolence for the strangers we pass in the street. The reason for this may be that the unit – the species as a whole – is too large. Species come in and out of existence too slowly for selection *between* different species to play much of a role in evolution. In contrast, selection *within* the species, between smaller, isolated breeding groups, happens much more often. These smaller groups do compete with each other and, in comparison with species, are relatively short-lived. The countervailing pressures of selection at the level of the individual or the gene would still apply, but less effectively. In some circumstances, evolution might be able to select for characteristics that benefit the group.

Here, if we look around us, we can easily accept that there is a 'passion in human minds' of love for, or devotion to, the group. To see it in a (relatively) harmless form, we need only go to a football match. Australians are as enthusiastic about football as any nationality, and almost every Australian child grows up supporting a football team. It is an affliction to which I am not immune, and which I have been unable to shake off, even as I grow older and presumably wiser. I know that it makes no difference at all to the larger scheme of things if Hawthorn, the team I have supported since childhood, wins or loses. I can even see that, since Hawthorn has been remarkably successful over the past decade, it is positively good when they are beaten by teams that have languished for years at the bottom of the ladder. This, surely, must gladden the hearts of the supporters of those lowly teams more than it disappoints Hawthorn's supporters, surfeited as they are with victories. Yet, when I am part of a crowd of Hawthorn supporters during a final, I don't take this larger perspective.

In *The Evolution of Love*, Sydney Mellon refers to the extraordinary feelings of solidarity and 'group love' that we may experience when we come together in certain ways. He mentions singing Christmas carols as an example. Again, I know exactly what he means. Although I am firmly non-religious, and lack even a Christian family background, when I stand with the other parents at the Carol Night held by my children's school (in Australia, even state schools have a Carol Night) the effect of everyone singing together can lead to a strong emotional response that makes me feel the importance of being part of that community. The same effect can occur with school songs, or even the national anthem. Mellon thinks that the way in which these emotions are enhanced and intensified when shared with a mass of others suggests that the experience triggers a genetic component of our nature, developed in the course of our evolution as a social primate.[19]

If parental love, taken to an extreme, has its dangers in rare cases, these feelings of group devotion are much more deadly, and their consequences are of global significance. In the form of unrestrained patriotism and nationalism, they have been responsible for the greatest crimes human beings have committed. Dictators like Hitler have skilfully captured these psychological forces, stirring up hatred of the outsider in order to weld individuals to the group. If you doubt the power of these methods, see the film made by Leni Riefenstahl of the 1934 Nazi Party Rally at Nuremberg. Even now, knowing that we are looking back at the rise of the movement that brought about all the bloodshed of World War II, that led to the destruction of so much of Europe, and that made Auschwitz possible, it is difficult to resist being drawn in by the potent symbols, the pageantry, the stirring music and the sense of unity and purpose shown by the enthusiastic, parading Nazis. The emotions on which Hitler was playing are so powerful that they still can make us set aside, for a time, our knowledge of what it actually is that we are watching. No wonder that, when experienced at first hand and without the benefit of hindsight, they led people to be ready to sacrifice their own lives and the lives of countless others for the sake of the *Volk*.

Any estimate of the extent to which these feelings of national and group loyalty are genetically based would be pure speculation. Since the same people under different cultural conditions may vary markedly in the fervour of their nationalism – compare any Western European nation in the thirties with the same nation today – cultural pressures obviously play a very large role in the expression of these feelings, and probably also in the extent to which they are actually felt. Even if, as most evolutionary theorists believe, competition between large groups of unrelated beings is not likely to play a major role in genetic evolution, it can more easily be a factor in cultural evolution. When we extend the notion of evolution to include 'cultural evolution', we are thinking not only of the evolution of particular physical organisms and the genes that give rise to them, but also of the evolution of cultural variations – in other words, of ways of living. As different societies adopt different ways of living, so an evolutionary process will lead to some surviving and spreading, and others dying out.

Cultural evolution is distinct from genetic evolution in two important respects. First, cultural change can spread through a group very rapidly. This means that cultural change can have an effect on the behaviour of the whole group within a single generation, and can improve the group's chances of survival within that time-frame. Genetic change, on the other hand, takes many generations to spread through a group, and before it can have an effect on the behaviour of the group as a whole, it would be likely to be wiped out in the individuals in which it appears, because they will be at a competitive disadvantage *vis a vis* other members of the group.

Second, whereas genetic change is random and hence blind, cultural change can be conscious and directed. Because of this, culture alone has the ability to reduce or even reverse the individual competitive disadvantage of devotion to the group. To go to war for one's country is to risk death – a severe disadvantage in any terms – but a warrior culture will treat those who take the risk and survive as heroes and will give them special privileges. Those who refuse to risk death for the sake of the group will be shunned as cowards. During World War I, when the British army still relied on volunteers, girls would stand on the streets of London giving out white feathers to men of military age who were not in uniform. The reproductive advantages of volunteering were thus made clear. Some other cultures have made it clearer still. When Native Americans of the Great Plains like the Cheyenne and the Arapaho were engaged in war, some warriors would take a solemn vow that they would fight to the death. Once they had done this, the laws governing relations with the other sex (which in other circumstances were very strict) no longer applied to them. In the days leading up to the battle these 'suicide warriors' could make love to as many willing women as they wished.[20] It is possible that in that brief period they would conceive as many children as they would have had if they had lived a normal lifespan. In any case, the custom must have gone some way towards ensuring that the genes of these heroic warriors were carried on to future generations.

Cultural evolution can work in different ways. We have seen that Edward O. Wilson explained the apparently selfless dedication of Mother Teresa of Calcutta by pointing out that, as a believing Christian, she would expect to be rewarded in heaven. How Wilson knows that, for Mother Teresa, providing consolation and comfort for others is not its own reward, I have no idea. Whatever the truth about Mother Teresa may be, though, we should recognize that belief in the soul, and in reward and punishment in the afterlife, may be favoured by cultural evolution precisely because it fosters altruism in this world. (Why else, one could ask, are such implausible beliefs so widespread?) Seen from an evolutionary perspective the truth or falsity of a belief does not in itself determine whether the belief will spread. More crucial is whether the belief helps or harms the believer. Usually, when we talk of the believer, we mean the individual – but as we have seen, with cultural evolution the crucial unit can also be the group. Generally, to have false beliefs is a disadvantage. Those who believe that they can fly off cliffs or kill lions with their bare hands leave few descendants and do not make much contribution to their society either. But when most members of a group believe that to die in battle for the survival of the group is to go straight to a realm of eternal bliss, the group will be more formidable in war than other groups who can offer their soldiers no comparable spur to self-sacrifice. Paradoxically, even the soldiers who hold this false belief may be less likely to die in war than the soldiers of other societies that lack the belief; for armies made up of soldiers who fight without fear of dying are more likely to be victorious, and victorious armies suffer fewer casualties than those that they rout.[21]

I have focused on heroic sacrifices, like the readiness to die in war, only because they provide dramatic illustrations of commitment to the group. Everyday ethical life includes innumerable minor sacrifices for the community, from putting your litter in the appropriate bin to taking part in a working bee at your children's school. The reward is intangible: sometimes it is the camaraderie of working together for a good cause; often it is no more than the avoidance of social disapproval. In whatever way these actions are encouraged, they show concern for others. In the next chapter we shall see how in Japan many of these intangible rewards serve to reinforce loyalty to the group and thereby gain a significantly greater commitment from each individual than could be expected in the West. Perhaps in this respect Japan has evolved a culture more suited to international economic competition.

Such intangible rewards should not be seen as negating the altruistic motivation of the individual. Richard Alexander, whom we encountered at the beginning of this chapter, labels social approval 'indirect reciprocity' and then uses this label as a basis for rejecting the claim that blood donors are altruistic. Because donors may feel a sense of obligation to contribute to the community, or may be aware of social approval for what they are doing, Alexander thinks that they are giving blood for the sake of the indirect benefits that they receive. Apparently he would be convinced that blood donors are really altruistic only if they kept their donations secret. One wonders what he would say about Germans who secretly helped Jewish victims of Nazi persecution, and certainly could expect no social approval (for details of these heroic actions, see Chapter 8). But one need not wonder long, because Alexander goes on to accept a suggestion from one of his colleagues that even secret acts 'require further examination because of the possibility that by convincing themselves that they are selfless, private donors may become better able to convey an appearance of selflessness to others'.[22]

In taking this line, Alexander is using an old ploy. Thomas Hobbes, the seventeenth century author of *Leviathan*, was notorious among his contemporaries for his cynical view of human nature. Like Alexander, although without his knowledge of evolutionary theory, Hobbes held that we always act out of self-interest. Once a friend observed him giving money to a beggar and asked Hobbes if what he had just done did not refute his own theory of human motivation. Hobbes replied that he had given money to the beggar not because it helped the beggar, but because it made him, Hobbes, glad to see the pleasure that the beggar obtained from the gift. This reply, like Alexander's view of selfless action, turns what appeared to be a challenging new idea into an unfalsifiable and hence uninteresting piece of dogma. Both Hobbes's and Alexander's views of human motivation are, in the end, entirely compatible with the existence of all the altruism (in the ordinary sense of the term) that anyone would ever want to argue for. After all, who cares what the 'real significance' of this kind of altruism might be, when we are interested in understanding how people can be motivated to act ethically. If blood donors are motivated by a sense of obligation to the community, or an awareness of social approval, this does not mean that their actions are not ethical, or even altruistic. To act ethically and altruistically, in the morally significant senses of these terms, is, among other things, to be moved by a sense of obligation to the community, or a desire to do what will meet with the approval of those whose opinions one respects. It would be absurd to deny that an action is ethical merely because people who carry out the action may in fact gain from it, if they are not motivated by the prospect of personal gain – and even more absurd if they are not even aware of this prospect. If Alexander *really* thinks that the existence of a possible biological explanation for an action must always lead us to deny the reality of our conscious motivation, one can only wonder if, before he makes love, he explains to his partner that the 'real significance' of his sexual desire is that the genes that lead people to have this kind of desire are more likely to survive into later generations. The existence of a biological explanation for what we do is quite compatible with the existence of a very different motive in our own minds. Conscious motivations and biological explanations apply on different levels.

Human beings often are selfish, but our biology does not force us to be so. It leads us, on the contrary, to care for our offspring, our wider kin, and, in certain circumstances, for larger groups too. As we shall see in subsequent chapters, this is only the beginning.

CHAPTER 6

How the Japanese Live

Japan: A successful social experiment?

In Chapter 4, I traced the development of the dominant ideas of the good life in Western, and then specifically American, society. Although the modern consumer ethic is significantly different from the earlier, more Protestant ethic of accumulating wealth, it retains the focus of that ethic on oneself, or at most, oneself and one's immediate family. Self-interest remains something for which one must strive competitively, against others, and the goal remains narrowly egoistic. So it is important to ask: can we live differently? Could we really make a radical shift in a less individualistic and less competitive direction? The ancient Greeks had a different idea of self-interest to our own, and so did Europe in the Middle Ages. Nomadic tribes such as the Aboriginal Australians or the Kung of the Kalahari have very different views of what it is to live a good life – since they must carry everything they possess, acquiring material goods cannot play a major role in their lives. Yet, it will be said by the modern defenders of Adam Smith, these examples from history or from cultures that have been pushed to the margins of our lands do not in any way contradict the claim that a modern capitalist society cannot thrive unless individuals aggressively and competitively pursue their own interests.

It is this that makes Japan such a fascinating test case. For if one thing is clear about Japan in the post-war period, it is that its economy has been phenomenally successful. A cluster of densely populated islands has become the feared rival of the larger and more resource-rich economies of the United States and the European Community. In this chapter I shall ask whether Japan represents a possible alternative to the way in which most people in the West think about their ultimate choices. There are not many other alternative models left. State socialism in Russia and Eastern Europe failed to provide a viable alternative to American-style capitalism. As soon as the iron fist of military power and KGB terror was released, few wanted to retain that form of society. There has also been a considerable blurring, in recent years, of differences between the American model and the capitalist economies of Western Europe, even of those nations like Sweden that have had long periods of social democratic government. Japan now stands alone as the leading candidate for the role of a successful alternative model economy in the modern world.

But *is* Japan different? In visiting Japan, a Westerner finds familiar Japanese cars, cameras and electrical goods; but alongside there is often an uneasy feeling of not quite understanding what is going on. Japanese expectations of social behaviour and personal relationships, aesthetic style, music, theatre – all are either clearly different, or else there is an ambiguity about the extent to which they resemble parallel practices in the West. The feeling of being in a foreign place is much stronger than it is when, for instance, an Australian goes to France, or a German travels to the United States. Even among those who are fluently bilingual, attempts to translate anything beyond the immediately practical soon lead to difficulties, because the two languages encapsulate different sets of ideas. In the business world, too, the Japanese appear to be different. Scores of books have sought to explain Japan's economic success. It is a commonplace, for example, that the Japanese are much more committed to their employer than in the West, that they will work much longer hours, and make greater sacrifices of their personal and family life for the sake of the corporation for which they work. But are these differences merely a veneer over a fundamentally similar human nature? Or do they really point to distinct conceptions of self-interest and different hopes about what life may bring?

In this chapter I shall present a view of Japanese culture that highlights some of the distinctive aspects of the way in which individual and group interests are seen in that society. I do not claim that the picture that emerges covers all aspects of Japanese society, nor do I deny that there are conflicting tendencies that can provide evidence for an alternative view. The subject of this book is neither Western nor Japanese culture, but conceptions of self-interest and their relationship to ideas of ethics. This chapter will therefore serve its purpose if it captures one way in which people think about self-interest in Japan, even if that is not the only way in which it is regarded.[1]

The corporation as an ethical community

The Japanese 'salaryman' or white-collar worker is at work by 8.30 or 9.00 in the morning like his European or American counterpart, but works much later, often not getting home until 10.00 p.m.[2] In 1985 a Ministry of Labour survey found that workers used only about half the vacation time to which they were entitled, and most work part of the weekends. Staying at home for four full weekends a month was considered scandalous.[3] Thus one might see the Japanese as succeeding simply because they embrace a more extreme form of the Protestant work ethic than do the descendants of the New England Puritans. But the difference between the two societies goes deeper than that.

If we take a historical view of Japanese ideas, the most striking distinction between Japanese and Western society is that for us the feudal era lies in the remote past, whereas in Japan it is relatively recent. In medieval Europe, the great age of feudalism was from the eleventh to the fourteenth centuries. In this system lord and serf were bound together in a close tie. The serf was not a free man; he was bound to the land, and the land was his lord's. He had rights to farm the lord's land, but was bound to give the lord a share of the crop. The lord's castle was a place of refuge for the serf and his family in time of strife, but the serf had to serve in the lord's army. Under such a system each had his or her station in life, and duties, obligations and entitlements that corresponded to it. The sense of belonging to a community was strong, but freedom and autonomy in the modern sense were unknown. The key virtue was loyalty; the loyalty of the serf and of the knights to their lord, and the loyalty of the lord to his king, who was first among the feudal lords of the land. It is easy to see that such a society would give rise to character traits and ideals very different from those we hold today under the free enterprise system. But, throughout Western Europe, serfdom was disappearing by the end of the fourteenth century, replaced by a system of free tenants and landless labourers. Hence, for us in the West, feudalism lies buried under 500 years of constant political, economic and religious change. Individual freedom and rights were exciting new challenges in the seventeenth and eighteenth centuries; now they have become part of the background rhetoric of the Western political system. This applies to economic freedom as well as to political freedom: we can scarcely conceive of a world in which we do not freely move around, working with one employer for a time and then switching to another if a higher salary or better job is offered.

In Japan the feudal system developed in the thirteenth century, and continued unabated until Commodore Perry arrived, uninvited, in the Bay of Edo in 1853. Backed by iron-clad gunships, Perry forced the shogun, or chief feudal lord, to open up the country to trade with the outside world. This humiliation led, in 1868, to the overthrow of the shogun, and the restoration of the *tenno*. (This term is usually translated as Emperor, although the position hovers between that of a Western monarch and that of a high priest, in some respects like the Pope, or perhaps better, the Dalai Lama.) Although the Emperors had never been deposed, they had not been effective heads of government for more than a thousand years. Under the shoguns they had become virtual prisoners, confined to the court in Kyoto, and reduced to purely ritual functions. The 'Meiji restoration', as the dramatic event of 1868 was known, after the name of the restored Emperor, was carried out in the name of traditional Japanese values, and to 'drive out the barbarians'. Ironically, it marks the beginning of modern Japan. The new government realized that if Japan was to avoid the fate of nearby China (recently defeated by the Western powers in the infamous Opium War) it would have to modernize. Once this momentous decision had been reached, it was pursued with extraordinary determination. The government sent representatives to all the most advanced nations to study and bring back not only Western technology, but also Western forms of government, social institutions, and dress. Japan learnt Western ways with such speed and success that in forty years it was able to wage war with modern weapons and defeat Russia, one of the great Western powers.

The speed of this transformation means that there are people still living in Japan today who can recall grandparents who had lived their formative years in feudal times. A British eyewitness to these events wrote in 1908:

> To have lived through the transition stage of modern Japan makes a man feel preternaturally old; for here he is in modern times with the air full of talk about bicycles and bacilli and 'spheres of influence', and yet he can himself distinctly remember the Middle Ages.[4]

Changes made so quickly do not go deep; they can thrive only if they are grafted onto existing rootstock. Though one cannot deny the dramatic changes that have taken place in Japan during the last century and a quarter, it would be equally mistaken to deny the continuing relevance of feudal ideas and traditions.

If loyalty is the virtue most prized in any feudal system, the Japanese samurai, or warrior caste, carried the ideal of devotion to one's lord to an extreme. Japan's most popular story, 'The Tale of the Forty-seven Roshi' serves as an example of these ideals in practice. The roshi were samurai in the service of Asano, the feudal lord of a province. Asano had been insulted by another lord, Kira, and in a rage, stabbed Kira, slightly wounding him. For this, Asano was ordered by the shogun, or head of government, to commit ritual suicide, which he obediently did. His *roshi* or *ronin* (the terms refer to samurai who have lost their master) were indignant that Kira had not been punished for his part in the quarrel, as customary law demanded. They determined to avenge their lord by killing Kira. To disarm the suspicions that Kira would naturally hold, they dispersed for a year, drinking and carousing, so that they were generally held in contempt as disloyal retainers. Then they gathered secretly together, captured Kira's castle and beheaded him, placing his head on the grave of their lord Asano. For this, they had to pay the expected price: on the orders of the shogun, they all committed ritual suicide. This tale, told over and over again in countless forms, dates from 1703. The *ronin*'s noble example was praised as the glory of the age. The story, still oft-repeated in Japanese movies and on television, is familiar to every Japanese from childhood on. It is constantly cited in modern Japan as a lesson in unconditional loyalty to the group and dedication without regard for the consequences to oneself.

Though the feudal lords and the samurai have gone, the collective way of thinking engendered by that age remains. This is not entirely accidental. Eiichi Shibusawa, who was involved in founding many Japanese companies, including the bank that is today Japan's largest, was a samurai before the abolition of feudalism. He transformed the feudal philosophy into a code to guide businessmen, seeing business as a long-term enterprise to be guided by standards of honour, justice and loyalty not all that different from the samurai codes.[5] Today every writer on Japanese business practices comments on the loyalty shown by employees to their corporation. The term *uchi*, literally 'inside', was used in feudal times for the household to which one's first loyalty was due; it is now employed also for the organization to which one belongs – and, in Japan, 'belongs' is a better term than 'works'. The same is true of another term, *daikazoku*, 'one great family', used in feudal times to refer to large related groups – 'clans' might be the closest Western notion. In the early days of Japanese capitalism, great business houses like Mitsui were, quite literally, feudal *daikazoku* – the head of the 'great family' was the leader of the business, and the several thousand workers were all drawn from members of the clan.[6] Later, as Thomas Rohlen notes in his anthropological study of the Japanese bank he calls by the fictitious name 'Uedagin', corporations were referred to as *daikazoku* in order to suggest that the firm, like the ideal Japanese family, 'is an entity in which the interests of members are secondary to the interests of the family as a whole'.

This notion of the company as a household or family would appear to Westerners to be either mere rhetoric, or unduly paternalistic and authoritarian. To the Japanese, however, it is appreciated as a way of bringing the traditional Japanese values of sympathy and human involvement into the company. It sets an ideal for personal relationships in the corporation: they should be warm, understanding and co-operative. Leaders, like parents, take an interest not only in how well a worker performs in the office, but also in his or her personal welfare. The younger generation of workers respect seniority, and know that, in time, they will assume responsibility for their juniors. In the case of Uedagin, the sense that the bank is a great family is strongly present at the annual ceremony for accepting new employees, that is, new members of the family. Speeches at this ceremony emphasize that it marks a turning point in the lives of the young trainees, with the responsibility their parents have had for ensuring their welfare now being transferred to the company. The parents of those who are being accepted into the bank (all of them either high school or university graduates) attend the ceremony, and one of their number gives a speech thanking the bank for accepting their children into the company and asking the bank to guide their still immature offspring. A representative of the trainees thanks the parents for their past care and upbringing, and thanks the bank for accepting them, and for the care and further training they will receive. On behalf of the trainees, the representative asks for guidance and discipline from the leaders of the company. The trainees then pledge their commitment to the bank, where most of them will work until their retirement.[7]

The family feeling thus conveyed to new members of the corporation is carefully fostered in many other ceremonies and gatherings. Japanese corporations often start the day with a 'morning-greeting ceremony' at which the section chief bows and greets the employees, who return the compliment. Sometimes there will be a little homily or pep-talk. There may also be a weekly assembly for the whole company, or in larger corporations, for a division. Perhaps once a month each section or smaller work group will hold a Sunday picnic, and twice a year the group will go away for an overnight stay at a nearby resort. At these activities the whole group will stay together, eating, drinking, singing, bathing and sleeping as a group (although men and women carry out the last two activities separately). Even the buses on which the group travels are equipped with a roving microphone, so that karaoke-style singing can take place during the journey.

Japanese companies have their own inspirational songs with rousing themes, to be sung both at formal ceremonies and on group excursions. Here, for example, is a verse from the Uedagin song:

> A falcon pierces the clouds,
> A bright new dawn is now breaking.
> The precious flower of our unity
> Blossoms here,
> Uedagin, Uedagin,
> Our pride in her name ever grows.[8]

In the West such songs would be an occasion either for mirth, or for the boredom that accompanies an empty ritual. No doubt there are some Japanese who have one of these two responses, but in most cases the songs are sung with enthusiasm and what appears to be genuine devotion. Mark Zimmerman, another American who worked in Japan, describes a meeting of employees of a construction company where the company song was sung four times, punctuated by bursts of cheering and much mutual backslapping, by young men whose eyes were glowing with pride. It was, Zimmerman reports, 'a very real demonstration of the employees' devotion to their company'.[9]

Thus if Japanese are willing to work longer hours with fewer holidays than most Westerners, a plausible explanation is not that they are a race with a genetic tendency to be workaholics, nor that they are even more anxious to get ahead than Westerners, but rather that they are bound by far stronger ties of loyalty to their corporation. Jack Seward, co-author of a book about Japanese business ethics called *Japan: The Hungry Guest*, provides a nice illustration of this. After Seward had returned to America after several years in Japan, a Japanese visitor to his home happened to see a television commercial for beer. The commercial showed men at work; then, when the five o'clock bell went off, the workers threw down their tools and ran to their pickups in order to get a beer. The Japanese visitor was shocked: 'Don't American workers feel any obligation to their company? They act as if they can't wait to get away from work . . . I would be ashamed to leave work so abruptly. If I did it often, my fellow workers would become very cold towards me. Besides, I feel that I have entrusted my life to the president of my company'. It was not the idleness of the American workers, nor their inordinate desire for beer that so disturbed the Japanese viewer, but their lack of commitment to their company and their fellow workers. Such a commercial would be impossible in Japan.[10]

A cynic might think that all this shows is that Japanese corporations are more skilful in exploiting their workers than corporations in the West. That thought misses the mark. As in the feudal system, nobility has its obligations. Once part of the corporation, the Japanese employee has a virtual guarantee of lifelong employment. Some corporations, like the Mazda facility in Hiroshima, are reported to have never laid off a worker.[11] Demotion is also rare. People who are erroneously promoted to levels of responsibility that are beyond their abilities tend to be moved to a position with an honourable title where they can do no harm: for example, 'researcher'.[12] This readiness to stand by employees whenever possible is in keeping with the ideal of the corporation as a family.

The family-like nature of the corporation is also reflected in the document that employees sign when they join a corporation. In contrast to a Western contract of employment, the Japanese document does not state the rights or duties of the employee, no salary is specified, nor does the document list any procedures for redress of grievances, for giving notice or for terminating employment. The document simply records, for example, that the bank recognizes the person named as a member of the bank, and the person in turn pledges to follow the rules of the organization. That is all that is needed. Contracts are for strangers who cannot trust each other. What is really important is implicit in all the ceremonies and traditions of the corporation: a mutual trust that both the corporate entity and the individual member will work for the good of all.

This desired mutuality of relationships is expressed by the Japanese term *wa*, usually but perhaps not quite adequately translated as harmony or concord. Rohlen writes that *wa* is 'undoubtedly the single most popular component in the mottos and names of companies across Japan' and takes the title of his book from Uedagin's motto, 'For Harmony and Strength'. He describes *wa* as 'the cooperation, trust, sharing, warmth, morale, and hard work of efficient, pleasant, and purposeful fellowship'. It is seen as an intrinsically desirable quality of human relationships, as well as a means to social improvement.[13] In large corporations, though the company creed may emphasize harmony across the entire corporation, the real sense of belonging, and of working in harmony with one's fellows, comes from the small work group, where workers in daily contact with each other are encouraged to respect each other as partners in a common enterprise. It is this that does most to explain why American-style clock-watching is unthinkable in Japan. At Uedagin, for example, the day's office work began at 8.30 and 'officially' ended at 5.00, but in fact would finish around 6.15. Often, however, this would not be the time to go home. Instead, there might be an office meeting to discuss a new sales campaign or some other proposal or problem. The meeting might finish at 7.30, when food and beer are brought in. As inhibitions disappear the conversation will become more animated and there may be singing, or individuals will tell humourous and risque stories. Such a party might close at 9.00 with a final toast to the success of the bank and the branch. Some of the men will then head off to a nearby bar for some more drinking and exchange of intimate details about their thoughts and lives. Rohlen comments:

> To the American observer accustomed to the homeward rush of employees at quitting time, these office meetings and parties that last long into the night seem at first profoundly exotic and inexplicable. In Uedagin offices, there is no set time when work ends, no time clock, and a reluctance to leave before the rest. Staying late is a common quality of office work. In some instances, the whole office will stay until the last person is finished.[14]

Not surprisingly, comparative studies have consistently shown that working is a more important part of life for Japanese workers – whether white-collar or blue-collar – than it is for their American counterparts.[15] All this means that, as one observer of labour-management relations in Japan puts it: 'Individuals belong, and they have goals that give clear-cut direction to their lives'.[16] That is no small matter.

For Western adults, the closest parallels to the attitudes and practices engendered towards corporations in Japan are to be found in team sports. The club songs, the comradeship, the striving for a common goal, the warm enveloping feeling of belonging – if we have ever shared in these feelings, we may be able to understand the way many Japanese feel about the company for which they work. The analogy extends also to the fact that the other face of harmony within the team is an intensely competitive attitude towards opposing teams – or in the Japanese business world, against competing companies. The emphasis on the importance of harmony *within* the corporation or other in-group in Japan should not mislead us into thinking that there is any lack of conflict and competition in Japanese society. The point is that this competition exists openly between corporations or similar institutions rather than within them.

In Japanese sport the concept of team spirit is taken much further than in Western sport. A few years ago, under the title 'You've Gotta Have "Wa"', *Sports Illustrated* described the problems of American baseballers playing with Japanese teams. Despite the generally higher standard of American baseball, American players were not always welcome with Japanese clubs because of their disruptive effect on the team's *wa*. This concept was explained for American sports fans as 'the Japanese ideal of unity, team play and no individual heroes – a concept that ex-US major leaguers playing in Japan have had a lot of trouble grasping'. In America, star players hold out for higher pay, and may feel they don't have to train as hard as the other players. In Japan, everyone does the same training, and demanding more money is seen as putting one's own interests before those of the team. In America, when coaches take players out of the game, a show of anger is considered normal; in

Japan, it is an almost unpardonable breach of discipline. When an American pitcher playing for the Yomiuri Giants kicked over trash cans and ripped up his uniform after being taken out of the game, the Giants published a set of rules of etiquette for foreign players, that included injunctions to 'Take good care of your uniform' and ended with 'Do not disturb the harmony of the team'.[17]

The harmony of the team is unlikely to survive if there is a sense that the benefits of the common effort are going disproportionately to one or two people. The reason why highly paid individual 'stars' do not fit well into Japanese baseball teams is also the reason why there are no Donald Trumps in Japanese business. To plaster one's name over one's assets in the largest possible letters would be, in Japan, the worst possible taste. It would also be asking for trouble. One of the most popular proverbs in Japan is: 'The nail that sticks up shall be hammered down'. In an insightful account of life in Japan, John Morley remarks that for the Japanese 'by far the most common cause of embarrassment . . . was not the fact that the person concerned had committed a faux pas or made a fool of himself but simply the fact that for a moment he had been *conspicuous*'.[18]

The sense that one should not stand out as an individual is developed at an early age. Any visitor to Japan will notice the large groups of school children, all dressed in identical uniforms and usually with their hair cut in the same way. (For Western visitors with teenage children, such behaviour is particularly astonishing.) A study of the behaviour of Japanese and American children in elementary school classrooms has shown that Japanese children are more strongly encouraged to think of themselves as a group. Japanese teachers were much more likely to address their remarks to all pupils, and to teach the class as a group, whereas American teachers were more likely to attend to individual children. American children initiated or attempted to initiate interaction with the teacher nine times more often than Japanese children.[19]

The habits of thought thus begun in childhood persist in later life. Japanese managers see the group as more important than the individual, and reward their workers in a manner designed to encourage them to interact with their groups, whereas American managers are more likely to reward workers on an individual basis.[20] Unlike Westerners, Japanese adults do not dress to impress. As Morley points out, it is impossible to tell from a glance at the average man on the train whether he is the company director or the storeroom clerk.[21] This is not to deny that rank is very important in Japan; it undoubtedly is, and the exchange of business cards, showing one's position in a company, is essential if Japanese are to know even such elementary things as the forms of politeness they use when speaking to each other. But while rank is important, displaying it is not.

Accordingly, in Japan, humility is not just a virtue, but a social necessity in every area of life, including business. As Seward and Van Zandt write in their study of Japanese business ethics:

> . . . humility is visible in the low public posture of the Japanese and is audible in their choice of honorifics in almost every sentence uttered. The businessman who is not ready to humble himself, to bow and kneel and repeat the verbal formulae of humility over and over again will not do well in commercial activities in Japan.[22]

Such a culture is at the opposite pole to the culture of Wall Street in the 1980s. Demanding higher salaries and bonuses as executives did during the boom years in America would be regarded, in Japan, as completely incompatible with a sense of working together in a shared and valued enterprise. Apart from the display of egoism involved, such a focus on boosting one's own pay shows contempt for the welfare of the company and the colleagues with whom one works. That there is a certain amount of insincerity in the Japanese show of self-effacement and deference is undeniable. Many who bow deeply and talk humbly may in fact feel themselves far superior to those they are addressing. But appearances do matter, especially to the Japanese, and the impossibility of showing off one's ability, rank or wealth goes a long way towards making everyone feel a valued part of the team.

In any case, apppearances are not entirely deceptive. The typical Japanese corporation does not focus primarily on making money, either for itself or for its individual members. In the tradition of

Shosan Suzuki, it is based, instead, on the idea that one should not aim at wealth, but rather work hard and do the job well; prosperity will then follow. As Rohlen says: 'The degree to which salaries, profits and material welfare are relegated to a minor place in the bank ideology is extraordinary to a Westerner'. In their place are ideals, not only of 'harmony and strength', of making the bank bigger and better, but also of contributing to a stronger and more prosperous Japan, and to improving the general welfare of society. Even distant goals of world peace and the betterment of underdeveloped countries are frequently mentioned among the goals of Uedagin. This may not translate into anything very tangible, but it does enhance the feeling of members of the bank that they are doing something worthwhile.[23] In referring to such broad goals, Japanese corporations are making the work, and hence the lives, of their employees more meaningful – something that is, as we shall see in the final chapter of this book, missing from the lives of many people in Western countries.

As for those at the very top, the earnings of heads of Japanese corporations are certainly ample, but as we saw in Chapter 3, the gap between the pay rates of ordinary workers and of chief executive officers in Japan is smaller than in almost any other country in the world, and much smaller than that in the United States.[24] When President Bush visited Tokyo in January 1992 the chief executives of Chrysler, Ford and General Motors came along in order to reinforce the President's plea for a better deal for American exports to Japan. The Japanese were able to point out that these three executives had received, in 1990, salaries and perks of more than $7.3 million; in contrast, the heads of Toyota, Honda and Nissan earned barely a quarter of that, a total of $1.8 million. Indeed, anyone who did not know the state of the world car market and had only the remuneration of the chiefs to go by, might gain the impression that it is the Americans, not the Japanese, who are making the more successful cars. In the year preceding the visit, however, sales of American cars were in a steep decline and more than 40,000 American autoworkers had lost their jobs. A Japanese-born academic teaching international business at New York's Baruch College pointed out that firing employees while one helped oneself to hefty bonuses would win no respect in Japan.

The self and the group

So *are* the Japanese different? Any generalization across an entire nation is risky, and individual exceptions are sure to abound. Fortunately, for the purposes of this book I do not need to answer so broad a question. The question relevant to this investigation is: can one find, in Japan, elements of a different conception of self-interest and of the relationship between the interests of self and others? Here the evidence points strongly to one answer: yes. As compared with their peers from Western cultures, Japanese white-collar workers have, probably implicitly rather than explicitly, made a different ultimate choice. Though they enjoy having new gadgets of many kinds, they are less likely than Westerners to see the meaning of their lives in terms of the acquisition of material possessions. They also have a much stronger sense of being part of a group. They are therefore less prone to think only or primarily of their own interests, and far more willing to put the interests of the group ahead of their own interests. Or at least – since it is very difficult to know what inward motivation people have – if they *do* think only or primarily of their own interests, they show sufficient self-discipline not to allow this to show in their demeanour or their behaviour. (All this may be true of blue-collar workers and other Japanese too, but the conclusion is well-founded only for the group from which the evidence has been drawn, and this is largely the white-collar workers in Japanese corporations.)

That this difference lies deeply embedded in Japanese culture and thought is suggested by the fact that it is reflected in the structure of the traditional Japanese home, and in the Japanese language. The ordinary Japanese home had no private rooms. If I lived in such a home, I could not regard the room in which I sleep as 'my bedroom'. It would just be a room in which I roll out a futon and go to sleep at night. In the morning I would put the bedding away and a small table might be moved to the centre of the room, creating a living space for all the family to use. Movable screens add to the flexibility of the space. No room has immobile furniture that designates it as having a particular function, or as being private space for a particular person. Bathing is often a communal activity. No wonder that households living in this way saw themselves as a single entity in a stronger sense than those in which a child can say to a parent or sibling: 'Get out of *my* room!'

This lack of a clearly defined sense of self is reflected in language in several ways. Morley notes an analogy between the term for one's home, household or group, *uchi*, and the Japanese concept of self:

> The Japanese carried his house around in his mouth and produced it in everyday conversation, using the word *uchi* to mean 'I', the representative of my house in the world outside. His self-awareness was naturally expressed as corporate individuality, hazy about quite what that included, very clear about what it did not.[25]

Robert Smith explains another aspect of the terms used for 'I' in Japanese:

> The large number of referents and the manner in which they are employed indicates that even the question 'Who is self; who is other?' is not unambiguously settled from the onset of interaction. There are, for example, terms that can be used for self-reference as well as for second-person and third-person reference. That is, some common terms such as *boku* or *temae* may mean 'I' or 'you' – they are interchangeable lexical items in the spoken language. In English usage, by contrast, the speaker stands at the center of the set of referents he or she will employ. Does this circumstance imply, then, that in Japan all interpersonal interaction takes place in a blur of ambiguity and confusion? Actually, it is sometimes so, but a safer conclusion is that the identification of self and other is always indeterminate in the sense that there is no fixed center from which, in effect, the individual asserts a non-contingent existence.[26]

In a footnote, Smith mentions one striking exception: 'Alone among the Japanese, the Emperor uses the first person referent *chin*'. Unlike most exceptions, this one really does prove the rule; for the Emperor stands for the whole, and his self-assertion is the group's assertion of its own importance, infinitely beyond that of any individual.

Professor Tomosaburo Yamauchi of the Osaka University of Education has referred to this feature of Japanese usage in a book the title of which may be translated as *Putting Oneself in Another's Shoes – The Moral Philosophy of Hare.*[27] Yamauchi points out that the usage of *boku* (and also *jibun*, another term that originally meant 'I') to mean 'you' occurs when one says something from the point of view of the hearer. Yamauchi then compares this feature of the Japanese language with the suggestion, in the writings of the English moral philosopher R. M. Hare, that an essential feature of moral thinking is our willingness to put ourselves in the position of others before making a moral judgment. If Yamauchi is right, it seems that this central aspect of moral thinking (on which I shall have more to say in Chapters 8 and 9) is to some extent built into Japanese linguistic usage. Such usage is, however, sometimes limited to the people within the group to which one belongs, in which case people's attitudes can be exclusive or hostile to others outside the group.

If we view society as the stage for an inevitable struggle between the interests of the individual and those of the group, we will be inclined to think that to elevate the importance of the group is to sacrifice the interests of the individual. This is not, however, the Japanese way of looking at things. In much Eastern thought, whether Confucian or Buddhist – and both traditions have been influential in Japan – the conflict between individual and group is essentially a false dilemma. The satisfaction of the individual is only to be found in commitment to the group. It is consistent with Zen, Japan's own contribution to Buddhist thought, that the individual should find personal fulfillment in devotion to duty and the development of self-discipline to the point at which one overcomes the desires that conflict with the good of the larger entity for which one is working. (The term 'fulfillment' is not quite strong enough to convey this idea. Some might say that what I have described is, in Zen, not only the way to 'fulfillment', but also to 'salvation'; but since Zen knows neither original sin nor hell, the Christian concept of salvation is singularly inappropriate. 'Fulfillment' will have to do, though it must be understood in a sense that goes very deep in the nature of our being.)

If this seems too philosophical to be of any relevance to the way employees think about their work for a corporation, consider the essay by the President of Uedagin that is given to every new member upon entering the bank. Entitled 'My Thoughts', it sets out a Buddhist attitude to life. Here is a passage that is a key, not only to the thoughts of the President, but to the understanding of a Japanese approach to the whole problem of self-interest and the nature of the good life:

> Buddha taught that the actions of the body are products of the spirit; therefore, first we must improve the spirit. A philosopher of the Ming dynasty said, 'If one's spirit is at peace one will not suffer discomfort. If one's spirit is strong one will never be concerned about material welfare'. These teachings emphasize spirit above all else . . .
> Buddha also said, 'All men live for something, that is the sum of it; however, some are mistaken and some are right in what they live for'. The mistaken ones think of themselves and are employed in trying to get rid of suffering, unhappiness, ill-fortune, and the like from their lives, but, in fact, they are seeking and inviting these very things into their lives.[28]

It is impossible to know how seriously new members of Uedagin take this advice on how to live; but what president of a Western company would even offer it?

Whether the distinctive aspects of Japanese ways of thinking about themselves and their group will persist in the face of greater awareness of other ways of doing things is impossible to say. There is some evidence that the past decade has seen an increasing emphasis on individualism and self-assertion.[29] Nevertheless, whatever the future holds for Japan, we know that a different society, as described in this chapter, has existed and has been highly successful in enhancing the welfare of its members.

To say that Japanese white-collar workers are, in comparison with Westerners, more likely to put the interests of the group ahead of their own interests, is not to say that their culture is better than that of the West. Maybe it is; maybe it is not. How would one compile such a balance sheet? On the positive side, it is obvious that the Japanese have been phenomenally successful in economic terms. A country of 124 million inhabitants, lacking oil or other mineral wealth, and with limited arable land, has become a dominant economic power, running an annual trading surplus of over $US100 billion. Japan also has a very low crime rate; Tokyo is often said to be the safest large city in the world. As we have seen, wealth tends to be relatively evenly distributed, and there are few really poor people in Japan; moreover even those doing menial tasks have a respected place in the group with which they work.

The negative side of the balance sheet might begin with the extraordinary pressures of Japanese life. This starts early: small children are under pressure to excel in primary school entrance tests so that they can get into a good primary school that will set them on the right educational path. Even kindergarten children often have special tutoring in reading and writing once kindergarten is over; and Japanese schoolchildren in primary and secondary school commonly spend several hours a day, after normal schooling, at a special 'cramming' school to ensure that they do well in their exams.

Once employed, we have already seen how little leisure time and vacation time Japanese can acceptably take. Official statistics for 1990 show that Japanese labourers worked an average of 400 hours a year more than their European counterparts – that is about eight extra hours a week. The real figure is likely to be higher still, since in Japan workers do not use time cards and are less likely to put in for overtime pay. In 1991 Akio Koiso, for thirty-one years an employee of Fuji bank, published *A Chronicle of a Fuji Bank Employee*, in which he told of branch managers pressuring subordinates to forego their vacations and work unpaid overtime. As Koiso put it: 'You get a stable salary and the smugness of bearing the name of an elite bank. But the price you pay is long, intense work hours, damaged health and the destruction of family life'.[30]

The Japanese have a special term – *karoshi* – to describe death from overwork. Attorneys, labour unions and others involved with *karoshi* estimate that at least 10,000 Japanese die every year from causes related to overwork. Death is an extreme response to overwork; but the destructive impact on family life mentioned by Koiso is inescapable. For many young Japanese children of office workers, it is a rare treat if father is home in time to see them before they go to bed. Only on Sunday can these children expect to see their father; otherwise, the mother runs what is effectively a single parent household.[31] Poll results published by *Time* in 1992 show that 88 percent of Japanese respondents admired the amount of leisure time available to American workers, and an almost identical figure admired America for its respect for family life.[32] The life of the Japanese office worker is premised on rigid sex roles, for if women were to work the same hours as men, who would spend time with the children and take care of domestic chores? The *Time* poll found that 68 percent of Japanese admired the treatment of women in America.

Also on the negative side is the adverse effect that a high level of group identification has on whoever or whatever is not part of the group: on both the individual, and on the larger, more universal perspective. The group puts pressure on the individual to conform, for those rare individuals who bring the wrath of the group on their heads will feel cut off from the most important aspect of their lives. The Japanese admire American freedom of expression and variety of lifestyles as much as they admire its leisure and respect for family life, according to the poll published in *Time*.

In short, if the corporation has taken over the mantle of the feudal lord, then the employees are its serfs: prosperous, well-treated, highly valued and respected serfs, to be sure, but tied to the corporation almost as securely as serfs were tied to their lord. No matter how willingly and enthusiastically members of the group may sing the company song and join in the company outings, we cannot help but wonder about the constraints on their ability to do otherwise. Most significant of all, for the impact of Japan upon the world, is the fact that devotion to the group and its members appears very largely to pre-empt the possibility of anything like equal concern for those outside the group, and for the larger whole. Morley observes that there is in Japanese ethics nothing corresponding to the key Christian injunction 'Thou shalt love thy neighbour as thyself'. In Japanese versions of the Bible the word 'neighbour' is translated by an uncommon Japanese word meaning 'the person next door', thus giving the rule 'very much the air of appropriation from some remote language'. The proper way to convey the meaning of the Christian commandment would have been to translate 'neighbour' by the Japanese word meaning 'outsider' – and then, says Morley, it 'would without exaggeration be an astonishing, a revolutionary concept in Japanese ethics'.[33]

This lack of concern for the outsider is dramatically illustrated by the samurai tradition known as 'trying out one's new sword', or *tsujigiri*. The Japanese term means, literally, 'crossroads cut'. For a sword to be acceptable to a samurai, it had to be capable of slicing right through an opponent, from the shoulder to the opposite flank, at a single blow. To go into battle with a sword that was not capable of doing this could bring dishonour. So, on obtaining a new sword, some samurai would test it by making a 'crossroads cut': that is, waiting at a crossroads until an unwary peasant, or any non-samurai wayfarer, happened to come along. Then, with a single stroke, he would try to slice the hapless person in two. The act was illegal, and liable to be severely punished, but it was not considered dishonourable.[34] Though such breathtaking disregard for the outsider lies far in the past, Japanese ethics is still deeply influenced by the idea that one's obligations to one's own group override those to strangers and to the public at large. Morley reports a Japanese sociologist as saying:

> Historically, the groundwork for any form of social structure other than the *uchi* [household, group] was never laid. Anything in the nature of a public morality, even the concept of 'public' itself, has failed to materialise in this country, and we are badly in need of it.

As evidence of this need, the sociologist goes on to cite the difficulty of arousing concern in Japan about such matters as mercury pollution and thalidomide:

> Putting it rather harshly, these cases were not matters of public concern, because it is difficult to mobilise support for an opinion

when those who support it remain unidentifiable, and this is unavoidably the case so long as you have no established word to address or refer to the general public.[35]

This passage helped to explain something about Japan that I had found both dismaying and mystifying. On three trips to Japan I have been involved with environmental and animal rights issues. On my first visit I was a witness for the defence of Dexter Cate, an American environmental activist who had released dolphins that Japanese fishermen had trapped in a net at Iki island. The fishermen had been planning to slaughter the dolphins, as they had done in previous years. Cate was charged with damaging the nets of the fishermen, and his Japanese/Hawaiian lawyer thought that it would be useful if the Japanese court could hear that Cate's actions were motivated by a coherent ethical view, held by respectable professors of philosophy such as myself. The court gave me a hearing that was not merely polite, but interested and respectful. Cate was convicted nevertheless. (Since he had already been waiting some months in gaol before his trial, he received no further penalty and was deported.)[36] On a subsequent trip I investigated Japanese attitudes to animals in general and to whales and dolphins in particular, interviewing people from the whaling and fishing industry, as well as Zen priests and one or two Japanese – the only ones I could find – who had supported the Western opposition to Japanese whaling and the killing of dolphins. On a third visit I met members of the Japanese Anti-Vivisection Society, who were trying to defend the interests of animals being used, virtually without any regulative protection, in Japanese laboratories. I also met a group of Japanese opposing a proposal by the City of Nagoya to dump rubbish on one of the few remaining large tidal mudflats in Japan, vital to thousands of migratory birds. Although there are very few foreigners living in Japan, on all these issues, foreigners or Japanese who had spent a considerable amount of time abroad were playing a prominent role. The few courageous Japanese who were trying to do something about the issue were clearly much more isolated than comparable groups in Western nations, and their breach with conformity was causing them far greater hardship. Some Japanese told me that their activities had led to a serious rupture with their families, who had been both angry and embarrassed by the fact that their daughter or son (much more often, daughter – were the sons preoccupied with their careers?) had publicly criticized something that other people were doing. For those who appeal to a broader concern than the interests of the group, Japanese society leaves no secure footing.

Japanese society demonstrates that the individualist conceptions of self-interest that prevail in the West are the outcome of Western history and culture, not a dictate of human nature. Yet the counterpart of this strong Japanese commitment to the group could well be the comparatively weak Japanese sense of responsibility for the public interest, or the interest of the global environment. Often individuals are unable to get along together until a common enemy appears; then the previously squabbling collection of individuals suddenly forms a remarkably cohesive unit, ready to battle together against the hostile and threatening world beyond. Though Japanese corporations are not exactly at war with rival corporations, there is still a strong element of this 'us against them' feeling in the group loyalty that prevails within the Japanese corporation. To that extent, while the Japanese alternative to our conception of self-interest offers important advantages over Western individualism, it falls short of the broader ethical view that is needed to bring about international justice and save the biosphere of our planet. For the same reason, it does not resolve the tension between individual interest and a genuinely ethical way of living. In the end, the pursuit of the collective interest of the group to which one happens to belong, regardless of the harm done to outsiders, is no more ethically justifiable than the single-minded pursuit of one's own more narrowly selfish interests. There is no shortage of historical examples to remind us how easily strong group identification spills over into atrocious behaviour to those outside the group: the most recent, still continuing as I write this, is the 'ethnic cleansing' of minorities in Bosnia-Herzegovina.

CHAPTER 7

Tit for Tat

Caring for those who care for us

In World War I, the Allied French and British forces faced the German army across a long front in Northern France. Both sides dug themselves into trenches from which they kept up a bombardment of the other side. When pitched battles were fought, casualties were enormous. The Allied High Command was willing to take heavy losses; they reasoned that since there were more French and British, combined, than Germans, as long as they killed at least one German soldier for every Allied soldier killed, they would win the war. National feeling and the propaganda of wartime fuelled hatred of the other side. The commanding officers strove to keep enmity at fever pitch, in order to keep up the morale of troops who had seen so many of their comrades die. Yet amidst the hatred, death and mud, an extraordinary system of co-operation known as 'live and let live' sprang up between Allied and German troops. Its essence was: I won't try to kill you as long as you don't try to kill me. For considerable periods, in several different sectors of the trenches, the British or French infantry aimed their shells where they did no harm, and the Germans could be relied upon to do the same. Troops could relax, and even stroll about quite openly in range of enemy machine guns, secure in the knowledge that the person behind the sights of the gun would not try to kill them. If something did go wrong – perhaps a unit was replaced by one that had not learned the system, or a zealous commanding officer decided to show the troops how it should be done – there was immediate retaliation.[1]

The extraordinary but well-documented existence of the 'live and let live' system during World War I is eloquent testimony to the possibilities of co-operation in what might seem to be the most adverse circumstances imaginable. We have already seen that our biology does not dictate that our ultimate choice be a narrowly selfish one. On the contrary, the way in which we have evolved has led to the existence of beings who care directly for their children, for other kin and to some extent for larger groups. The example of Japan shows how far a culture can reinforce concern for the group. The aim of this chapter is to show how our evolution has allowed a propensity for another kind of concern for others, and how human cultures everywhere have developed this aspect of our nature.

In a large, anonymous society that often appears to live by the rule of looking after number one, it is easy to forget how much of an everyday experience helping and being helped by others can be in other societies. The contrast became especially vivid for the inhabitants of Tristan da Cunha, a tiny and remote island in the South Atlantic Ocean. In 1961 the population of this island consisted of 264 people, mostly descendants of European sailors, who spoke English and belonged to the Church of England. Their quiet, agriculturally based life came to an abrupt halt in September 1961 when their island – which consists of the tip of a volcano that rises from the ocean floor – erupted, spitting out hot ashes. The British Navy evacuated the entire population and took them to England, where they settled in housing with modern conveniences and were helped to find work. Within two years, almost all of them returned to Tristan, despite the burnt-out homes and hard conditions they faced there. But a few found conditions on the island so difficult that they went back to England. There they were visited by Peter Munch, an anthropologist who had studied their way of life both on Tristan and in England. He found that those who went back to England a second time were even more discontented with life there than they had been on their first forced visit. Then the entire island community had been transplanted; now the few who had chosen to return to England were living among strangers. As one Tristaner said:

> No, the people on Tristan, they's jus' like one family and they live happy and one help t'other, and if I's out in my farm and doin' my potatoes, and someone's finish' his'n, he'll come along an' give me a hand, an' the next day he got something to do, I go 'n give *him* a hand, so we all help 'nother. On Tristan they's jus' like brothers 'n sisters.[2]

To see how these helping relationships work, here is an imaginary example:

Max is a small peasant farmer with a crop ready to harvest. The rainclouds are building on the horizon. Unless Max gets some help, it will rain before he can bring in the harvest. The grain that he has not harvested will spoil. So Max asks Lyn, his neighbour, whose crop is not yet ripe, if she will help him to harvest his crop. In return, he offers to help her when her crop is ready. Max will be better off if Lyn agrees to help him. But will Lyn be better off if she helps? She will, if this means that Max will help her, because she often also has trouble getting her harvest in before it rains. But can she rely on Max's promise to help her? How does she know that, after she has helped him to harvest his crop, he will not stand by and laugh when she asks him for help? If she cannot be even moderately confident that Max will help her, it is not in her interest to help him. She could use her time better by pulling out some weeds that hamper the growth of her crop. Max's problem is that, if he is to get his crop harvested before it spoils, he must somehow get Lyn to believe that if she helps him, he will help her.

In some societies, Max and Lyn could enter into a formal agreement, and, if Max broke the agreement, Lyn would be entitled to some form of compensation or damages. But if Max and Lyn live in a society which lacks such means of making a binding agreement, Max's best chance is to win Lyn's trust. If he has a reputation for being trustworthy, this should not be a problem. How does he get such a reputation? In a small-scale community like Tristan da Cunha, in which everyone knows everyone else, the best way to do this is by actually being trustworthy; that is, by honouring one's commitments to others, and generally being a member of the community in good standing with others.

Max might try to gain a good reputation another way; he might try to deceive others into thinking he is trustworthy when in reality he is not. But – again, in small communities with little change in membership – this is unlikely to work. In those conditions – and they are the conditions that have prevailed for most of the period in which human beings and other social primates have existed – honesty really is the best policy.

In the early eighties Robert Axelrod, an American social theorist, made a remarkable discovery about the nature of co-operation. The full significance of Axelrod's result is still not properly appreciated outside a narrow circle of specialists. It has the potential to change not only our personal lives, but the world of international politics as well.

To understand what Axelrod found, we first need to know something about the problem in which he was interested – a well-known puzzle about co-operation called the Prisoner's Dilemma. The name comes from the way in which the puzzle is usually presented: an imaginary choice facing a prisoner. There are many versions. Here is mine:

You and another prisoner are languishing in separate cells of the Ruritanian Police Headquarters. The police are trying to get you both to confess to plotting against the state. An interrogator comes to your cell, pours you a glass of Ruritanian wine, gives you a cigarette, and in tones of beguiling friendliness, offers you a deal.

'Confess to the crime!' he says, 'And if your friend in the other cell . . .'

You protest that you have never met the prisoner in the other cell, but the interrogator brushes your objection aside and continues: 'So much the better, then, if he is no friend of yours; for as I was about to say, if you confess, and he does not, we shall use your confession to lock him away for ten years. Your reward will be that you shall go free. On the other hand, if you are so stupid as to refuse to confess, and the 'friend' in the other cell does confess, you will be the one who goes to prison for ten years, and he will be released.'

You think about this for a while, and realize that you don't yet have enough information to decide, so you ask:

'What if we both confess?'

'Then, because we didn't really need your confession, you won't go free. But, seeing as how you were trying to help us, you'll each get only eight years.'

'And if neither of us confesses?'

A scowl passes over the face of your interrogator, and you fear that he is about to strike you. But he controls himself, and grumbles that, then, since they will lack the evidence for a conviction, they won't be able to keep you very long. But then he adds:

'We don't give up easily. We can still keep you here another six months, interrogating you, before those bleeding hearts at Amnesty International can put enough pressure on our government to get you out of here. So think about it: whether your buddy confesses or not, you'll be better off if you confess than if you don't. And my colleague is telling the other guy the same thing, right now.'

You think over what the interrogator has said and realize that he is right. Whatever the stranger in the other cell does, you will be better off if you confess. For if he does confess, your choice is between confessing too, and getting eight years in gaol, or not confessing, and spending ten years behind bars. On the other hand, if the other prisoner does not confess, your choice is between confessing, and going free, or not confessing, and spending another six months in the cells. So it looks like you should confess. But then another thought occurs to you. The other prisoner is in exactly the same situation as you are. If it is rational for you to confess, it will also be rational for him to confess. So you will both end up with eight years in gaol. Whereas, if neither of you confessed, you would both be free in six months. How can it be that the choice that seems rational for each of you, individually – that is, to confess – will make you both worse off than you would have been if you had decided not to confess? What should you do?

There is no solution to the Prisoner's Dilemma. From a purely self-interested point of view (one that takes no account of the interests of the other prisoner) it *is* rational for each prisoner to confess – and if each does what it is rational to do from a self-interested point of view, they will each be worse off than they would have been if they had chosen differently. The dilemma proves that when each of us individually chooses what is in our own interest, we can each turn out to be worse off than we would each have been if we had both made a choice that is in our collective interest.

You are unlikely ever to find yourself in the situation of the Ruritanian prisoners, but there are many everyday illustrations of the general rule that the Prisoner's Dilemma proves. Anyone who has spent some time in rush hour traffic knows that, while it may be in your individual interest to take your car to town (since the buses also get held up by the traffic, and they don't run very often anyway) it would be in the interests of everyone if you could all collectively decide to go by bus, since then the bus company could afford to run a much more frequent service, and without the traffic, you would get to work in half the time.

The situation of Max and Lyn, in the example just given, is similar to that of the prisoners in some respects, but different in others. They will both be better off if they co-operate, because otherwise each will lose the grain he or she is unable to reap before it rains. But is it rational for each, individually, to co-operate? If Lyn helps Max with his harvest, and then calls on Max to help her when she needs to get her crop in, Max might be tempted to think that it is not in his interests to help. For he will have already benefited from Lyn's help, and he could more usefully spend his time getting rid of some weeds before he plants his next crop. But now let us put ourselves in Lyn's position. Suppose that Lyn is thinking about whether she should help Max with his harvest. If she realizes that, since Max's harvest will be gathered first, it will not be in his interest to help her with her harvest, and for that reason he may not do so, she will not help him in the first place. Thus, as in the case of the prisoners, both Max and Lyn will be better off if they co-operate, but it is doubtful whether it will be rational for either of them to do so.

If we think of the prisoner's decision *not* to confess as a form of co-operation with the other prisoner – that is, adopting a strategy that means working together, rather than against each other – then it is easy to see the parallel between the Prisoner's Dilemma and what we might call the Peasant's Dilemma. They are both versions of a common problem, the Co-operator's Dilemma. But there is also a crucial difference between the two versions. The Prisoner's Dilemma is a once-in-a-lifetime situation. You and the other prisoner must each decide, just once, whether to co-operate with the other prisoner or not to do so. You and the other prisoner will, presumably, never be in that position again. In that respect, the answer you give to the interrogator in your cell will have no further effects on your life, other than those that the interrogator has spelled out for you. Max and Lyn, on the other hand, are neighbours and are likely to remain neighbours all of their lives. As predictably as the seasons themselves, they will need help to bring in their harvest, not only this year, but for many years to come. This provides a vital additional factor for each of them to take into account when they work out what is in their own interests. Now Max knows that if Lyn helps him, and he does not return the favour, she will surely refuse to help him next year, and probably for many years to come. While Max may get a short-term benefit from the weeding he can do instead of helping Lyn, in the long run he will be much worse off. So it will be in his interest to help Lyn; and Lyn, knowing that this will be the case, will also know that it is in her interest to help Max. Thus the logic of the Co-operator's Dilemma is dramatically different when it is going to be repeated indefinitely, instead of being a one-off situation.

Now we have enough background to see what Axelrod did. He thought of the Prisoner's Dilemma as a game, in which the aim is to spend the least possible time in gaol. To make this work, he set up a round-robin tournament, with many different players. Each player must play the game 200 times with one player. Each game involves deciding whether to co-operate with the other player, by keeping silent, or to defect, and confess. How many years you spend in gaol as a result of that decision depends on what the other player does, in accordance with the offer made to you by the Ruritanian police, as in the story above. The difference is that having done this once, you do it again, and so on. Each time that you do it, the situation is different, because you know what your opponent did before. Once you have played your 200 games with one player, you move on to the next, and so on, until everyone has played the required number of games with everyone else. At the end, we add up the total number of years each player has spent in gaol.

We can think of a variety of possible strategies that you might adopt in order to win the tournament. For example, you might always keep silent. We could call that strategy Always Co-operate. Or you might adopt the extremely selfish strategy Never Co-operate. You might try a more complicated strategy, say, co-operating for the first ten games, but not co-operating after that. You might also devise a strategy that is sensitive to what your opponent does: for example, co-operate only if the other player has co-operated in the previous game. Axelrod wanted to know if one strategy would generally do better than any other strategy. If it did, maybe it would also be useful in real-life situations, in which we, or our governments, must decide whether to co-operate or not with others who may or may not co-operate themselves. So he announced a Prisoner's Dilemma tournament, along the lines just sketched. Invitations were sent to people carrying out research in areas related to strategies for making decisions. The invitation set out the rules of the competition, and asked entrants to submit, in a form that could be run on a computer, the strategy that they thought would win.

Fourteen entries came in, some of them quite elaborate. The computer pitted them all against each other. The winner turned out to be the shortest and simplest strategy submitted. It went like this:

a. On the first move, co-operate.

b. On every subsequent move, do whatever the other player did on his or her previous move.

This strategy was called Tit for Tat, because it paid the other players back for what they did. If they were nice and co-operated, it co-operated. If they were selfish and did not, they got a selfish, unco-operative response back on the next turn.

That such a childish strategy should win must have caused some discomfort to the many experts who had spent a long time devising much more sophisticated and complicated strategies. Axelrod decided to hold a second, larger tournament, to see if any entrant, knowing that Tit for Tat would be entered again, and knowing how well it had done previously, anyone could come up with a better strategy. This time sixty-two entries were received. The tournament was run. Tit for Tat won again.[3]

Why did Tit for Tat do so well? One reason is that it is what Axelrod calls a 'nice' strategy: by this, he means a strategy which is never the first to try to act in an unco-operative way. Despite being nice, Tit for Tat actually does better than 'mean' strategies that are the first to be selfish. This is not only true of Tit for Tat; in general, in Axelrod's tournament, nice strategies did far better than strategies that were not nice.

This leads to a significant discovery about the role that unselfish behaviour can play in enhancing one's prospects of surviving and leaving descendents. Axelrod shows precisely why beings who act in an unselfish manner can do as well as, or even better than, those who behave completely selfishly. There are three key findings:

1. In doing better for itself, Tit for Tat also helps all other nice strategies to do better. In other words, the total number of years spent in gaol by Tit for Tat *and* other nice strategies against whom Tit for Tat plays will be the minimum possible, because these strategies will all begin by co-operating, and will continue to do so. In general, nice strategies support each other.

2. In sharp contrast to nice strategies, mean strategies spoil each

other's chances of success when they play against each other. Mean strategies playing against each other all end up doing very badly.

3. When nice and mean strategies are matched against each other, nice strategies will do well as long as they are provoked to retaliate by the first selfish action of another.

To understand the significance of these findings for the evolution of unselfish behaviour, we have to stop thinking of them as computer programs or strategies for playing games, and instead think of them as ways in which animals might behave. They would have to be social animals, living in a stable group, with the ability to recognize other members of the group and remember their previous cooperative or unco-operative actions. Human beings, throughout their evolutionary history, have been social animals of this kind. Chimpanzees and gorillas, many species of monkey, elephants, wolves, and several other social mammals would also satisfy these requirements. The question then becomes: if some analogue of the Prisoner's Dilemma occurs quite frequently in real life, would animals be more likely to survive and reproduce if they always go for their own immediate advantage? Or would they do better if they behave 'nicely', giving up some immediate advantage in order to co-operate with another animal?

The answer can be derived from the three key findings above. First, in a group of animals all behaving nicely, each of them would do well. Second, in a group of mean animals, each of them would do badly. Third, and most importantly, when some animals in a group are nice and others are mean, the nice ones would continue to do well, as long as they stop co-operating immediately when they discover that another animal is mean.

The reason for this third conclusion needs to be spelled out more fully. When mean animals interact with nice animals, the mean ones do better on the first encounter, because the nice ones give up their immediate advantage in order to be co-operative, whereas the mean ones do not. But since this is only one encounter, in stable groups it would not make much difference over the long run. It can be outweighed by the fact that, as long as a reasonable proportion of the group are nice, nice animals will do better than mean animals in their second and subsequent encounters with other nice animals, because they will reap the benefits of co-operation, whereas the mean animals will not.

So far, so good. Too good, in fact. Somewhere, in this evolutionary equivalent of the Garden of Eden, the serpent must be lurking. As in the Bible story, innocence opens the way for it. If nice animals live in a group with mean ones and behave nicely without discriminating between those animals who return the favour and those who do not, the mean animals gain an advantage. They benefit from co-operation without giving up anything in return. A vicious spiral commences. Initially the mean animals may be few, but they will now reproduce at a higher rate than the nice ones. Gradually nice animals will meet fewer nice animals, and the chances for reaping the benefits of co-operation will be reduced. In the end, animals who behave nicely will disappear from the group.

We can put this more plainly still. To be nice to someone who is not nice to you is to allow yourself to be a sucker. Where there are suckers, cheats prosper.[4] Conversely, if there are no suckers, cheats do badly. If all nice animals withdraw co-operation as soon as they detect a lack of co-operation on the other side – in other words, as soon as they notice that they are dealing with a cheat – mean animals will have few opportunities to exploit suckers. So the thought that we encountered in Chapter 2 – 'I don't want to be the only sucker' – is a healthy one. To be a sucker is bad, not only for oneself, but for everyone. Fortunately this does not mean that we have to be a cheat ourselves in order to do well. The saving element in the situation is that if a proportion of the animals in a group behave in a Tit for Tat kind of way, they can keep out the cheats. Such a society may no longer be paradise, because love and kindness can no longer be unconstrained; but it is still a lot better for all than life in a group dominated by mean animals.

This result amounts to nothing less than an experimental refutation of Jesus's celebrated teaching about turning the other cheek. Most of us think that turning the other cheek is a noble ideal, even if too idealistic for this world. Consequently, we admire those who are prepared to act on it. If they are prepared to be struck on both cheeks, we think, they are the *only* ones who are likely to be worse off. Now we know that this is not so. To turn the other cheek is to teach would-be cheats that cheating pays. There is not much attraction in an ethic of turning the other cheek if the resulting hardship falls not only on those who allow themselves to be struck, but on everyone else as a whole.

What happens if a group starts off with mostly mean members? Can a virtuous spiral get going? Yes, it can, as long as there is at least a small cluster of nice animals, and they interact mostly with each other. Then they can benefit from co-operating, while not allowing themselves to be exploited. The mean animals will be left to interact mostly with other mean animals, and will do badly. How does the cluster of individuals begin to co-operate? As we have seen, there can be advantages in altruism towards kin, and genes that lead to kin altruism will be favoured by the process of evolution. So initially, members of the cluster might all be related, and co-operation might evolve for that reason. Thus co-operation can emerge even in a world where at first almost everyone acts for immediate, short-term advantage – as happened among the entrenched troops during the World War I. And such co-operation will spread, as long as there is a stable group of people who are better off, as a result of their co-operation, than others who do not co-operate.

This is a striking result. With Tit for Tat, we can spiral in a virtuous direction only. In the right conditions, Tit for Tat behaviour can eliminate mean behaviour, while mean behaviour finds it difficult to dislodge Tit for Tat behaviour. As Axelrod puts it: 'the gear wheels of social evolution have a ratchet.'[5]

It may still seem that we have come very little distance from narrow self-interest. Maybe 'nice' behaviour is advantageous, but if so, aren't those who are being nice merely more enlightened egoists? This objection makes a mistake that is similar to the misunderstanding I mentioned in Chapter 5 in connection with altruism towards kin. Our feelings of love towards our brothers and sisters are no less genuine because we can explain how such feelings evolved: it is still true that we help our siblings because we care about them, not because of the degree of genetic overlap between us. Similarly, the fact that co-operation is the best policy does not mean that those who are co-operative are necessarily being co-operative *because* they desire to gain an advantage. Sometimes this will be true. Presumably it was true in the 'live and let live' system.

But at other times it will not be. Some of us just are the kind of beings who develop warm feelings towards those who show kindness towards us.

Consider friendship. Typically, friends help each other. Presumably this usually means that each is better off than he or she would have been without the aid of a friend. So is friendship and all the emotions that belong to it – love, loyalty, solidarity, gratitude and so on – just a charade, a mere cloak thrown over naked self-interest? Of course not. There are some who regard their friends in a calculatingly egoistic way, but most of us do not. Most of us like our friends, and enjoy spending time with them. This turns out to be an effective way of bringing about co-operation. Many other animals also co-operate, and also form bonds with other, unrelated members of the group. Between these friends, co-operative behaviour takes place. Some animals share food. Others defend their friends against attack. Chimpanzees and many other primates spend a lot of time grooming each other, removing parasites and dirt from parts that one cannot reach oneself. Our pleasure in being close to our friends may have evolved because it brings us benefits, but friendly feelings are no less genuine for that.

One more point on this topic of friendship and co-operation: in a small, stable society in which everyone knows everyone else, cheats will not prosper. But the less well we know the people with whom we live, work and deal, the greater the opportunities for some of them to benefit by deceit. Richard Christie, a psychologist from Columbia University in New York, developed a way of measuring a character trait he called 'Machiavellianism', which involved the ability to manipulate and deceive others. His work pre-dates the interest in evolutionary explanations of social behaviour, but it shows, as this evolutionary model predicts, that there are some who get on by manipulating and cheating others to their own advantage, and others who will not adopt such tactics. In a test of several hundred Spanish students, it was found that those who showed a high degree of Machiavellianism tended to come from the more industrialized and developed parts of the country. An American study found that Machiavellianism was more pronounced among those who had spent their adolescence in a large city.[6] In ecological terms, we could say that interactions with strangers create a niche for those who can take advantage of the co-operative instincts of others, receiving the benefit of help, but failing to give help themselves when it will no longer benefit them to do so. This niche only exists, however, because many offers to co-operate are genuine. Like a parasitic growth that needs a healthy tree from which to feed, cheats weaken the co-operative bond on which their way of earning a living depends. Thus the cynical view that everyone is in some sense a cheat has the logic of the relationship backwards. If everyone were a cheat, no-one would trust anyone, and there would be no opportunity to cheat.

Doing better with Tit for Tat

In almost every facet of our lives, we are faced with decisions that are structured like repeated versions of the Prisoner's Dilemma. In personal relationships, in business relationships, in politics and in relations between governments, we must decide whether to co-operate with another individual, potential business partner or client, political ally or foreign government. Each side may be tempted to try to reap the benefit of co-operation without paying the price; but if both do it, they will both be worse off than they would have been if they had all co-operated. Axelrod's findings can be applied in ways that make it possible for all parties to achieve better results than they would have achieved otherwise. In the previous section we saw the role played by the elements of Tit for Tat in ensuring its success in the tournaments. Now I shall re-state these elements as rules for use by anyone in a wide variety of everyday situations:

1. Begin by being ready to co-operate. Greet the world with a friendly face, think the best of strangers and show kindness towards them, unless you have reason to believe the contrary. Tit for Tat suggests that this will pay off for you as well as for others.

Obviously there are limits to how much one can risk at a first encounter. I often lend books to people whom I do not know well; usually I get them back. Since back issues of academic journals are often impossible to replace, I don't lend them, except to people I know well. In entering into a new business relationship it is equally obvious that risks should be kept low; but whatever the deal that is struck, one should give full value on the assumption that the other party will do the same.

Because Tit for Tat works only when there is likely to be a continuing relationship between you and the other party, both parties can benefit by finding a way to ensure that the relationship between them will be a lasting one. Marriage served precisely this function of providing a basis for a lifetime of wholehearted co-operation, as long as divorce was impossible, socially unacceptable, or very difficult to obtain. The easy, Hollywood-style acceptance of a life involving several divorces and remarriages has undermined this important function of the marriage ceremony. To go through a ceremony of marriage without even intending to make a long-term commitment is utterly pointless, a mere relic of an age in which to have sex without the blessing of the Church was thought to be sinful, and to have children out of wedlock was to disadvantage them. In societies not dominated by conservative forms of religion, these beliefs are disappearing, and we are better off without them. Should the institution of marriage disappear with them? There are signs that it will, as more and more couples live together without getting married.

There are, of course, many ways of making clear the seriousness of a commitment to the other partner, apart from the religious or legal nature of the marriage bond itself. Pooling finances and putting time and energy into the joint home is one; it means that if the relationship breaks up, the mutual investment will be lost. In my own marriage, I felt that it was the decision to conceive a child together, rather than the decision to get married, that created the firmest commitment. I do not mean that my wife-to-be and I conceived, or even sought to conceive, a child before we got married. We were not so unconventional; four years passed between our marriage and the decision to have our first child. Despite the good relationship we had built up during this period and the commitment we had made to each other, before we had a child, staying together seemed optional. Since we did not regard divorce as contrary to any divine or moral law, if our feelings towards each other changed, we could each go our own way. Our decision to have a child closed that option; it could still be opened again, but only with much greater difficulty. (I stress that this is a point about the possibilities of making a binding commitment, rather than about the nature or quality of our relationship.) Our child linked our futures in a much more binding way than any other form of commitment could do, because once a loving bond has developed between parents and child, there is no way of undoing the link between the parents cleanly and completely. No matter how much either or both partners may want to end the relationship and begin afresh, the existence of their mutual child makes it impossible for them to do so.

2. *Do good to those who do good to you, and harm to those who harm you.* In following Tit for Tat we must steer a course between two great dangers: the danger of getting into an unending series of mutual – and mutually destructive – paybacks, and the danger of being exploited. We start by being friendly and co-operative. But once it is clear that the other party is not being equally co-operative, it is time to change our own policy. How swiftly should we change? In the tournaments Axelrod ran there was a program called Tit for Two Tats that forgave the first instance of unco-operative behaviour, and only retaliated if the failure to co-operate was repeated. It did very well in the first tournament, but not in the second, where there were more programs able to exploit its forgiving nature.

The most momentous historical example of a failure to abide by this second crucial Tit for Tat principle is the policy of appeasement pursued by Britain and France as Hitler progressively tore up the Treaty of Versailles. He began by rebuilding the German army. If the Allies had been following a Tit for Tat policy they would have retaliated in some way, but they did nothing. In 1936 Hitler marched his soldiers into the Rhineland, which the Treaty had made a demilitarized zone. Here, even an exponent of Tit for Two Tats would have acted, but again the Allies did nothing. A similar lack of response greeted Hitler's annexation of Austria in 1938. Before the year was out, he demanded the Sudetenland, the

German-speaking regions of Czechoslovakia. For a time it appeared that the Allies had had enough; but at Munich, they again yielded all that the German dictator had demanded. Giving in to unilateral force in this way simply enhanced Hitler's belief that he could achieve what he wanted; it also contributed to his growing reputation with his own people as a leader of genius. Had the Allies stood firm against the remilitarization of the Rhineland, for instance, they would have had an easy victory against a relatively unprepared enemy. When the Allies finally committed themselves to the defence of Poland, war came on much worse terms for them. By being too forgiving, by following what proved to be a policy of Tit for About Five Tats, the British and French governments ensured only that when war came, it would be a far greater catastrophe than it would have been if it had come earlier. Several factors played a role here, especially the guilt felt by many in Britain and France over the harshness of the Versailles Treaty, and a firm desire, very understandable after the slaughter of World War I, to avoid war at all costs. Nevertheless, with the benefit of hindsight, it is clear how tragic a misjudgment it was to allow someone prepared to use unilateral force to achieve what he wanted at no cost at all.

In other situations it may be difficult to apply Tit for Tat at all. The involvement of America and its Allies in the war in Vietnam was often justified by pointed references to the need to avoid the mistake of appeasing communism, as Nazism had been appeased. Behind this thought lay the idea that international communism was a single entity that had advanced across Asia, conquering China, North Korea, North Vietnam, and was now threatening to spread through South Vietnam to Thailand and Malaysia. But this was wrong; the war in Vietnam was more a local conflict than a testing ground for the forces of international communism, and the communist victory in Vietnam did not lead, as the hawks had said it would, to the 'dominoes' of Thailand, Malaysia and Indonesia also falling to communism.

The example of Vietnam shows that Tit for Tat is no substitute for a detailed and accurate understanding of the particular facts of a situation. Even then, it will not bring about the utopia of a world without the use of force, but it will, if intelligently applied and well understood, make war rare, for it will mean that war does not pay. Thus despite the scepticism that greeted President Bush's hailing of the United Nations stand against Iraqi aggression as inaugurating a 'new world order', it is not absurd to see a collective determination to resist clear cases of aggression as the basis for a new world order, based essentially on the simple but powerful principle of Tit for Tat. There is, however, still one great threat to this prospect. Tit for Tat is a rule that does well in a situation of continuing relationships. If the evil that can be visited on the other party is so great that the other party cannot retaliate at all, Tit for Tat cannot apply. Similarly, if to retaliate would only ensure the destruction of both parties, it will not make sense to retaliate, even if one can do so. The existence of nuclear weapons makes both of these possibilities real. Along with everything else they put in jeopardy, nuclear weapons thus threaten the best basis we have for regulating relationships between nations.

3. Keep it simple. Tit for Tat is a very simple rule. There are advantages in keeping one's behaviour simple; it makes it easy for the other party to see what is going on. Game theorists use the term Zero-sum Game to describe a game in which if anyone gains, others must lose the equivalent amount. Playing poker for money is, in financial terms, a Zero-sum Game. At the end of an evening's poker, the sum of the winnings of those who are ahead, less the losses of those who are behind, must equal zero. If life were a Zero-sum Game, playing by a simple rule would be a disadvantage, because one could do better for oneself only by making the other player do worse. (In poker you try to win by misleading the other players about your intentions.) In many real-life situations, however, both parties will gain from co-operation, and they will do better if they understand each other from the start. Then they can know how to achieve co-operation. Each will also do better if the other parties know that he or she is not open to being exploited. To be open and straightforward about your policy can thus be in your own interest, for it makes it easier for others to see what you are doing, and to co-operate with you for mutual benefit.

Should Tit for Tat be applied within closer personal relationships?

To suggest that it should seems petty and coldly calculating. Surely lovers don't have to play Prisoner's Dilemma games with each other; nor do close friends. Or consider bringing up children: shouldn't parents respond to their children from love and devotion, rather than in the calculating way suggested by Tit for Tat?

It is true that between lovers, in a family, or with close personal friends, where each genuinely cares for the well-being of the other, the question of reciprocity scarcely arises. To put it more technically, in Prisoner's Dilemma games, caring about the welfare of the other player changes the way in which we assess the outcomes. If each prisoner in the Ruritanian gaol cares as much for the welfare of the other prisoner as he cares for his own, he would make his decision so as to achieve not the shortest time in gaol for himself, but the lowest total number of years to be spent in gaol by both of them. Refusing to confess produces a lower total whatever the other prisoner does (if the other prisoner confesses it produces a total of ten years in gaol, rather than sixteen when both confess; and if the other prisoner does not confess it produces a total of one year, rather than ten when one confesses and the other does not). Therefore the altruistic prisoner would refuse to confess, and if both prisoners were altruistic they would both be better off than they would have been if neither of them had cared about how long the other spent in gaol. So lovers, families and close personal friends who care as much for the welfare of the other lover, family member or friend as they do for their own welfare, do not get into Prisoner's Dilemma-type situations with each other.

Genuine concern for others is, then, the complete solution to the Prisoner's Dilemma; it dissolves the dilemma altogether. Where possible, we do well to try to extend it beyond family and close personal friends. We often invite children to put themselves in the place of another. 'How would you like it if she did that to you?' is a commonly heard explanation of why, for example, your daughter should not take another girl's toy. This teaches an important moral point, that others feel hurt or aggrieved, just as we do. If fellow-feeling is sufficiently strong, then there is no need for Tit for Tat; but when it is not, Tit for Tat has a role, even in close personal or family relationships. Especially with children, it is vital that, as a minimum, they come to understand that reciprocity works for the benefit of both parties to a relationship. So when my teenage daughter slouches off to watch television instead of doing her share of the household chores, loving fatherly forgiveness may not be best for her, or for anyone else in the family. Instead, it might be more in her interests, as well as in mine, to let her know that the next time she wants to be driven to her friend's place, she may find me otherwise occupied. It may make me feel bad to do it, but it helps her to appreciate that other people do not exist only for her own convenience.

In the larger society, outside the family and personal relationships, Tit for Tat plays a central role in regulating the way we interact with others. Modern urban life, however, is a much more difficult environment in which to pursue Tit for Tat than the computerized world of Axelrod's tournaments. We can only apply the strategy if we know who is co-operating with us and who is not. The computers have no problem in figuring out who the other player is, or what the other player is doing, because the program tells them. Nor is this much of a problem for Max and Lyn in their stable relationship, engaged in a task that can hardly be disguised. There is scope for subtle forms of cheating even in a small-scale society. People on a co-operative food gathering trip may quietly gulp down the tastiest berries they find when no-one else looking. Coping with these minor forms of cheating, however, is a trifling problem compared with those we face in everyday life in large cities. The city forces us to interact constantly with people whom we have never seen before, and will probably never see again; it is hardly surprising that it lacks the cosy security of village life in which no-one locks their doors. Nor should we wonder at the fact that when we seat ourselves in protective steel shells and hurtle around the roads in a manner inherently liable to kill or injure others, some people behave in a less co-operative manner than they do when they are relating to people face-to-face.

We can think of a system of taxation as a gigantic, annually repeated Prisoner's Dilemma. We all want (at least some of) the government services financed out of taxation, but each of us would prefer not to pay his or her share. The difficulty in applying Tit for

Tat is that those who do not co-operate are not easily detected. Thus not paying your fair share of taxation can be a winning strategy for each individual to pursue. To change the pay-off we must make the penalties for detection so large that (taking into account the odds against detection) tax evasion ceases to be a worthwhile gamble. We can do this either by increasing the penalties, or by improving the rate of detection, or by doing both at the same time. If we can succeed we will eliminate the Prisoner's Dilemma entirely. The change in pay-offs does not have to be strictly financial. Adding public embarrassment to the fines can make not co-operating still less attractive. In other circumstances, the embarrassment itself may be enough. Changing the pay-offs will not eliminate tax evasion altogether: people commit all sorts of crimes, the consequences of which are predictably damaging to their own interests. To reduce tax evaders to those unable to judge where their own interests lie would, however, be a significant advance on the present situation in many countries.

Much of our system of justice can be explained in the same way. Justice is not, as often thought, a sacrosanct moral principle imposed on us by a divine being, nor is it somehow engraved into the bedrock of the universe. Justice is neither more nor less than a set of conceptual tools for making Tit for Tat work in the real world. As such, it needs to be used with discretion. 'Let justice be done, though the heavens fall' is an ancient saying, but one that invests justice with a shade too much significance. How absolute we ought to be about justice will depend on the circumstances. If, as may happen in rare circumstances, justice works to no-one's benefit, both in the short and the long-term, to adhere to it is pointless.

In his compilation of knowledge about the moral codes of different societies, Edward Westermarck concluded: 'To requite a benefit, or to be grateful to him who bestows it, is probably everywhere, at least under certain circumstances, regarded as a duty'.[7] This duty of gratitude leads us to respond in kind to favours done for us; the corresponding ideas of moral resentment, moral indignation, retribution, and revenge suggest how we are to respond when someone harms us. All of these ideas are aspects of reciprocity. Reciprocity is Cicero's 'first demand of duty',[8] the 'single thread' of the Confucian way,[9] and according to the American sociologist Alvin Gouldner, one of the few moral ideas that can claim to have universal acceptance in practically every society known to us.[10] (Obligations to one's kin, especially of parents to their children, are, as we saw in Chapter 5, also endorsed in every known society; kinship and reciprocity are the two strongest, and perhaps the only, claimants to the title of universally accepted moral principle.)

In this respect, the constancy of the human situation is more impressive than the variations often pointed to by ethical relativists. Polybius, a Greek historian, wrote more than 2,000 years ago that:

> . . . when a man who has been helped when in danger by another does not show gratitude to his preserver, but even goes to the length of attempting to do him injury, it is clear that those who become aware of it will naturally be displeased and offended by such conduct, sharing the resentment of their injured neighbor and imagining themselves in the same situation. From all this there arises in everyone a notion of the meaning and theory of duty, which is the beginning and end of justice.[11]

In the true spirit of Tit for Tat, the celebrated code of Hammurabi of Babylon proclaimed justice to consist in 'an eye for an eye and a tooth for a tooth'. (The rule held only between members of the aristocracy; for injuries to freemen or slaves, fines were sufficient.)[12] But is taking out the eye of the perpetrator appropriate compensation for the loss of one's own eye? Here we begin to debate what is or is not fair or just. Perhaps I don't want to put your eye out, but would rather have some more useful compensation for the injury you caused me. What if you didn't put out my eye, but started a fire that burnt my crop, and you, being a shiftless person, don't have a crop of your own anyway? Even if we have an agreed concept of fairness, our lack of impartiality compounds the difficulties of applying it. The feeling that we have been short-changed can lead to retaliation that in turn provokes more serious retaliation, until, like the famous Hatfields and McCoys, we have a full-blown feud echoing down the years and even over several generations.[13] To avoid this we need a concept of impartiality, and a system that will deliver impartial decisions about what constitutes fair dealing. From this it is a short step to the society as a whole taking over and enforcing some aspects of justice, including the task of seeing that serious offenders are appropriately punished.

4. Be forgiving. Tit for Tat means always being ready to forget and forgive the past. No matter how black a past the other party may have, all that is needed to make Tit for Tat co-operate is a single co-operative act by the other. This makes it easier to break out of patterns of mutually damaging recriminations. It also avoids complications, and makes it easier for the other party to see exactly what the policy is. In real life, we are reluctant to forget the past, because it serves as a guide to the future. If the other party offers to co-operate, we have to judge if the offer is sincere. When past co-operative overtures have turned out to be followed by attempts to exploit us, we may well be more reluctant to commit ourselves than whether past offers have been genuine. With this reservation, though, the success of Tit for Tat shows the value of remaining open to the possibility of beginning or resuming a co-operative and mutually beneficial relationship with those who have, in the past, been unco-operative.

5. Don't be envious. The final factor contributing to the success of Tit for Tat is that it does not mind others doing as well or better than it does. Tit for Tat did better overall because it promoted co-operative situations more often than any other strategy. Had it been envious, it would have tried to overcome the gain that the other player may have got on that single occasion when Tit for Tat made a co-operative move but the other player was selfish. But Tit for Tat could have done this only by being selfish, and that would have led to mutual retaliation and fewer co-operative interactions.

In a Zero-sum Game, it makes sense to be envious. But even poker is only a Zero-sum Game in theory, and not always in real life. If we are more interested in having an entertaining evening than in whether we win or lose a few dollars, we may all gain from the game, irrespective of whether we end up ahead or behind. Life is not a Zero-sum Game. We do better if we are not envious. This is true both psychologically and in terms of Tit for Tat strategy. Strategically, the best co-operative partners we can have are ones who will rejoice in our success, as well as in their own. Deeply envious people are therefore likely to miss out on opportunities for mutually beneficial co-operation. They can try to keep their envious nature secret, but this is not easy to do. Even if they do succeed in this, however, they will pay a psychological cost. Envy is not a pleasant emotion to have. It is intrinsically opposed to contentment, essentially a preoccupation with unfulfilled wants, and this is hardly likely to lead to happiness. If we describe a man as deeply envious, we conjure up a picture of someone who is miserable, unable to enjoy what he has, and obsessed rather with what he has not. Sometimes this takes extreme forms, and drives people to ruin themselves. The Wall Street banker Dennis Levine seems to have been driven by envy. According to a former colleague at Drexel Burnham Lambert, Levine 'bitched endlessly that while he was earning in the six figures, his clients were making nine. "Next to them", Dennis used to say, "I feel like a pisher"'. The way Levine found to move his already ample income into the next bracket ended in gaol both for him and for those with whom he exchanged inside information.

There is no doubt that envy can be a strong motivating force. It can make people strive for positions of high status, or for material wealth. No doubt this is why it survives from one generation to the next, despite its obvious disadvantages both for the envious person and for others. Unfortunately, because it is such a strong motivating force, those who want to sell us their products often appeal, subtly or not so subtly, to the element of envy that is in many of us. They foster a climate of envy and a conception of self-interest based on ranking ourselves relative to others. That, in turn, undermines out tendency to co-operate for mutual benefit.

Self-interest and ethics: An interim conclusion

Societies evolve ethical rules in order to make co-operation more reliable and more durable. The results benefit everyone in the society, both collectively and as individuals. Adopting an initially friendly and co-operative stance, entering into long-term relationships, but not allowing oneself to be exploited, being straightforward and open, avoiding envy – these are not foreign edicts that command us to subdue our own inclinations and turn away from the pursuit of our best interests. They are sound recommendations for anyone seeking a happy and fulfilling life as a social being.

If we now draw into this picture points made in Chapter 5 about the ethical significance of family and kinship, we can see that a great deal of ethics fits very well with an evolutionary account of our evolved social nature. In some of the most central areas of ethical behaviour, our desires and our ethics are in harmony. In our life with our family and kin, and with our lovers, friends, partners and colleagues, very often self-interest and ethics will point in the same direction. By these means we can eliminate at least a part of the conflict between ethics and self-interest. To that extent, our ultimate choice of how to live is made less difficult. We can choose to live ethically, and at the same time live in a manner that satisfies many of our most important needs as a human being. On the other hand, the areas of ethics we have been discussing in this chapter and in Chapter 5 are by no means the whole of ethics. The remaining chapters of this book turn to a distinct and much more demanding aspect of ethics, and also to some deeper questions about the true nature of self-interest.

CHAPTER 8

Living ethically

Heroes

Yad Vashem is situated on a hilltop outside Jerusalem. Established by the Israeli Government to commemorate the victims of the Holocaust and those who came to their aid, it is a shrine, a museum, and a research centre. Leading toward the museum is a long, tree-lined avenue, the Allee des Justes, or Avenue of the Righteous. Each tree commemorates a non-Jewish person who risked her or his life in order to save a Jew during the Nazi period. Only those who gave help without expectation of reward or benefit are deemed worthy of inclusion among the Righteous. Before a tree is planted a special committee, headed by a Judge, scrutinizes all the available evidence concerning the individual who has been suggested for commemoration. Notwithstanding this strict test, the Avenue of the Righteous is not long enough to contain all the trees that need to be planted. The trees overflow onto a nearby hillside. There are now more than 6,000 of them. There must be many more rescuers of Jews from the Nazis who have never been identified. Estimates range from 50,000 to 500,000, but we will never really know. Harold Schulweis, who started a foundation that honours and assists such people, has pointed out that there are no Simon Wiesenthals to search out those who hid, fed and saved the hunted. Yad Vashem, with a limited budget, can play only a passive role in reviewing evidence about people nominated by survivors. Many who were helped did not, in the end, survive; others prefer not to relive painful memories, and have not come forward, or in any case could not identify their rescuers.

Perhaps the most famous of those commemorated at Yad Vashem is Raoul Wallenberg. In the early years of World War II, as the Nazis extended their rule across Europe, Wallenberg was leading a comfortable life as a Swedish businessman. Since Sweden was neutral, Wallenberg travelled extensively throughout Germany and to its ally, Hungary, in order to sell his firm's line of specialty foods. But he was disturbed at what he saw and heard of the persecution of the Jews. One of his friends described him as depressed, and added, 'I had the feeling he wanted to do something more worthwhile with his life'. In 1944, the scarcely credible news of the systematic extermination of the Jews began to build up to such a degree that it could no longer be ignored. The American Government asked the Swedish Government if, as a neutral nation, it could expand its diplomatic staff in Hungary, where there were still 750,000 Jews. It was thought that a strong diplomatic staff might somehow put pressure on the nominally independent Hungarian government to resist the deportation of Hungarian Jews to Auschwitz. The Swedish Government agreed. Wallenberg was asked to go. In Budapest he found that Adolf Eichmann, who had been appointed by Himmler to administer the 'Final Solution', was determined to show his superiors just how ruthlessly efficient he could be in wiping out the Hungarian Jewish community. Wallenberg succeeded in persuading the Hungarian Government to refuse Nazi pressure for further deportations of Jews, and for a brief interlude it seemed that he could return to Sweden, his mission accomplished. Then the Nazis overthrew the Hungarian government and installed in its place a puppet regime led by the Hungarian 'Arrow Cross' Nazi party. The deportations began again. Wallenberg issued 'Swedish Protective Passes' to thousands of Jews, declaring them to have connections with Sweden, and to be under the protective custody of the Swedish Government. At times he stood between the

Nazis and their intended victims, saying that the Jews were protected by the Swedish Government, and the Nazis would have to shoot him first if they wanted to take them away. As the Red Army advanced on Budapest, the situation began to disintegrate. Other neutral diplomats left, but the danger remained that the Nazis and their Arrow Cross puppets would carry out a final massacre of the Jewish ghetto. Wallenberg remained in Budapest, risking falling bombs and the hatred of trigger-happy German SS and Hungarian Arrow Cross officers. He worked to get Jews to safer hiding places, and then to let the Nazi leaders know that if a massacre took place, he would personally see to it that they were hanged as war criminals. At the end of the war, 120,000 Jews were still alive in Budapest; directly or indirectly, most of them owed their lives to Wallenberg. Tragically, when the fighting in Hungary was over, Wallenberg himself disappeared and is presumed to have been killed, not by the Germans or the Arrow Cross, but by the Soviet secret police.[1]

Oskar Schindler was, like Wallenberg, a businessman, but of very different character and background. Schindler was an ethnic German from Moravia, in Czechoslovakia. Initially enthusiastic for the Nazi cause and the incorporation of the Czech provinces into Germany, he moved into Poland after the invading Nazi armies, and took over a factory in Cracow, formerly Jewish-owned, that made enamel ware. As the Nazis began taking the Jews of Cracow to the death camps, Schindler protected his Jewish workers, using as a justification the claim that his factory was producing goods essential for the war effort. On the railway platforms, as Jews were being herded into the cattle-trucks that would take them to the extermination camps, he would bribe or intimidate SS officials into releasing some that he said belonged to, or had skills that were needed for, his factory. He used his own money on the black market, buying food to supplement the inadequate rations his workers received. He even travelled secretly to Budapest in order to meet with members of an underground network who could get news of the Nazi genocide to the outside world. Near the end of the war, as the Russian army advanced across Poland, he moved his factory and all his workers to a new 'labour camp' he constructed at

Brinnlitz in Moravia. It was the only labour camp in Nazi Europe where Jews were not beaten, shot, or worked or starved to death. All of this was very risky; twice Schindler was arrested by the Gestapo, but bluffed his way out of their cells. By the end of the war, at least 1,200 of Schindler's Jewish workers had survived; without Schindler they would almost certainly have died.

Schindler exemplifies the way in which people who otherwise show no signs of special distinction prove capable of heroic altruism under the appropriate circumstances. Schindler drank heavily and liked to gamble. (Once, playing cards with the brutal Nazi commandant of a forced labour camp, he wagered all his evening's winnings for the commandant's Jewish servant, saying that he needed a well-trained maid. He won, and thus saved the woman's life.) After the war Schindler had an undistinguished career, failing in a succession of business ventures, from fur breeding to running a cement works.[2]

The stories of Wallenberg and Schindler are now well known, but there are thousands of other cases of people who took risks and made sacrifices to help strangers. Those documented at Yad Vashem include: a Berlin couple with three children who moved out of one of the two rooms of their apartment, so that a Jewish family could live in the other room; a wealthy German who lost most of his money through his efforts to help Jews; and a Dutch mother of eight who, during the winter of 1944, when food was scarce, often went hungry, and rationed her children's food too, so that their Jewish guests could survive. Samuel Oliner was a twelve-year-old boy when the Nazis decided to liquidate the ghetto of Bobowa, the Polish town in which he was living. His mother told him to run away; he escaped from the ghetto, and was befriended by a Polish peasant woman who had once done some business with his father. She helped him assume a Polish identity, and arranged for him to work as an agricultural labourer. Forty-five years later Oliner, then a professor at Humboldt State University in California, co-authored *The Altruistic Personality*, a study of the circumstances and characteristics of those who rescued Jews.[3]

I know from my own parents, Jews who lived in Vienna until 1938, that for each of these heroic stories there are many more that show less dramatic, but still significant, instances of altruism. In my parents' escape from Nazi Europe, the altruism of a virtual stranger proved more effective than ties of kinship. When Hitler marched into Vienna my newly-wedded parents sought to emigrate; but where could they go? To obtain an entry visa, countries like the United States and Australia required that one be sponsored by a resident, who would guarantee that the new immigrants would be of good behaviour and would not be a burden on the state. My father had an uncle who, several years earlier, had emigrated to the United States. He wrote seeking sponsorship. The uncle replied that he was very willing to sponsor my father, but since he had never met my mother, he was not willing to extend the sponsorship to her! In desperation my mother turned to an Australian whom she had met only once, through a mutual acquaintance, when he was a tourist in Vienna. He had not met my father at all; but he respond-ed immediately to my mother's request, arranged the necessary papers, met my parents on the wharf when their ship arrived, and did everything he could to make them feel welcome in their new country.

Sadly, my parents' efforts to persuade their own parents to leave Vienna were not heeded with sufficient speed. My mother's father, for example, was a teacher at Vienna's leading academic high school, until the school was ordered to dismiss all Jewish teachers. Despite the loss of employment, he believed that as a veteran of the World War I, wounded in battle and decorated for gallantry, he and his wife would be safe from any attack on their person or lives. Until 1943 my grandparents continued to live in Vienna, under increasingly difficult conditions, until they were sent to concentra-tion camps, which only my maternal grandmother survived. Even during the grim years of the war prior to 1943, however, we know from letters that my parents received that some non-Jews visited them, to bring news and comfort. When my grandfather became nervous about possessing his ceremonial sword (because Jews had for some time been forbidden to keep weapons), a friend of my mother hid the sword under her coat and threw it into a canal. This woman was also a schoolteacher; her refusal to join the Nazi Party cost her any chance of promotion. Non-Jewish former pupils of my grandfather continued to visit him in his flat, and one refused to accept a university chair because he would then have been compelled to support Nazi doctrines. These were not heroic, life-saving acts, but they were also not without a certain risk. The important point, for our purposes, is that all the social pressure on these people was pushing them in the opposite direction: to have nothing to do with Jews, and certainly not to help them in any way. Yet they did what they thought right, not what was easiest to do, or would bring them the most benefit.

Primo Levi was an Italian chemist who was sent to Auschwitz because he was Jewish. He survived, and wrote *If This is a Man*, an extraordinarily telling account of his life as a slave on rations that were not sufficient to sustain life. He was saved from death by Lorenzo, a non-Jewish Italian who was working for the Germans as a civilian on an industrial project for which the labour of the prisoners was being used. I cannot do better than close this section with Levi's reflections on what Lorenzo did for him:

> In concrete terms it amounts to little: an Italian civilian worker brought me a piece of bread and the remainder of his ration every day for six months; he gave me a vest of his, full of patches; he wrote a postcard on my behalf and brought me the reply. For all this he neither asked nor accepted any reward, because he was good and simple and did not think that one did good for a reward.
>
> . . . I believe that it was really due to Lorenzo that I am alive today; and not so much for his material aid, as for his having constantly reminded me by his presence, by his natural and plain manner of being good, that there still existed a just world outside our own, something and someone still pure and whole, not corrupt, not savage, extraneous to hatred and terror; something difficult to define, a remote possibility of good, but for which it was worth surviving.
>
> The personages in these pages are not men. Their humanity is buried, or they themselves have buried it, under an offence received or inflicted on someone else. The evil and insane SS men, the Kapos, the politicals, the criminals, the prominents, great and small, down to the indifferent slave Haftlinge

[prisoners], all the grades of the mad hierarchy created by the Germans paradoxically fraternized in a uniform internal desolation.

But Lorenzo was a man; his humanity was pure and uncontaminated, he was outside this world of negation. Thanks to Lorenzo, I managed not to forget that I myself was a man.[4]

A green shoot

We must, of course, be thankful for the fact that today we can help strangers without dreading the knock of the Gestapo on our door. We should not imagine, however, that the era of heroism is over. Those who took part in the 'velvet revolution' that overthrew communism in Czechoslovakia, and in the parallel movement for democracy in East Germany, took great personal risks and were not motivated by thoughts of personal gain. The same can be said of the thousands who turned out to surround the Russian Parliament in defence of Boris Yeltsin in his resistance to the hard-liners' coup that deposed Mikhail Gorbachev. The supreme contemporary image of this kind of courage, however, comes not from Europe, but from China. It is a picture that appeared on television and in newspapers around the world: a lone Chinese student standing in front of a column of tanks rolling towards Tiananmen Square.

In liberal democracies, living an ethical life does not involve this kind of risk, but there is no shortage of opportunities for ethical commitment to worthwhile causes. My involvement in the animal liberation movement has brought me into contact with thousands of people who have made a fundamental decision on ethical grounds: they have changed their diet, given up meat, or, in some cases, abstained from *all* animal products. This is a decision that affects your life every day. Moreover, in a society in which most people continue to eat meat, becoming a vegetarian inevitably has an impact on how others think about you. Yet thousands of people have done this, not because they believe that they will be healthier or live longer on such a diet – although this may be the case – but because they became convinced that there is no ethical justification for the way in which animals are treated when they are raised for food. For example, Mrs A. Cardoso wrote from Los Angeles:

> I received your book, *Animal Liberation*, two weeks ago . . . I
> thought you would like to know that overnight it changed my
> thinking and I instantly changed my eating habits to that of the
> vegetarian . . . Thank you for making me aware of our selfishness.

There have been many letters like this. Some of the writers had no
particular interest in the treatment of animals before they more or
less accidentally came into contact with the issue. Typical of these is
Alan Skelly, a high school teacher from the Bahamas:

> As a high school teacher I was asked to become involved in the
> general studies taught to grade eleven. I was asked to prepare
> three consecutive lessons on any social topic. My wife had been
> given a small leaflet, 'Animal Rights', by a child in her class. I
> wrote to the organization, People for the Ethical Treatment of
> Animals, in Washington, DC and received on hire the video
> 'Animal Rights'. This video has had such an impact upon my
> wife and I that we are now vegetarians and committed to animal
> liberation. They also sent me a copy of your book, *Animal Lib-
> eration* . . . Please be aware that fourteen years after the publi-
> cation of your book you are responsible for the radicalization
> and commitment of my wife and I to animal liberation. Perhaps
> next month when I show PETA's video to 100 eleventh grade
> students I may also extend others' moral boundaries.

Some of the people who write tell me of particular difficulties they
may have; how they can't get non-leather hiking boots, or see no
practical alternative to killing mice that get into their house. One
had a retail fur and leather shop when he became convinced that
we ought not to be killing animals for their skins – he has had problems convincing his partner to change the nature of the business!
Others want to know what to feed their dogs and cats, or whether I
think prawns can feel pain. Some practise their new diets alone,
others work together with groups trying to change the way animals
are treated. A few risk their own freedom, breaking into laboratories in order to document the pain and suffering occurring there,
and perhaps to release a few animals from it. Wherever they draw

the line, they all provide significant evidence that ethical argument can change people's lives. Once they were convinced that it is wrong to rear hens in small wire cages to produce eggs more cheaply, or to put pigs in stalls too narrow for them to turn around, these people decided that they had to bring about a moral revolution in their own lives.

Animal liberation is one of many causes that rely on the readiness of people to make an ethical commitment. For two gay Americans, the cause was the outbreak of AIDS. Jim Corti, a medical nurse, and Martin Delaney, a corporate consultant, were horrified to discover that American regulations prevented their HIV-positive friends from receiving novel drugs that appeared to offer some hope for people with AIDS. They drove to Mexico, where the drugs were available, and smuggled them back into the USA. Soon they found themselves running an illegal worldwide operation, smuggling drugs and fighting government bureaucracies that sought to protect people dying from an incurable disease against drugs that were not proven safe and effective. Eventually, after taking considerable risks and doing a lot of hard work, they succeeded in changing government policies so that AIDS patients – and all those with terminal diseases – have quicker access to experimental treatments.[5]

Australia's most memorable wilderness struggle took place in 1982 and 1983, when 2,600 people sat in front of bulldozers that were being used to begin construction of a dam on the Franklin river, in south-west Tasmania. The Franklin was Tasmania's last wild river, and the dam, to be built to generate electricity, would flood dramatic gorges and rapids, obliterate Aboriginal heritage sites, destroy Huon Pines that had taken 2,000 years to grow, and drown the animals that lived in the forests. The blockaders came from all over Australia, some travelling thousands of kilometres at their own expense from Queensland and Western Australia. They included teachers, doctors, public servants, scientists, farmers, clerks, engineers and taxi drivers. Almost half were arrested by police, mostly charged with trespass. A team of twenty lawyers, all volunteers, helped with court proceedings. Nearly 450 people refused to accept bail conditions, and spent between two and twenty-six days in gaol. Professor David Bellamy, the world-renowned English botanist, travelled around the world to take part in the blockade, and was duly arrested. Interviewed later in the local police lock-up, he said:

> It was the most uplifting thing I have ever been part of, to see such a broad cross-section of society peacefully demonstrating in quite inhospitable weather against the destruction of something they all believed in.[6]

Ethical commitment, no matter how strong, is not always rewarded; but this time it was. The blockade made the Franklin dam a national issue, and contributed to the election of a federal Labor government pledged to stop it. The Franklin still runs free.

These exciting struggles exemplify one aspect of a commitment to living ethically; but to focus too much on them can be misleading. Ethics appears in our lives in much more ordinary, everyday ways. As I was writing this chapter, my mail brought me the newsletter of the Australian Conservation Foundation, Australia's leading conservation lobby group. It included an article by the Foundation's fund-raising co-ordinator, in which he reported on a trip to thank a donor who had regularly sent donations of $1,000 or more. When he reached the address he thought something must be wrong; he was in front of a very modest suburban home. But there was no mistake: David Allsop, an employee of the state department of public works, donates 50 percent of his income to environmental causes. David had previously worked as a campaigner himself, and said he found it deeply satisfying now to be able to provide the financial support for others to campaign.[7]

There is something uplifting about ethical commitment, whether or not we share the objectives. No doubt some who read these pages will think that it is wrong to release animals from laboratories, no matter what the animals might suffer; others will think that everyone ought to abide by the decisions of the state's planning procedures on whether or not a new dam should go ahead. They may think that those who take the opposite view are not acting ethically at all. Yet they should be able to recognize the unselfish commitment of those who took part in these actions. In the abortion controversy, for example, I can acknowledge the actions of opponents of abortion as ethically motivated, even while I disagree with them about the point from which human life ought to be protected, and deplore their insensitivity to the feelings of young pregnant women who are harassed when going to clinics that provide abortions.

In contrast to most of the examples given so far, I shall now consider some in which unselfish, ethical action is a much quieter, more ordinary event, but no less significant for that. Maimonides, the greatest Jewish moral thinker of the medieval period, drew up a 'Golden Ladder of Charity'. The lowest level of charity, he said, is to give reluctantly; the second lowest is to give cheerfully but not in proportion to the distress of the person in need; the third level is to give cheerfully and proportionately, but only when asked; the fourth to give cheerfully, proportionately, without being asked, but to put the gift into the poor person's hand, thus causing him to feel shame; the fifth is to give so that one does not know whom one benefits, but they know who their benefactor is; the sixth is to know whom we benefit, but to remain unknown to them; and the seventh is to give so that one does not know whom one benefits and they do not know who benefits them. Above this highly meritorious seventh level Maimonides placed only the anticipation of the need for charity, and its prevention by assisting others to earn their own livelihood so as not to need charity at all.[8] It is striking that, 800 years after Maimonides graded charity in this way, many ordinary citizens take part in what he would classify as the highest possible level of charity, at least where prevention is not possible. This happens at the voluntary blood banks that are – in Britain, Australia, Canada and many European countries – the only source of supply for the very large amount of human blood needed for medical purposes. I have already briefly mentioned, in Chapter 5, this widespread instance of ethical conduct. The gift of blood is in one sense a very intimate one (the blood that is flowing in my body will later be inside the body of another); and in another sense a very remote one (I will never know who receives my blood, nor will they know from whom the blood came). It is relatively easy to give blood. Every healthy person, rich or poor, can give it, without risk. Yet to the recipient, the gift can be as precious as life itself.

It is true that only a minority of the population (in Britain, about 6 percent of people eligible to donate) actually do donate.[9] It is also true that to give blood is not much of a sacrifice. It takes an hour or so, involves a slight prick, and may make you feel a little weak for the next few hours, but that is all. How many people, a sceptic might ask, would be prepared to make a *real* sacrifice so that a stranger could live?

If the willingness to undergo anaesthesia and stay overnight in hospital is enough of a real sacrifice, we now know that hundreds of thousands of people *are* prepared to do this. In recent years, bone marrow donor registries have been established in about twenty-five countries. In the USA, about 650,000 people have registered and 1,300 have donated. Figures in some other countries are comparable. For instance, in France, 63,000 have registered, and 350 have donated; England has had 180,000 registrations and 700 donations to date; in Canada, 36,000 have registered, and 83 have donated; while Denmark's registrations total 10,000, with five donations. Approximately 25,000 Australians have registered on the Australian Bone Marrow Donor Registry, and at the time of writing, ten have already donated bone marrow.[10] With calm deliberation, in a situation untouched by nationalism or the hysteria of war, and with no prospect of any tangible reward, a number of ordinary citizens are prepared to go to considerable lengths to help a stranger.

We should not be surprised about this willingness to help. As the American author Alfie Kohn puts it in a cheery book called *The Brighter Side of Human Nature*:

> It is the heroic acts that turn up in the newspaper ('Man Dives into Pond to Save Drowning Child') and upstage the dozens of less memorable prosocial behaviors that each of us witnesses and performs in a given week. In my experience, cars do not spin their wheels on the ice for very long before someone stops to give a push. We disrupt our schedules to visit sick friends, stop to give directions to lost travelers, ask crying people if there

is anything we can do to help ... All of this, it should be stressed, is particularly remarkable in light of the fact that we are socialized in an ethic of competitive individualism. Like a green shoot forcing its way up between the concrete slabs of a city sidewalk, evidence of human caring and helping defies this culture's ambivalence about – if not outright discouragement of – such activity.[11]

Countless voluntary charities depend on public donations; and most also rely on something that, for many of us, is even harder to give: our own time. American surveys indicate that nearly 90 percent of Americans give money to charitable causes, including 20 million families who give at least 5 percent of their income to charity. Eighty million Americans – nearly half the adult population – volunteer their time, contributing a total of 15 billion hours of volunteer work in 1988.[12]

We act ethically as consumers, too. When the public learnt that the use of aerosols containing CFCs damages the ozone layer, the sale of those products fell significantly, before any legal phase-out had come into effect. Consumers had gone to the trouble of reading the labels, and choosing products without the harmful chemicals, even though each of them could have chosen not to be bothered. Leading advertising agency J. Walter Thompson surveyed American consumers in 1990 and found that 82 percent indicated that they were prepared to pay more for environmentally-friendly products. Between a third and half said that they had already made some environmental choices with their spending dollars. For example, 54 percent said that they had already stopped using aerosol sprays.[13]

The Council on Economic Priorities is a United States organization that rates companies on their corporate citizenship records. The aspects rated are giving to charity, supporting the advancement of women and members of minority groups, animal testing, military contracts, community outreach, nuclear power, involvement with South Africa, environmental impact, and family benefits. The results are published annually in a paperback that has sold 800,000 copies. Presumably many of those who buy the book are interested in supporting companies that have a good record on ethical issues.

Many of the millions of customers who have helped to make The Body Shop a successful international cosmetics chain go there because they want to make sure that when they buy cosmetics, they are not supporting animal testing or causing damage to the environment. From small beginnings, the organization has grown at an average rate of 50 percent per annum, and sales are now around $150 million a year. Similarly, mutual investment funds that restrict their investments to corporations that satisfy ethical guidelines have become much more significant in the last decade, as people become concerned about the ethical impact of their investments and not only about the financial return they may gain.[14]

These examples of ethical conduct have focused on ethical acts that help strangers, or the community as a whole, or nonhuman animals, or the preservation of wilderness, because these are the easiest to identify as altruistic, and therefore as ethical. But most of our daily lives, and hence most of our ethical choices, involve people with whom we have some relationship. The family is the setting for much of our ethical decision-making; so is the workplace. When we are in long-standing relationships with people it is less easy to see clearly whether we do what we do because it is right, or because we want, for all sorts of reasons, to preserve the relationship. We may also know that the other person will have opportunities to pay us back – to assist us, or to make life difficult for us – according to how we behave toward him or her. In such relationships, ethics and self-interest are inextricably mingled, along with love, affection, gratitude and many other central human feelings. The ethical aspect may still be significant.

Why do people act ethically?

In Chapter 5 I referred to the cynical view that if only we probe deeply enough, we will find that self-interest lurks somewhere beneath the surface of every ethical action. In contrast to this view, we saw that evolutionary theory, properly understood predicts that we will be concerned for the welfare of our kin, members of our group, and those with whom we may enter into reciprocal relationships. Now we have seen that many people act ethically in circumstances that cannot be explained in any of these ways. Oskar

Schindler was not furthering his own interests, nor those of his kin or of his group, when he bribed and cajoled SS officers to protect Jewish prisoners from deportation to the death camps. To a successful non-Jewish German businessman, the abject and helpless Jewish prisoners of the SS would hardly have been promising subjects with whom to begin a reciprocal relationship. (Real life has unpredictable twists; as it happened, many years after the war, when Schindler was struggling to find a career for himself, some of those whose lives he had saved were able to help him; but in 1942, as far as anyone could possibly tell, the prudent thing for Schindler to do would have been to keep his mind on his business, or relax with the wine, women and gambling that he obviously enjoyed.) Similar things can be said about other rescuers in thousands of well-documented cases. The point is sufficiently established, though, by the more humdrum example of blood donation. Since this is an institution that continues to thrive, it is easier to investigate.

Richard Titmuss, a distinguished British social researcher, published the results of a study of nearly 4,000 British blood donors in a splendid book called *The Gift Relationship*. He asked his sample of donors why they first gave blood, and why they continued to give. Overwhelmingly, people from all levels of education and income answered that they were trying to help others. Here is one example, from a young married woman who worked as a machine operator:

> You can't get blood from supermarkets and chain stores. People themselves must come forward, sick people can't get out of bed to ask you for a pint to save their life, so I came forward in hope to help somebody who needs blood.

A maintenance fitter said simply:

> No man is an island.

A bank manager wrote:

> I felt it was a small contribution that I could make to the welfare of humanity.

And a widow on a pension answered:

> Because I am fortunate in having good health myself and like to
> think my blood can help someone else back to health, and I felt
> this was a wonderful service I wanted to be part of.[15]

Aristotle suggested that we become virtuous by practising virtue, in
much the same way as we become players of the lyre, a kind of
ancient harp, by playing the lyre. In some respects this seems a
strange idea, but it is supported by further research on the motivation of blood donors. Professor Ernie Lightman, of the University of
Toronto, surveyed 2,000 voluntary blood donors, and found that
their first donation was prompted by some outside event, such as an
appeal from a blood bank for more donors, the fact that friends or
colleagues were donating, or the convenience of a place to donate.
As time passed, however, these external motivators became less significant, and 'ideas such as a sense of duty and support for the
work of the Red Cross, along with a general desire to help' became
more important. Lightman concludes that 'with repeated performance of a voluntary act over time, the sense of personal, moral
obligation assumed increasing importance'. Researchers at the University of Wisconsin have also studied the motivation of blood
donors, and found that the greater the number of donations the
donors have made, the less likely they were to say that they were
prompted to give by the expectations of others, and the more likely
to say that they were motivated by a sense of moral obligation and
responsibility to the community. So maybe Aristotle was right: the
more we practise virtue, for whatever reason, the more likely we are
to become virtuous in an inner sense as well.[16]

Altruistic action is easy to recognize as ethical, but much ethical
behaviour is quite compatible with regard for one's own interests.
Here is one last example, this time from my own experience. As a
teenager, I worked during the summer holidays in my father's
office. It was a small family business, importing coffee and tea.
Among the correspondence I had to read were, occasionally, letters
that my father sent out to the exporters from whom he had pur-
chased goods, reminding them that they had not yet sent him

invoices for goods dispatched a considerable time ago. Sometimes it was clear, from the length of time that had elapsed, that something had slipped through the system in the 'accounts payable' section of the exporter's business. If the exporters were large firms, they might never have noticed their mistake; for us, on the other hand, since we worked on gross profit margins of 3 percent, one or two 'free' consignments would have made more profit than a month's normal trading. So why not, I asked my father, let the exporters look after their own problems? If they remembered to ask for their money, well and good, if they did not, better still! His reply was that that was not how decent people did business; and anyway, to send these reminders built up trust, which was vital for any business relationship, and would in the long run rebound to our profit. The answer, in other words, hovered between references to an ethical ideal of how one ought to behave (what it is to be virtuous in business, one might say) and a justification in terms of long-term self-interest. Despite this ambivalence, my father was clearly acting ethically.

Ethics is everywhere in our daily lives. It lies behind many of our choices, whether personal or political, or bridging the division between the two. Sometimes it comes easily and naturally to us; in other circumstances, it can be very demanding. But ethics intrudes into our conscious lives only occasionally, and often in a confused way. If we are to make properly considered ultimate choices, we must first become more aware of the ethical ramifications of the way we live. Only then is it possible to make ethics a more conscious and coherent part of everyday life.

CHAPTER 9

The nature of ethics

A broader perspective

Those who act ethically stand for an alternative way of living, at odds with the narrow, accumulative and competitive pursuit of self-interest that, as we have seen, has come to dominate the West, and is now unchallenged in the former communist nations as well. I want to consider why one might choose this ethical alternative. Before we can discuss this question, however, we need to get clear what it is to act ethically. The nature of ethics is often misunderstood. Ethics cannot be reduced to a simple set of rules, like 'do not tell lies', 'do not kill', or 'do not have sexual relations except with someone to whom you are married'. Rules are useful for educating children, and as a handy guidebook when it is difficult for us to think carefully and calmly. In some ways they are like recipes. If you are an inexperienced cook, recipes are essential; even for the experienced cook they are normally to be followed, but a good cook knows when and how to adapt. Just as no cookbook will ever cover all the circumstances in which you may need to produce a palatable meal, so life itself is too varied for any finite set of rules to be an absolute source of moral wisdom.

This analogy should not be pushed too far. It may take a while for a budding chef to get to the point at which she or he can independently assess a recipe, and decide how it should be improved. We are all entitled, however, to think for ourselves about ethics. The moral rules still being taught in most societies are often not the ones that we most need to teach our children today. The tension between self-interest and ethics that is at the core of this book exists independently of religious, or more specifically Christian, ethics; but the traditional Christian emphasis on the denial of harmless bodily pleasures, especially sexual pleasures, bears a heavy responsibility for increasing that tension until, in many people, it reaches breaking point, with the outcome either an abandonment of ethics, or a sense of guilt and defilement.

There is much talk today of the decline in ethics. Very often what those who talk about this really mean is that there has been a decline in the observance of certain ethical rules. I don't know if there really has been a decline in obedience to these rules. (Does anyone? No doubt someone can produce a survey showing that today more people say that they tell lies than did ten years ago; but maybe people have just become more honest in reporting that they lie.) In any case, *if* there has been such a decline, it does not mean that there has been a decline in ethics, but only that there has been a decline in obedience to these rules. Is that a good thing, or a bad thing? It all depends. Have people been breaking the rules because they don't care about ethics at all, and are interested only in satisfying their own short-term desires? Or have they been breaking them because they realize that obeying the rule is, in certain circumstances, likely to do more harm than good, for everyone affected by it? That may be an ethical thing to do.

It is also often said that ethics is 'all very well in theory but no good in practice'. But we cannot rest content with an ethics that is unsuited to the rough-and-tumble of everyday life. If someone proposes an ethic so noble that to try to live by it would be a disaster for everyone, then – no matter who has proposed it – it is *not* a noble ethic at all, it is a stupid one that ought to be firmly rejected. Ethics is practical, or it is not really ethical. If it is no good in practice, it is no good in theory either. Getting rid of the idea that an ethical life must consist of absolute obedience to some short and simple set of moral rules makes it easier to avoid the trap of an unworkable ethic. An understanding of ethics that allows us to take into account the special circumstances in which we find ourselves is already a major step towards attaining an ethics that we really can use to guide our lives.

So don't think of an ethical approach to life as one in which every time we are about to enjoy ourselves, an image of a stone tablet drops from some section of our mind, engraved with a commandment saying 'Thou shalt not!' And don't think of it as a mere ideal that is irrelevant to what we are doing here and now. How then *should* we think of it? We should think of an ethical life as a life that results from a positive choice of goals and the means by which they may be achieved. But this is still too vague. What if my chosen goal is to live a life of ease and luxury? Is that an ethical end? If not, why not? If so, are any means that I might use to achieve my end also ethical, so long as they will help me to gain it?

Suppose that I choose my own happiness as my goal. I pursue this goal in an efficient manner. Am I living an ethical life? In other words, can I be both purely egoistic and at the same time ethical? Here is one reason – not necessarily the only reason – for saying that I may not be. In pursuing my own happiness, I may interfere with others pursuing their own happiness. Perhaps I have not even thought about this possibility. Perhaps, having thought about it, I have dismissed it as irrelevant, since after all it is *my* happiness that I care about, not anyone else's. In both of these cases I have not made an ethical choice. To act ethically is to act in a way that one can recommend and justify to others – that, at least, seems to be part of the very meaning of the term. How can I recommend and justify to others actions that are based only on the goal of increasing my own happiness? Why should other people think that my happiness is more important than theirs? They may agree that I have some reason to further my own happiness, but that very reasoning would lead them to further their own interests, not mine – and that is just what I do not want to recommend to them, because if they are as single-minded in defending their own interests as I am in defending mine, they may interfere with my pursuit of my own interests.

The point just made does not show that it is *irrational* to be solely concerned with one's own interest, disregarding the impact one has on others. It shows only that it cannot be ethical to live such a life. Since this conclusion depends on the meaning of 'ethics', no recommendation about what it is or is not reasonable or rational to do can follow from it. Some philosophers have tried to argue that there is something illogical about saying: 'I know that, ethically speaking, I ought to do this, but I can't decide whether to do it'. But the arguments that purport to show that this is illogical all end up trying to deduce conclusions about what it is reasonable to do from the meanings of words like 'good' or 'ought'. That particular philosophical conjuring trick was exposed long ago.[1] You can define 'good' or 'ought' in any way you choose. It is always possible for me to say, without committing any logical mistake: 'If that is what "good" means, then I don't care about doing what is good'. To choose to disregard ethical considerations entirely might not be a *wise* choice, but that is very different from saying that it is an incoherent or self-contradictory choice.[2]

To live ethically is to think about things beyond one's own interests. When I think ethically I become just one being, with needs and desires of my own, certainly, but living among others who also have needs and desires. When we are acting ethically, we should be able to justify what we are doing, and this justification must be of a kind that could, in principle, convince any reasonable being. That this is a fundamental requirement for ethics has been recognized since ancient times, and in different cultures[3], but it has been given its most precise form by R. M. Hare, formerly professor of moral philosophy at the University of Oxford. As Hare puts it, if our judgments are to be moral, they must be 'universalizable'. By this he means, not that they must hold in all possible situations, but that we must be prepared to prescribe them independently of the role that we occupy – and that includes prescribing them independently of whether we gain or lose by their application. Essentially, this means that in considering whether I ought to do something I must, if I am thinking ethically, imagine myself in the situation of all those affected by my action (with the preferences that they have). At the most fundamental level of ethical thinking, I must consider the interests of my enemies as well as my friends, and of strangers as well as my family. Only if, after taking fully into account the interests and preferences of all these people, I still think that the action is better than any alternative open to me, can I genuinely say that I ought to do it. At the same time I must not ignore the long-term effects of fostering family ties, of establishing and promoting reciprocal relationships, and of allowing wrongdoers to benefit from their wrongdoing. No-one can, in everyday life, carry out so complex a process of thinking on the occasion of every moral choice; hence the desirability of moral rules, not as repositories of absolute moral truth, but as generally reliable guides for normal circumstances. Hare's explication of the nature of ethical thinking allows us to take account of all the facts relevant to ethical behaviour that were discussed in earlier chapters of this book, while at the same time it shows why ethical thinking limits the extent to which we may put our own needs and our own happiness – or that of our family, or even of our race or our nation – ahead of the happiness of these other beings.[4] To live ethically is to look at the world with a broader perspective, and to act accordingly.

The gender of ethics

To say that ethical judgments could, in principle, be accepted by anyone raises a question that has been the subject of much discussion in the past decade: is ethics gendered? It has long been thought that there are differences in the way males and females approach ethics. For most of history, women's nature has been seen as more inclined to what we might call the domestic virtues, and less suited to a broad perspective. Thus in *Emile*, Rousseau summarizes a woman's duties as: 'the obedience and fidelity which she owes to her husband, the tenderness and care due to her children'.[5] Men, but not women, should understand and participate in civic affairs and politics, because 'a woman's reason is practical . . . The search for abstract and speculative truth, for principles and axioms of science, for all that tends to wide generalisation, is beyond a woman's grasp'.[6] Hegel took a similar view: women's ethical judgment was limited to the customary ethical life of home and family; the world of affairs, of civil society and of the more abstract realm of universal morality was for men. Freud brought this tradition into the present century, saying that women 'show less sense of justice than men' and 'are more often influenced in their judgments by feelings of affection or hostility'.[7]

Since Mary Wollstonecraft wrote her pioneering *A Vindication of the Rights of Woman* in 1792, there has been a strand of feminist thought that argues strongly, against Rousseau and those who think in his mould, that there are no distinctively male or female virtues: ethics is universal. A quite distinct strand of feminist thought, however, came to the fore in the early days of the struggle for women's suffrage. In advocating votes for women, some feminists argued that women *do* have a distinctive approach to many ethical and political issues, and that it is precisely for this reason that their influence should be more strongly felt in politics. It is male ambition and aggression, this argument ran, that is responsible for the follies of war, with all the suffering that this brings. Women, on the other hand, were said to be more nurturing and more caring. In *Women and Labour*, published in 1911, Olive Schreiner suggested that having experienced pregnancy, childbirth and the rearing of children, women will view the 'waste' of life in war differently from men.[8]

Such views became unpopular in the seventies, during the resurgence of the modern feminist movement, when any talk of natural or innate psychological differences between the sexes was ideologically suspect. More recently, however, some feminists have revived the idea that women see ethics differently from men. Much of the impetus for this change has come from Carol Gilligan's study, *In a Different Voice: Psychological Theory and Women's Development*. Gilligan reacted against the work of the Harvard psychologist Lawrence Kohlberg, who spent his working life studying the moral development of children. He did this by asking children what they would do in a number of moral dilemmas, and grading their level of moral development by the answers they give. In one dilemma, a man called Heinz has a wife who will die unless she can get a drug that he cannot afford. The druggist refuses to give the drug to Heinz. Should Heinz steal the drug in order to save his wife? Jake, an eleven-year-old boy, answers that Heinz should steal the drug, and then face the consequences. Jake, according to Kohlberg, thus shows his understanding of social rules and his ability to rank principles about respect for property, and respect for human life. On the other hand Amy, a girl of the same age as Jake, focuses more on the relationship between Heinz and his wife, and also criticizes the druggist for not helping someone who is dying. She suggests that Heinz should persist in trying to talk to the druggist, to see if they can come up with a solution to the problem. Kohlberg regards the boy's answer as indicative of a higher stage of moral development, because it considers the problem at a more abstract level, and refers to a system of rules and principles. Gilligan points out that Amy sees the moral universe in less abstract, more personal terms, emphasizing relationships and responsibilities between people. This may be different from the way in which Jake sees morality, but it is not therefore inferior or at a lower stage of development.[9]

In *Caring: A Feminine Approach to Ethics and Moral Education*, Nel Noddings defends a view in some respects like that of Gilligan. She argues that women are less inclined than men to see ethics in terms of abstract rules and principles. Women, Noddings thinks, are more likely to respond directly to specific situations on the basis of an attitude of caring. For women, the relationships in which they are involved are central to their perception of the situation. At one point Noddings develops this view into a criticism of my own argument that we should extend the basic moral principle of equal consideration of interests to all beings who have interests, that is, to all sentient creatures. This is, in Noddings's view, an example of an abstract and distinctively male attitude to ethics; the feminine approach she espouses would not lead us to have duties to *all* animals, but rather to particular ones, such as our companion animals, with whom we are in some kind of relationship. On this basis Noddings rejects my view that where we have adequate alternatives to eating animal flesh, we should be vegetarians. Noddings refers approvingly to the reluctance one might feel for eating a named farmyard animal like Daisy the cow, but thinks our obligations not to eat animals go no further.[10]

Here I think Noddings goes astray, not only in her specific ethical judgments, but also in her characterization of a feminist approach to ethics. I cannot prove Gilligan and Noddings wrong when they claim that women are less inclined to think in terms of abstract ethical rules and principles than men, though the basis on which they make this claim is flimsy, and it is ironic that they should come close to agreeing with Rousseau's clearly sexist view that women do not reason abstractly.[11] Other feminists take a different stance. Alison Jaggar, for instance, has argued that 'feminist ethics' does not need to be 'feminine ethics'; she also rejects biological determinism, emphasizing that not all women are feminists, while some men are.[12] In any case, when it comes to how one lives, women do not limit their ethical concerns to those with whom they have some relationship. On the contrary, there is evidence to suggest that women are, if anything, *more* universal in their ethical concern than men, and readier to take a long-term view. The popular Canadian environmentalist and broadcaster David Suzuki notes, in his book *Inventing the Future*, that in his experience 'women are disproportionately represented in the environmental movement'. The same is true of the animal liberation movement. From the nineteenth century until the present day, women have clearly outnumbered men in groups trying to stop the exploitation of animals. Recently at the local animal liberation group with which I work, we decided to check the sex ratio of its membership. To our surprise, we found that over 80 percent of our members are female. Curious about this, I wrote to People for the Ethical Treatment of Animals, a Washington, DC-based organization that has more members than any other group pursuing the goal of equal consideration for animals. They told me that they had discovered a similar preponderance of women when they last examined their list of supporters.[13]

Suzuki explains the large number of women in the environmental movement by reference to the fact that women have been excluded from much of the power structure in our society, and so have less at stake in the status quo than men. This means, Suzuki thinks, that they can see through our social myths with greater clarity than men. There may be something in this, but to be involved in the environmental movement one also needs a concern for the long-term care of the planet and the species who live on it. Similarly, people are drawn to the animal liberation movement very largely because they care about the suffering of animals. Is it possible that, on the whole, women do care more strongly than men about the suffering of others? Are they, perhaps, the more ethical gender? All such generalizations will certainly have exceptions, and should be treated with caution, but I suspect that there is some truth in this one. Unlike mainstream party politics, success in campaigns for animals offers little in the way of career prospects, and does not bring benefits for the campaigners, beyond their knowledge that they have helped to reduce the suffering of other beings. Although other explanations are certainly possible, the predominance of women in the environmental and animal movements therefore suggests a greater readiness to work for larger goals, and not just to help oneself or one's own kind. Interestingly, Carol Gilligan quotes from a woman who expresses exactly this commitment to a universal ethic:

> I have a very strong sense of being responsible to the world, that I can't just live for my enjoyment, but just the fact of being in the world gives me an obligation to do what I can to make the world a better place to live in, no matter how small a scale that may be on.[14]

In earlier chapters of this book I have stressed the importance of family, kin and reciprocal relationships. In the previous section of this chapter I have referred to the importance of a broader perspective, too, and I shall develop that idea in the next chapter; but that broader perspective must be able to recognize the central place that personal relationships have in human ethical life. The generalized concern for the entire world expressed in the last quotation is exactly what the world needs if it is to overcome its problems. The next question is: if someone is choosing how to live, and doesn't already have that sense of responsibility to the world, are there good reasons why he or she should take on so universal an ethical commitment?

Jesus and Kant: Two views on why we ought to live ethically

My father believed that to remind his suppliers to send out their invoices was both right, and likely to prove profitable in the long run. I don't know whether he really thought that in each instance it was likely to bring some benefit, or if he was referring in a more general way to the benefits of adopting a scrupulously honest approach to one's dealings with customers. Nor do I know whether he had chosen honesty because he believed it to be the best policy, or if he would have chosen it even if convinced that, in the long run, it would harm his business.

These questions reflect a deep division about how the ethical life may be justified or recommended when we are making an ultimate choice about how to live. For most of the history of Western civilization, Christianity has had a monopoly on our thinking about why we should do what is right. The answer it gives is that we should do what is right in this world so as to have a better fate in the next. The early Christians did not think that this world was of much significance in itself. They expected that it would soon end, that the Day of Judgment was close at hand. After all, as Jesus had said:

> I tell you this; there are some standing here who will not taste death before they have seen the Son of Man coming in his kingdom.[15]

And if that prediction had already been falsified by the end of the first century after Jesus, Christians could still remember his advice:

> Hold yourself ready, therefore, because the Son of Man will come at the time you least expect him.[16]

Though belief in the imminence of the Second Coming ebbed, the view persisted that this world is significant only as a preparation for the next, the world in which we will slough off our mortal bodies and live forever. The meaning of this world therefore lies in the fact that it is part of God's plan. Our role in it is to act for the greater glory of God. If we need a further reason for acting morally, that can easily be found in the promise of heavenly joy if we do so, and the threat of hellish torments if we do not. These rewards and punishments are often played down by sophisticated modern

Christians who are uncomfortable with so crudely self-interested an answer to the question of why we should do what is right. But the threat of reward and punishment was a central feature of Christian moral teaching until quite recently. It began with Jesus, whom the Gospels portray as preaching a morality of self-interest. We are often told that Jesus said, in his celebrated Sermon on the Mount:

> . . . when you do some act of charity, do not announce it with a flourish of trumpets, as the hypocrites do in synagogue and in the streets to win admiration from men.

This may sound like an anticipation of Maimonides' Golden Ladder of Charity; but the remainder of the passage, in which Jesus tells us why we should not behave in this way, is less elevating:

> I tell you this: they have their reward already. No; when you do some act of charity, do not let your left hand know what your right hand is doing; your good deed must be secret, and your Father who sees what is done in secret will reward you.[17]

Throughout the sermon, Jesus hammers home the same message: about loving your enemies, about praying in private, about forgiving others the wrongs they have done, about fasting, about judging others, and more generally, about doing 'the will of my heavenly father'. In each case, the reward of heaven is held out as an incentive – a reward, moreover, that, unlike treasure on earth, cannot grow rusty, or be stolen by thieves.[18]

For the next eighteen centuries, there was no challenge to the Christian warning of the danger of eternal punishment. Christian theologians debated whether noble non-Christians like Virgil would have to go to hell, and worried over the fate of infants who died before being baptized, and who therefore would still be in a state of Original Sin when the Day of Judgment came. For the illiterate masses, Christian painters vividly depicted the sufferings of the damned, tormented by devils and roasted by the flames of hellfire, while in heaven the righteous sprouted wings and played their harps. Eighteen centuries was quite long enough to leave a lasting impression on the Western mind.

As the eighteenth century enlightenment gradually loosened the hold of Christianity on our moral thinking, Immanuel Kant, the greatest of German philosophers, presented a very different picture of morality. Kant sought to reconstruct the Christian conception of morality in a manner that made it independent of teachings about heaven and hell, and largely independent even of belief in God. Instead he relied on reason, to the exclusion of everything else. According to Kant, we act morally only when we have put aside all motives stemming from our desires or inclinations. If duty is not to be 'everywhere an empty delusion', then 'bare conformity to universal law as such' must serve as the motive for moral action. By 'universal law' Kant meant the moral law – and in particular his famous 'categorical imperative' that tells us to act only in accordance with principles that we would be ready and willing to enact into universal laws. Thus he was saying that we must do our duty for duty's sake. The blood donor who is moved to give by a simple desire to help her fellow-humans is not acting morally unless she can put aside that desire, and be motivated only by the thought that to help another human being is her duty, in accordance with the moral law.

Understandably, many modern thinkers who consider themselves Kantians seek to deny that so cold and rigid a view can be what Kant really meant. So here is an extraordinary passage that leaves little doubt:

> To help others where one can is a duty, and besides this there are many spirits of so sympathetic a temper that, without any further motive of vanity or self-interest, they find an inner pleasure in spreading happiness around them and can take delight in the contentment of others as their own work. Yet I maintain that in such a case an action of this kind, however right and however amiable it may be, has still no genuinely moral worth . . . for its maxim lacks moral content, namely the performance of such actions, not from inclination, but *from duty*.

According to Kant, it is only when such a person somehow loses 'all sympathy with the fate of others', so that the person is no longer moved by any inclinations, but acts for the sake of duty alone, that 'for the first time his action has its genuine moral worth'. [19]

Here is a doctrine that might wring a grimace of recognition from an early Christian saint mortifying his flesh in the desert. In one sense Kant's view is diametrically opposed to the idea we considered in Chapter 2, that morality is a game for suckers; and yet the two views have in common the assumption that to act morally we must deny our own best interests for the sake of our moral duty. The difference is that those who think morality is a game for suckers see this assumption as a reason for holding morality in contempt, whereas for Kant, it merely shows how pure and rare true moral worth is. Kant's position offers a bleak prospect of the human condition. We grasp the moral law because as reasoning beings, we are inevitably aware of it and in awe of it, but we find it fundamentally hostile to our nature as physical, desiring beings. We may yearn to bring about harmony between the moral law and our desires, but we can never succeed.

In many non-Western societies, such a view of human nature would be greeted with baffled incomprehension. In Buddhist ethics, for instance, the source of goodness must be sought within one's own nature, not as something imposed from outside. Even among the ancient Greeks, the idea that what we ought to do could be contrary to *all* our desires would have caused bewilderment. That Kant's doctrine was taken seriously, and often even accepted by his European readers suggests that it reflects an element of the distinctive moral consciousness with which generations have grown up in Western Europe. It is, in fact, the element to which the term 'morality' (rather than 'ethics') most naturally applies today, for morality is linked more closely with the idea of a moral law, and carries the implication that we ought to feel guilty when we fail to meet its standards.

Let us look a bit more closely at this idea of morality. Why on earth would anyone ever believe that to give blood has *more* worth when the donor gives out of duty, without any inclination to help others, than when the donor gives because he or she feels 'an inner pleasure in spreading happiness', or is drawn to the blood bank by sympathy with the plight of those in need of the blood?

Here is one possible reason. We praise or blame people with an eye, directly or indirectly, towards getting them and others to act in the ways we want them to act. For people who enjoy spreading happiness, or who are moved to act by strong feelings of sympathy for the needs of others, praise for giving blood is superfluous. All these people need to know is that they can easily give blood, and that people will suffer if there is a shortage of blood. Then they will give. Moral praise and blame really come into their own only when we are faced with people who take no pleasure in making others happy, and are lacking in sympathy for those in need. Then morality gives us a lever with which we may be able to move them to do the right thing, despite the absence of any inherent desire to do it. In other words, by suggesting that duty for duty's sake has some special moral worth, we are making up for a deficiency in motive for doing the right thing.

Moral worth, in Kant's sense of the term, is a kind of all-purpose glue that society can use to fill the cracks in the ethical fabric of society. If there were no cracks – if we all enjoyed doing what needs to be done, and helping others for its own sake – we would not need it; but such a utopia remains out of reach. That is why the notion of moral worth is so useful. A woman may lack generous inclinations, but if she sees it as her duty to aid those in distress, she will do so. A man may harbour prejudices against those of a different racial group, yet if he accepts that it is his duty to avoid racial discrimination, he will do so. There are limits to what can be accomplished by this kind of artificial substitute for more natural inclinations. Qualities like warmth of personality, spontaneity, creativity and so on cannot be promoted by a morality that tells us to do our duty for its own sake. A dutiful father may provide for his children as carefully as any other father, but he cannot love them for duty's sake. Nevertheless, a morality of 'duty for duty's sake' is useful enough to make it easy to understand why a society might promote it.

Useful as it might be, there is something about this conception of morality that should make us uneasy. No matter how much we encourage people to do their duty for its own sake, the real purpose behind this encouragement is to get them to do their duty because of the good consequences that will flow from their doing so. That is why, if we are to retain the special moral worth of duty for duty's sake, we cannot allow anyone to inquire too closely into the reason *why* one should do one's duty. We have to say, as the British philosopher F. H. Bradley was later to put it, that 'to ask for the Why? is simple immorality . . . we desert a moral point of view, we degrade and prostitute virtue, when to those who do not love her for herself we bring ourselves to recommend her for the sake of her pleasures'.[20] This is fine rhetoric, but hardly a convincing response. If those who insist on duty for its own sake spurn all support from inclination or self-interest, they entrench forever the division between morality and self-interest (no matter how broadly we conceive of self-interest). They leave morality a closed system. If you accept 'the voice of moral consciousness', then you will also accept that you should not inquire further. For those who are not already committed to living as duty dictates, however, the basic question of how we are to live becomes unanswerable, because morality, one of the chief contenders, has turned in on itself and refused to offer an answer at all. If you do not accept the moral point of view, then on this account there is no way in which you can be given a reason that will lead you to accept it.

Sceptics deride morality as something that society foists upon us for its own sake. If by 'morality' we mean the view that moral worth is to be found only in action done for the sake of duty, they seem to be right. To put it bluntly: on this view, morality is a fraud. Unchallenged, it may be socially useful, but the gains are achieved at a high risk, for once questioned, this conception of morality has no means of resisting the sceptical challenge. Thus the sceptics score an undeservedly easy triumph.

The Kantian conception of morality is dangerous in another way. Without guidance from human benevolence and sympathy, a strong sense of duty can lead to rigid moral fanaticism. A startling example of just how far this can go emerged at the trial of Adolph Eichmann, held in Jerusalem in 1961. According to the official record of his pre-trial police examination, at one point Eichmann, the former chief administrator of the Holocaust, 'suddenly declared with great emphasis that he had lived his whole life according to Kant's moral precepts, and especially according to a Kantian definition of duty'. During the trial, one of the judges questioned Eichmann about this, and Eichmann replied: 'I meant by my remark about Kant that the principle of my will must always be such that it can become the principle of general laws'. Eichmann also cited, in support of his Kantian attitude to his duty, the fact that out of the millions of cases that passed through his hands, he allowed sympathy to sway him from the path of duty on only two occasions. The implication clearly is that on other occasions he felt sympathy for the Jews he was sending to the gas chambers, but because he believed one should do one's duty unaffected by sympathy, he steadfastly stuck to his duty, instead of being tempted to bend the rules and help the Jews.[21]

Eichmann seems not to have been the only Nazi who steeled himself for appalling acts by focusing on duty and crushing more normal instincts. In a speech to the SS *Einsatzgruppen*, special squads appointed to carry out the killing of groups of Jews, Heinrich Himmler told his troops that they were called upon to fulfil a 'repulsive duty' and that he would not like it if they did such a thing gladly. He had recently witnessed the machine-gunning of about 100 Jews and had, he said, 'been aroused to the depths of my soul' by what he had seen; but he was obeying the highest law by doing his duty.[22]

So let us throw out, once and for all, Kant's idea that moral worth is to be found only when we do our duty for the sake of doing our duty. (It is because this idea has pervaded our notion of morality for so long, and so successfully, that I prefer to use the term 'ethics' rather than 'morality'.) We should also reconsider the assumption – shared by both Kant and the sceptics who regard ethics as a game for suckers – that ethics and our natural inclinations are always liable to conflict. Then we can construct an account of ethics that builds on, instead of turning away from, our own nature as social beings.

Beyond Jesus and Kant: The search for an ultimate answer

Jesus recommended obedience to God's command in order to avoid damnation, whereas the Kantian conception of morality carries with it the implication that we must recommend morality entirely for its own sake, without any suggestion that 'honesty is the best policy' or even that we may find fulfillment in commitment to an ethical life. We have rejected the views of both Jesus and Kant, but the ultimate question 'why should we act ethically?' is still in need of an answer. The decision to live an ethical life places some limits on what we can do. We might want to do things that we know we cannot justify from an universalizable point of view. Why not do them anyway?

Kant's mistaken insistence on the idea that we should do our duty for its own sake was an understandable reaction against a traditional view of reward and punishment that he found contemptible. Because the Christian view had so long dominated all Western thought, the dawning of a secular age in which many do not believe in God, or in a life after death, has come as a shock. If God goes, what else goes with him? Some thought that morality without God was an impossibility. Dostoyevsky wrote, in *The Brothers Karamazov*, that if there is no God, 'everything is permitted'. That thought struck a chord with those who believed that the meaning of this world lies in its part in God's plan. Without God there can be no providence watching over us, no divine plan for the world, and hence no meaning to our lives. On a more individual basis, if the reason for doing what is right is to go to heaven rather than hell, the end of belief in a life after death seems to spell the end of any reason for doing what is right. Kierkegaard wrote:

> If man had no eternal consciousness, if, at the bottom of everything, there were merely a wild, seething force producing everything, both large and trifling, in the storm of dark passions, if the bottomless void that nothing can fill underlay all things, what would life be but despair?[23]

It was not only for Christians that the decline of religious belief gave rise to a problem about ethics. For many atheists and agnostics raised in a Christian culture, ethics seemed to be a mere appendage of religion, and one that could not survive without it. For the existentialist philosophers of the mid-twentieth century like Jean-Paul Sartre, the rejection of God meant that we are alone in the world. We must choose, but all our choices are arbitrary. There are no rules, no right or wrong. All that remains, for Sartre, is to choose 'authentically' and avoid a life of 'bad faith'. But if all choice is arbitrary, how can one choose one alternative over another? Even a preference for authenticity over bad faith needs some kind of justification.

A quite different group of twentieth century philosophers came to a similar conclusion by a different route. 'Theology and Absolute Ethics', wrote Frank Ramsey, a brilliant Cambridge philosopher who died in 1930 at the age of twenty-six, 'are two famous subjects which we have realized to have no real objects'.[24] That attitude, spoken with the confidence of youth and a modern scientific outlook, expresses the view of ethics taken by the logical positivists, a group of thinkers that began with the celebrated 'Vienna Circle' and spread to the English-speaking world as a result of Wittgenstein's *Tractatus* and A. J. Ayer's forthright manifesto, *Language, Truth and Logic*. Ayer denied that any assertion can be meaningful unless there is, at least in principle, some way in which its truth can be verified. Since judgments that an action is ethically right or wrong cannot be verified such judgments are, on Ayer's view, no more than expressions of our subjective feelings. Supporters of the objectivity of ethics have been on the defensive ever since.

I share Ramsey's view of theology and, to a degree, I also share his view of 'absolute' (by which he means 'objective') ethics. We cannot set a super-computer to calculate the answer to 'life, the universe and everything', as Douglas Adams imagines in his entertaining *Hitchhiker's Guide to the Galaxy*. If the universe has not been constructed in accordance with any plan, it has no meaning to be discovered. There is no value inherent in it, independently of the existence of sentient beings who prefer some states of affairs to others. Ethics is no part of the structure of the universe, in the way that atoms are. But in the absence of belief in God, what other options are there for finding a basis for ethics? Is it possible to study the nature of ethics in a secular fashion and find some philosophical grounding for how we should live?

The quest is both an ancient and a universal one, so for those willing to look back to the pre-Christian era, or outside Christianity to a different culture, there are alternative accounts of the meaning of life and the place of ethical behaviour in it. Among the most ancient of all surviving literary works is the epic of Gilgamesh, King of Uruk, in ancient Sumer (now southern Iraq) during the third millenium before the Christian era. Gilgamesh is first introduced as a brutal tyrant ruling by force, bullying men and raping virginal girls before they marry. Then Gilgamesh begins to worry about his own mortality, and since he had defeated all other opponents, determines to defeat death. Travelling far to find the answer, he pauses for refreshment at an ale house, where the barmaid tells him to accept mortality and make the most of the pleasures life can offer:

> Gilgamesh, let your belly be full.
> Be merry every day and night.
> Make each day a day of joy.
> Dance, play, by day and by night.
> Wear clean clothes.
> Let your head be washed and your body bathed with water.
> Cherish the little child who grasps your hand.
> Let your wife rejoice in your arms
> For this is the destiny of mankind.

But Gilgamesh rejects this hedonistic counsel, and after further adventures, returns to Uruk still mortal, but committed to the welfare of his people. He becomes a great king, building the walls of Uruk that provided security for his people, refurbishing the temples, and making his kingdom more fertile, prosperous and peaceful. The underlying message is that we find the good life, the most satisfying life, in carrying out our ethical responsibilities as best we can.[25]

Eastern traditions offer other answers. Like Gilgamesh, Siddhartha Gotama was a prince who had known the life of luxury and ease. According to legend this young man, brought up in a sheltered courtly atmosphere in Northern India, left the palace grounds one day and encountered an old man, a sick man, and the dead body of a man. Shocked at sights he had never seen before, he asked the driver of his carriage for an explanation, and was told that it is a fate that comes to all people. Then the prince met a wandering holy man, with shaven head and tattered robe. This man, he learnt, had chosen to live a homeless life. The prince went back to his palace. That night he could take no pleasure in the girls brought to his bed. Instead he lay pondering the meaning of what he had seen. The next day he left the palace, exchanged his princely robes for those of a beggar, and went seeking an answer to the dilemma of living in a world with so much suffering in it. The answer that he found, after many years searching, struck his followers as so wise that they called him the Enlightened One: the Buddha. In Buddha's teaching, the four sublime virtues are loving kindness, compassion, sympathetic joy, and equanimity. The first three show the strongly outwardly-directed nature of Buddhism, and its concern for all sentient creatures; the third and fourth reflect the fact that this concern for others is linked to an inner life that is both joyful and calm. Buddhism is not a religion, in the standard Western sense; it does not teach belief in any god or gods, and the Buddha certainly never regarded himself as a god, or a being to whom one should pray. Buddhists do, however, use techniques of meditation to reach states in which their deep sense of self is taken over and replaced by a stronger feeling of being part of a larger whole. This feeling of oneness with others and the universe is, at the same time, a feeling of joy and zest for life. Thus Buddhism attempts to solve the antagonism of self and other by finding the deepest fulfillment of the self in a state of mind dominated by feelings of kindness towards others. In this state the enlightened person acts on the basis of these feelings for the good of all, without thought of further reward.

Yet the Buddhist tradition must be counted as a failure in social terms. Instead of challenging conventional practices, Buddhism has accommodated itself to the status quo. Take, for example, the oft-cited 'first precept' of Buddhism: harmlessness or not-killing towards all sentient beings. In Japan one is reminded of this precept every time one visits an historic Buddhist temple, because it is printed on the back of the admission ticket. Yet when I visited Japan some years ago to study Japanese attitudes to animals, I found that very few Japanese Buddhists were vegetarians. Only in a few of the stricter sects did the monks refrain from meat, and even then they did not expect their lay followers to do so. Buddhist priests even bless the Japanese whaling fleet before it sails off to bring death to Antarctic whales. Roshi Philip Kapleau, author of the classic *Three Pillars of Zen*, recounts that during his own training in Japan meat was widely eaten, as it was at a monastery where he lived in Burma. The monks excused this action by claiming that the animals 'were not killed for them' and so they supposedly had no responsibility for their deaths![26] As we saw in Chapter 6, Buddhist ideas do have some influence on the goals that Japanese people set themselves in life. Nevertheless, on the whole, there and in other Buddhist countries, only a tiny minority of those who call themselves Buddhists really live the compassionate ethical life presented in the story of Buddha's life and teachings.

In the pre-Christian Western tradition, as we saw in Chapter 1, Socrates attempted to answer Glaucon's challenge by claiming that only the good person is really happy. To do so, he argued that the good person is one who has the parts of his or her soul in the proper relationship to each other. In the *Phaedrus*, Plato puts forward the same view by picturing reason as a charioteer, commanding the two horses of spirit and appetite. Socrates and Plato held that nobody does wrong willingly; people do wrong only if their reason is unable to control their spirit (that is, emotions like anger or pride) or their appetite (for example greed or lust). To this Aristotle made the sensible comment that the doctrine is 'manifestly at odds with the observed facts'. The assumption that Socrates and Plato make is that to know what is good is already to seek to bring it about. They drew no distinction between knowing what is good and deciding to do it. Though not in itself convincing, this idea began a long line of philosophical thought designed to show that if only we reason correctly, and are not swayed by desires to act contrary to our reason, we will freely choose what is right. Kant belongs in this broad tradition, even though Socrates and Plato saw the choice of a good life not as a sacrifice of one's own interests in the name of duty, but as the wise choice of a life that was more successful, and hence happier, than the life that was not lived so wisely.

David Hume, the great eighteenth century Scottish philosopher, has in modern times been the source of the most fundamental opposition to the Kantian tradition in ethics. Hume held that every reason for doing anything has to connect with some desire or emotion we have, if it is to have any effect on our behaviour. (The view of ethics taken by logical positivists like A. J. Ayer in *Language, Truth and Logic* is a recognizable philosophical descendant of Hume's position.) If Hume is right, the only way to answer the question: 'What should I do?' is by asking, first: 'What do you *really* want to do?' Hume hoped that the answer would mostly, if not always, be that one wanted to do what was good or right, not (as Kant would have insisted) because it is one's duty, but because of the naturally sociable and sympathetic desires human beings have. Hume belongs to a school of British philosophy that recommends the ethical life on the basis of enlightened self-interest. In contrast to Hobbes's pessimism, philosophers like the Earl of Shaftesbury, Bishop Butler (a Bishop of decidedly secular tendencies, as far as his moral argument was concerned) and David Hume all took a much more positive view of human nature. They saw human beings as naturally sociable and benevolent creatures, and therefore argued that we find real happiness in the development and satisfaction of this side of our nature. They stressed the rewards of a noble character, a good reputation and an easy conscience. They urged us to follow our natural affections for others, and wrote of the joy of true friendship, based on openness and honesty. They also pointed to the probability that wrong-doing will be detected.[27]

On the whole, those who belong to this school of thought hold that human beings are more strongly motivated by feelings of benevolence and sympathy for others than they are by more hostile emotions. Fortunately, therefore, in doing what we want to do, most of us, most of the time, will also do what is good for others.

By the nineteenth century, however, a more pessimistic outlook prevailed Jeremy Bentham, the founding father of utilitarianism, thought that nature has placed us all under two masters, pleasure and pain, and we will do whatever brings us the most pleasure and the least pain. To make sure that there was no conflict between what maximized pleasure and minimized pain for the individual, and for society as a whole, Bentham thought the law was needed, backed up by a system of reward and punishment. For a later utilitarian philosopher, Henry Sidgwick, the impossibility of reconciling one's own happiness and right conduct threatened the whole foundations of ethics. At the end of the first edition of his classic work *The Methods of Ethics*, after 473 pages of dense philosophical thought, Sidgwick wrote:

> The old immoral paradox, 'that my performance of Social Duty is good not for me, but for others' cannot be completely refuted by empirical arguments; nay, the more we study these arguments the more we are forced to admit, that if we have these alone to rely on, there must be some cases in which the paradox is true. And yet we cannot but admit . . . that it is ultimately reasonable to seek one's own happiness . . . the Cosmos of Duty is thus really reduced to a Chaos; and the prolonged effort of the human intellect to frame a perfect ideal of rational conduct is seen to have been foredoomed to inevitable failure.

Is Sidgwick right? Is 'the prolonged effort of the human intellect' – from the writer of the epic of Gilgamesh onwards – to answer the question with which this book is concerned really 'foredoomed to inevitable failure'? That conclusion might well seem to be the one that best fits the selfish, thoughtless, violent and often simply irrational behaviour that takes up so large a portion of the evening television news services. This is the other extreme from the shining examples of heroically ethical behaviour with which this chapter began. The remaining chapters will provide some grounds for hoping that it is too extreme a view, and that there may be some kind of answer, if only a partial one, to Sidgwick's 'old immoral paradox'.

CHAPTER 10

Living to some purpose

The myth of Sisyphus and the meaning of life

According to an ancient Greek myth, Sisyphus betrayed the secrets of the gods to mortal men. For this the gods condemned him to push a huge stone to the top of a hill; as he neared the peak the effort became too much for him, and the stone rolled all the way down to the bottom. Sisyphus then had to begin his task again . . . but the same thing would happen, and Sisyphus must labour with his stone for eternity. The myth of Sisyphus serves as a bleak metaphor for the meaninglessness of human existence. Each day we work to feed ourselves and our family, and as soon as the task is done, it must begin all over again. We reproduce, and our children must take over the same task. Nothing is ever achieved, and it will never end, until our species is extinct.

The French existentialist writer Albert Camus wrote an essay on the myth of Sisyphus. It begins with a famous line: 'There is but one truly serious philosophical problem, and that is suicide'. Camus continues: 'Judging whether life is or is not worth living amounts to answering the fundamental question of philosophy'.[1] Perhaps it does, in the sense that if we judge life not to be worth living – and act accordingly – we will not be in a position to ask any further philosophical questions. But we should add (and Camus would have agreed) that it is not so much a matter of passively *judging* whether life is or is not worth living, but of consciously *choosing* a way of living that is worth living. Even Sisyphus, Camus maintains, can do this. So the essay that began by facing us with the prospect of suicide ends on a positive note:

> There is no fate that cannot be surmounted by scorn . . . The struggle itself toward the heights is enough to fill a man's heart. One must imagine Sisyphus happy'.[2]

In the concluding chapter of his book *Good and Evil*, Richard Taylor, an American philosopher, also draws upon the myth of Sisyphus in order to explore the nature of the meaning of life.[3] Taylor asks an ingenious question: in what way would the fate of Sisyphus need to be altered, in order to put meaning into his life? Taylor considers two possibilities. The first is that instead of endlessly trying to get the same stone to the top of the hill, with nothing to show for his labours, Sisyphus might succeed in pushing different stones to the top of the hill, and there construct a noble temple. The second is that, although Sisyphus continues to push only the same stone, and always in vain, the gods, in a perversely merciful mood, implant in him a fierce desire to do just what they have condemned him to do – push stones!

Taylor's two possibilities for putting meaning into the life of Sisyphus derive from two different views of the basis of ethics. On the first, we can live a meaningful life by working toward goals that are objectively worthwhile. To build a temple that endures and adds beauty to the world is such a goal. This view of ethics presupposes that there are objective values, in accordance with which we can judge as good (among other things) the creation of great works of art like the temples of ancient Greece. The second possibility finds meaning, not in anything objective, but in something internal to ourselves – our motivation. Here it is our desires that determine whether what we do is worthwhile. *Anything* can be a meaningful activity, on this view, if we want to do it. On this view, pushing a rock up a hill, only to see it roll down as we near the top, starting again, and doing the same thing forever, is neither more nor less meaningful than building a temple, because the presupposition here is that there is no such thing as objective value or meaning, independently of what we desire. Meaning is subjective: an activity will have meaning for me if it happens to tally with my desires; otherwise it will not.

Taylor favours the subjectivist approach. He thinks that the only thing that can give meaning to our lives is our own inner desire, our own will. In taking this view he is in keeping with the dominant spirit of the twentieth century, as expressed by existentialists, by logical positivists and by many contemporary philosophers who would not accept either of these labels, but would agree that since the universe as a whole has no meaning, we are free to give our own meaning, not to the universe as a whole, but to our own lives. Yet this very freedom can lead to a problematic view of value that lies behind some of the dissatisfaction felt with life even in the most affluent circumstances. The everyday problems of this view of value are worth exploring in more detail.

Of housewives, Aboriginal Australians and caged hens

As a magazine writer in 1950s America, Betty Friedan interviewed many women who were living the classic American dream: they were young and healthy, they lived in fine suburban homes, their husbands had well-paid jobs, their children went to school, their housework was made easier by many labour-saving appliances and (we can add with the benefit of hindsight) no-one worried about drugs or AIDS. This was the Good Life, in the most prosperous country in the world, and these women should surely have been the envy of anyone who has ever lacked comfort, leisure and financial security. Yet when Friedan talked to them, she found that they had a problem. They didn't have a name for it, and nor did Friedan, so she called it 'the problem that has no name'. The problem formed the core of Friedan's *The Feminine Mystique*, the book that more than any other single work triggered the modern feminist movement. In it women describe the problem in their own words. Here is a 23-year-old mother:

I ask myself why I am so dissatisfied. I've got my health, fine children, a lovely new home, enough money . . . It's as if ever since you were a little girl, there's always been somebody or something that will take care of your life: your parents, or college, or falling in love, or having a child, or moving to a new house. Then you wake up one morning and there's nothing to look forward to.[4]

The magazines and television soaps of the time tried to tell women that the role of wife and mother was the most fulfilling there can be. After all, compared to women in earlier periods, or in other countries today the American housewife of the fifties had it easy. 'Having it easy', however, was little consolation; in reality it was precisely the problem. This kind of life was supposed to be all that a woman needed for fulfillment, but when she had achieved everything she was supposed to want, her life plan came to a dead stop. The suburban housewife lives an isolated existence in her comfortable home, equipped with labour-saving devices that allow her to complete her daily chores in an hour or two. In another hour at the supermarket she can gather the week's food supply for the entire family. Her only role is to bring up a family, and her children soon spend all day at school, and much of the rest of their time watching television. Nothing else seems worth achieving.

Consider a quite different way of living. Over the past forty years, several groups of Australian Aboriginals who subsisted by hunting and gathering in remote desert areas have come into contact with Western civilization. Through this contact they have access to reliable supplies of food, steel axes, clothes, and many other goods. If quality of life depended on quantity of material possessions, this contact would be bound to improve the quality of life of the Aboriginal groups. Yet observers are agreed that it has had exactly the opposite effect. We do not have to idealize the nomadic Aboriginal life in order to recognize that it provides many opportunities for finding satisfaction in the tasks of obtaining the necessities of life. Richard Gould, an American anthropologist who lived with an Australian Aboriginal hunter-gatherer group, found that:

> . . . the daily lives of the nomadic Aborigines are essentially
> harmonious and rewarding. An individual grows up realising
> what is expected of him. By acquiring and developing practical
> knowledge and skill he learns to fulfil these expectations and is
> rewarded immediately by his own satisfaction in achievement
> and in the long run by the esteem of his kin.[5]

When food comes from a shop, bought with a government welfare
cheque provided by a well-meaning social worker eager to see that
all Australians get what they are legally entitled to receive, the skills
and knowledge acquired over a lifetime are immediately devalued.
The result is deeply demoralizing. Almost everything that the members of the nomadic group used to spend their days doing has lost
its point. It is no wonder that alcohol often becomes a major problem, and even when it does not, these formerly nomadic Aboriginals
appear to be at a loss for anything to do.

The modern housewife in her tidy household and the Aboriginal
Australian sitting on the dusty ground outside the store are suffering from the same malaise: the elimination of purpose from their
lives. The need for purpose lies deep in our nature. We can observe
it in other animals, especially those who, like us, are social mammals. The tiger, restlessly pacing back and forth behind the bars of
a small concrete cell, is fortunately becoming a less common sight
at the zoo. But the monkeys still kept in barren metal cages in
laboratories, or the pigs confined for months on factory farms in
stalls too small to allow them even to pace back and forth, are suffering from the same problem. When you provide a sow with food
and a warm dry place to lie down, you have not provided her with
everything she needs. Such animals exhibit what ethologists call
'stereotypical behaviour' – they restlessly gnaw at the bars of their
pen, or stand rocking their heads back and forth. They are trying to
make up for the absence of purposive activity in their lives. Even
the caged factory farm hen devours her daily nutritional needs in a
few minutes pecking at the feed with which she is supplied and then
is left with nothing at all to do. As a result she will restlessly peck at
her companions, and all factory farm hens are now 'debeaked' to
stop them killing each other. Some relatively more enlightened

keepers of animals now mix the day's food with straw or other inedible material and scatter it across the floor of the cage, so that the animal must work to find it. Hens kept indoors can be given food that is very finely ground; then instead of getting their daily food intake in a few minutes, it may take them several hours. On the modern view of work and leisure, as we apply it to humans, these devices make the animals work harder, reduce their leisure time, and so should make them worse off; but observation shows that the animals' welfare is improved. Of course, such strategems are at best a poor imitation of the wide variety of activities that animals have available to them in their natural conditions. They do not make it acceptable to keep animals in barren cages; but their relative success should make us re-examine our attitude to work and leisure. It is clear that our quest for a purpose to our lives has its roots a long way back in our evolutionary history, and will not easily be eliminated.

There is one short cut to overcoming the need for purpose. For the pharmaceutical industry, an existential void is a marketing opportunity. In the sixties, suburban doctors started prescribing tranquillizers in increasing quantities to housewives who came to them feeling depressed. As the Rolling Stones sang in 'Mother's Little Helper':

> Kids are different today, I hear every mother say
> Mother needs something today to calm her down
> And though she's not really ill, there's a little yellow pill
> She goes running for the shelter of her mother's little helper
> And it helps her on her way
> Gets her through her busy day
> Doctor please, some more of these
> Outside the door she took four more
> What a drag it is getting old.

That is one way of 'solving' the dissatisfaction caused by a loss of purpose: turn the dissatisfied housewife into a contented zombie. It solves the problem only in the sense that alcohol solves the problems Australian Aboriginals have in adjusting to Western civilization, and crack and other drugs solve the problems of unemployed Americans living in urban slums.

Not quite as addictive as heroin, less harmful than alcohol, but still problematic from an environmental perspective, is that other great modern tranquillizer, going shopping. Many people readily admit that shopping is not so much a means to obtain goods that they need, but rather their major recreational activity. A large dose of it seems to help overcome depression. Shopping is a modern substitute for more traditional hunter-gatherer activities. The shopping mall has replaced the old hunting grounds. Like gathering roots, seeds and berries in an arid environment, shopping can take a large portion of the day. It allows for the development of specialized forms of knowledge and skill. (How do you select the right items to gather? Where and when are the genuine bargains to be found?) Shopping can even pass as purposeful activity; its leisure component can be disguised or denied, in a way that it cannot if one spends the day playing golf.

Why was it mostly women who experienced such a loss of purpose in the fifties? At that time most men, but relatively few women, worked in jobs that held out the prospect of a promotion, an increase in responsibility and power. This is still often the case, if not quite to the same extent. So when one morning a man wakes up and asks himself, 'Is this all there is to my life?' he can quieten the doubts by thinking about that coming glorious day when he gets to move up to a more important position, with higher pay and more responsibility. That is why, as both employers and unions have found, a career structure, a ladder leading upwards, is often more crucial for job satisfaction than actual rates of pay. In contrast, for a housewife there is no promotion. Romance will fade, and the children will need their mother less and less. No wonder that many American housewives, once they had everything they were supposed to want, felt the meaningless of their existence more acutely than their husbands did.

The struggle to win

Some people – typically men – find their purpose by taking a competitive attitude to life. In the first chapter of this book I

referred to the moment in the movie *Wall Street* when Bud Fox
challenges Gordon Gekko's lust for more and more money, asking:
'How much is enough?' Here is Gekko's answer:

> It's not a question of enough, pal. It's a zero-sum game. Some-
> body wins, somebody loses.

The reply will touch a familiar chord with anyone who knows how
the big names of the eighties think, talk and write. In the first chapter of his second book, *Surviving at the Top*, Donald Trump reports
on what has happened since his first book by writing of his 'victories' and of the lessons that have taught him 'not to take the
winning for granted'. A few pages on, he compares himself with 'a
professional prize fighter'. Later, in a more introspective mood, he
remarks:

> I'm sometimes too competitive for my own good. If someone is
> going around labeling people winners and losers, I want to play
> the game and, of course, come out on the right side.[6]

Thorstein Veblen, the crusty turn-of-the-century American sociologist of Norwegian stock who wrote *The Theory of the Leisure Class*
would have smiled at the way in which people like Trump displayed
their wealth, buying absurdly luxurious yachts in which they seldom had time to sail, or palatial country residences they rarely visited. It was Veblen who coined the term 'conspicuous consumption'
to describe consumption that has the purpose of displaying one's
wealth, and thus enhancing one's relative status. Veblen held that,
once needs for subsistence and a reasonable degree of physical comfort have been satisfied, the motive that lies at the root of the desire
to own is 'emulation' – the desire to equal or surpass others. Property becomes 'the most easily recognized evidence of a reputable
degree of success as distinguished from heroic or signal achievement'. It therefore becomes 'the conventional basis of esteem'.[7]
Conspicuous consumption, if it is to be effective in enhancing the
consumer's fame, must be 'an expenditure of superfluities . . . it
must be wasteful'. (Veblen dryly adds that in a work of economic

theory such as his, 'the use of the word "waste" as a technical term
. . . implies no deprecation of the motives or of the ends sought by
the consumer under this canon of conspicuous waste'.)[8] The canons
of 'pecuniary taste' dictate that 'marks of superfluous costliness'
are indications of worth, and goods will be unattractive if 'they
show too thrifty an adaptation to the mechanical end sought'.[9] The
result is a striving that can never be satisfied:

> . . . the end sought by accumulation is to rank high in compari-
> son with the rest of the community in point of pecuniary
> strength. So long as the comparison is distinctly unfavorable to
> himself, the normal, average individual will live in chronic dis-
> satisfaction with his present lot; and when he has reached what
> may be called the normal pecuniary standard of the community,
> or of his class in the community, this chronic dissatisfaction will
> give place to a restless straining to place a wider and ever-
> widening pecuniary interval between himself and this average
> standard. The invidious comparison can never become so favor-
> able to the individual making it that he would not gladly rate
> himself still higher relatively to his competitors in the struggle
> for pecuniary reputability.

If, by nature or by socialization, men are more likely to engage in
this striving for status than women, that is at once their burden,
and their means of escaping the need to face questions about the
meaning of their lives. They can go on accumulating wealth since,
as Veblen adds:

> In the nature of the case, the desire for wealth can scarcely be
> satiated in any individual instance . . . [10]

This matches a remark that Michael Lewis reports in *Liar's Poker*.
When he was a rising bond trader at Salomon Brothers, one of his
colleagues said to him:

> You don't get rich in this business, you only attain new levels of
> relative poverty. You think Gutfreund [Salomon's chief execu-
> tive] feels rich? I'll bet not.[11]

Indeed, John Gutfreund's wife, Susan, famous for her exotic dinner parties, reportedly once concluded an account of the problems of maintaining proper staff for their New York and Paris residences by complaining: 'It's so expensive to be rich!'[12] In *Bonfire of the Vanities*, Tom Wolfe ridiculed the lifestyle of people like the Gutfreunds. In one devastating scene the bond trader Sherman McCoy and his wife, Judy, are invited to a dinner on Fifth Avenue, six blocks from where they live. Judy's dress made walking impossible; a taxi is out of the question too:

> What would they do *after* the party? How could they walk *out* of the Bavardages' building and have all the world, *tout le monde*, see them standing out in the street, the McCoys, that game couple, their hands up in the air, bravely, desperately, pathetically trying to hail a taxi?

So the McCoys hire a limousine and driver to drive them six blocks, wait four hours, and then drive them six blocks home, at a cost of $197.20. But this does not ensure happiness:

> ... the driver couldn't pull up to the sidewalk near the entrance, because so many limousines were in the way. He had to double-park. Sherman and Judy had to thread their way between the limousines . . . Envy . . . envy . . . From the license plates Sherman could tell that these limousines were not hired. They were *owned* by those whose sleek hides were hauled here in them. A chauffeur, a good one willing to work long hours and late hours, cost $36,000 a year, minimum; garage space, maintenance, insurance, would cost another $14,000 at least; a total of $50,000, none of it deductible. *I make a million dollars a year – and yet I can't afford that!*[13]

Acquisition without limit is another form of escape from meaninglessness. But it is an escape-hole that suggests a fundamental lack of wisdom. By 'wisdom', I mean the product of reflection with some intelligence and self-awareness about what is important in life; 'practical wisdom' adds to this the ability to act accordingly. The goal of emulation described by Veblen cannot possibly satisfy a reflective mind, and seems not even to satisfy those who do not reflect on what they are doing.

As Veblen suggests, behind the desire for acquisition lies a competitive urge. Already in the seventies, Michael Maccoby, who had studied both psychoanalysis and social science, sensed the rise of a new style of business executive. After interviewing 250 managers from twelve major American corporations, he concluded that for many of these executives, business life was about winning – for themselves, for their unit, or for their corporation. He wrote a book about what he had found, and called it after the new style of executive: *The Gamesman*. But the book was no celebration of the rising competitive executive dedicated to winning. Instead it contained a warning that if life is regarded simply as a game, then eventually a time will come when it ceases to matter:

> Once his youth, vigor, and even the thrill in winning are lost, [the gamesman] becomes depressed and goalless, questioning the purpose of his life. No longer energized by the team struggle and unable to dedicate himself to something he believes in beyond himself, which might be the corporation or alternatively the larger society, he finds himself starkly alone.[14]

Michael Milken seems to have been a classic example of a supreme winner who gained little satisfaction from winning. When Milken was at the height of his success, a legend around the financial world with a personal fortune of a billion dollars, one of his colleagues told Connie Bruck: 'Nothing is good enough for Michael. He is the most unhappy person I know. He never has enough . . . He drives everything – more, more, more deals'. In 1986 one longtime buyer of Milken's junk bonds told Bruck that 'there seemed to be less and less joy in Milken – something that had been part of him in the early years – and more compulsion'.[15]

In a critical study of the emphasis on competition in Western society, Alfie Kohn found that many sporting competitors report feeling empty after achieving the greatest possible success in their chosen sport. Here is Dallas Cowboys coach Tom Landry:

... even after you've just won the Super Bowl – *especially* after you've just won the Super Bowl – *there's always next year.* If 'Winning isn't everything. It's the only thing' then 'the only thing' is nothing – emptiness, the nightmare of life without ultimate meaning.[16]

Harvey Ruben, author of a book called *Competing* and an enthusiast for competition, concedes that: 'The discovery, ultimately, that "making it" is often a hollow gain is one of the most traumatic events that the successful competitor can experience'. Stuart Walker, a sailing boat racer and another author of a book about winning and competing, says:

> Winning doesn't satisfy us – we need to do it again, and again. The taste of success seems merely to whet the appetite for more. When we lose, the compulsion to seek future success is overpowering; the need to get out on the course the following weekend is irresistible. We cannot quit when we are ahead, after we've won, and we certainly cannot quit when we're behind, after we've lost. We are addicted.[17]

Here is the best available answer to one of the questions I asked in Chapter 1. Why did Ivan Boesky risk everything for a few million dollars, when he already had more than he could ever spend? In 1992, six years after Boesky pleaded guilty to insider trading, his estranged wife Seema broke her silence and spoke about Ivan Boesky's motives in an interview with Barbara Walters for the American ABC network's *20/20* program. Walters asked whether Ivan Boesky was a man who craved luxury. Seema Boesky thought not, pointing out that he worked around the clock, seven days a week, and never took a day off to enjoy his money. She then recalled that when, in 1982, *Forbes* magazine first listed Boesky among the wealthiest people in the US, he was upset. She assumed he disliked the publicity, and made some remark to that effect. Boesky replied:

> That's not what's upsetting me. We're no one. We're nowhere. We're at the bottom of the list and I promise you I won't shame

you like that again ever. We will not remain at the bottom of that list.[18]

The craving to win, whether in business or in sport, is the modern version of the labours of Sisyphus – a sentence to never-ending labour without a goal. It is an addiction that had Boesky hooked, and that ruined him. But even if he had not been ruined by it, ultimately – win or lose – he would have found his craving insatiable.

The inward turn

Many people think that if their lives are not fulfilling, something must be wrong with them. So they turn to psychotherapy. In the twenty years to 1976, the number of Americans seeing mental health professionals trebled. The pattern began with young, urban, well-educated professionals, but spread to other sectors of society.[19] I could not help noticing this when I took up a visiting appointment in the Department of Philosophy at New York University in 1973. Until my arrival in New York, I had never known anyone who was seeing a psychotherapist as much as once a week; but as I became acquainted with a circle of New York professors and their spouses, I soon found that many of them were in *daily* psychoanalysis. Five days a week, eleven months of the year, they had an appointment for one hour, not to be broken under any circumstances short of a life or death emergency. They could not go on holiday unless their analyst was taking a holiday at the same time. (Often both partners were in analysis with different analysts; but fortunately shrinks all go on holidays in August, so couples could still go away together.) Nor did all of this come cheap. Some of my colleagues, well-paid, successful academics, were handing over a quarter of their annual salary to their analysts! This was for people who, as far as I could tell, were neither more nor less disturbed than those not in analysis, and apart from their commitment to analysis, they seemed no different from the people I had known in Oxford or Melbourne. I asked my friends why they were doing this. They said that they felt repressed, or had unresolved psychological tensions, or found life meaningless. I wanted to pick them up and shake them. These people were intelligent, talented, wealthy, and living in one of the world's most exciting cities. They were at the centre of the greatest communications hub in history. The *New York Times* was informing them every day of the state of the real world. They knew, for example, that in several developing countries, there were families that did not know where the next day's food was coming from, and children who were growing up physically and mentally stunted by malnutrition. They knew, too, that the planet could produce enough food for every human being to be adequately fed, but that it was so unequally distributed as to make laughable any talk of justice between nations. (For example, in 1973 the per capita Gross National Product of the United States was $6,200, and of Mali, $70.[20]) If these able, affluent New Yorkers had only got off their analysts' couches, stopped thinking about their own problems, and gone out to do something about the real problems faced by less fortunate people in Bangladesh or Ethiopia – or even in Manhattan, a few subway stops north – they would have forgotten their own problems and maybe made the world a better place as well.

In looking inwards for solutions to their problems, people are seeking the mysterious substance that, in Taylor's second possible way of adding meaning to the life of Sisyphus, the gods put into Sisyphus in order to make him *want* to push stones up the hill. In suggesting that the solution lies, instead, in getting out into the world and doing something worthwhile, I am siding with the alternative solution, which does not change what Sisyphus is like, but allows him to change the external world by building a temple. As yet, I offer no philosophical justification for taking this apparently objectivist stance. For the moment, it is enough that, in practice, it seems to work.

People spend years in psychoanalysis, often quite fruitlessly, because psychoanalysts are schooled in Freudian dogma that teaches them to locate problems within the patient's own unconscious states, and to try to resolve these problems by introspection. Thus patients are directed to look inwards when they should be looking outwards. Viktor Frankl, a non-Freudian psychotherapist, tells the story of an American diplomat who came to see him at his Vienna clinic, wanting to continue analysis he had begun five years previously in New York. Frankl asked the diplomat why he had started analysis in the first place, and the diplomat said that he had been discontented with his career, finding it very difficult to support the American foreign policy of the time. His Freudian analyst had responded by repeatedly telling him that the problem was that the US Government and his superiors were nothing but father images; he was dissatisfied with his work because he unconsiously hated his father. The analyst's solution, therefore, was that the patient should become more aware of his unconscious feelings for his father, and should try to reconcile himself with his father. Frankl disagreed. He concluded that the diplomat did not need psychotherapy at all. He was simply unhappy because he could find no meaning in his work. So Frankl suggested a change of employment. The diplomat took his advice. He enjoyed his new career from the start, and when Frankl saw him five years later, he was continuing to do so.[21]

The error of looking inwards for meaning is so common that Robert Bellah and his colleagues, in planning the study that resulted in their book *Habits of the Heart*, chose therapy, alongside love and marriage, as a significant aspect of American life to examine. As they say in their preface:

> In thinking about private life, we decided to study love and marriage, one of the oldest ways in which people give form to their private lives, and therapy, a newer, but increasingly important, way in which middle-class Americans find meaning in the private sphere.[22]

The therapist, then, has a new role: not merely to help those who are mentally ill, but also to bring meaning into the lives of middle-class Americans.

Another indicator of the widespread acceptance of a psychotherapeutic approach to life is the astonishingly enduring popularity of M. Scott Peck's book *The Road Less Travelled*. As I write these lines, in June 1992, this book has been on the *New York Times* Bestseller List for 436 weeks, or more than eight years. Peck, a psychiatrist, recommends psychotherapy, not only as a means of treating mental illness, but as a 'short cut to personal growth'. While admitting that 'it is possible to achieve personal growth without employing psychotherapy', he suggests that 'often the task is unnecessarily tedious, lengthy and difficult'. Comparing the use of psychotherapy as a means to personal growth with the use of a hammer and nails to build a house, he urges that 'It generally makes sense to utilize available tools as a short cut'.[23]

I find this analogy doubtful; the short cut is very likely to turn into a long blind alley. The occupational disease of therapists, to which few are immune, is an excessive focus on the self, a condition often found in conjunction with a superficial subjectivism about values that effectively disqualifies the therapist from wholeheartedly taking an ethical stand. As the authors of *Habits of the Heart* report:

> the therapeutic self . . . is defined by its own wants and satisfactions . . . Its social virtues are largely limited to empathic communication, truth-telling and equitable negotiation . . . the therapeutically inclined fear any statement of right or wrong that is not prefaced by a subjective disclaimer such as 'I think' or 'it feels to me' because they believe moral judgments are based on purely subjective feelings and cannot meaningfully be discussed.[24]

A Gestalt therapist sketched the transition from 'morality' to its therapeutic successor:

> The question 'Is this right or wrong?' becomes 'Is this going to work for me now?' Individuals must answer it in light of their own wants.[25]

Note here the inability to see the value of any purpose beyond the self, a characteristic that this therapist shares with a more popular writer who also distrusts morality. In *Looking Out for # 1*, Robert J. Ringer writes:

> In deciding whether it's right to look out for Number One, I suggest that the first thing you do is eliminate from consideration all unsolicited moral opinions of others . . . You should concern yourself only with whether looking out for Number One is moral from your own rational, aware viewpoint . . . I perhaps can best

answer the question *Is it right?* by asking you one: Can you see any rational reason why you *shouldn't* try to make your life more pleasurable and less painful, so long as you do not forcibly interfere with the rights of others?[26]

I include Ringer among those who reduce everything to the internal view of the self, because that is the general tenor of his book, as the title suggests; but note how Ringer quietly slips in the proviso about not forcibly interfering with the rights of others. It would be interesting to know what 'rational reason' he can see for not forcibly interfering with the rights of others, as long as it 'makes your life more pleasurable and less painful'. Once Ringer accepts that there is one moral requirement that is not grounded in pleasure or pain for yourself, why should he not accept that there are others too?

Like *Looking Out for # 1*, Gail Sheehy's *Passages: Predictable Crises of Adult Life* was a very popular self-help book of the seventies. It appealed to a considerably more sophisticated readership than Ringer's, but similarly focused on the individual self as the source of all validity. Here is Sheehy's advice for coping with mid-life crisis:

> The most important words in midlife are – Let Go. Let it happen to you. Let it happen to your partner. Let the feelings. Let the changes.
>
> You can't take everything with you when you leave on the midlife journey. You are moving away. Away from institutional claims and other people's agenda. Away from external valuations and accreditations, in search of an inner validation. You are moving out of roles and into the self . . . To reach the clearing beyond, we must stay with the weightless journey through uncertainty.[27]

To think critically about the values and standards that you accept is fine; but to imagine that you can 'let go', become 'weightless' and simply find your own standards in your 'self' is to repeat the psychoanalysts' mistake of looking inwards rather than to the reality in which we live, a reality that provides both opportunities and limits for our actions. If our lives are to have any meaning beyond the fantasy of our own imagination, we must lock into that reality and consider what claims it makes upon us. We live for a time and then die. Our lives can be pleasurable or painful, but if we want them to have some meaning as well, we cannot create this meaning out of our subjective experiences alone. There can be no meaning to a life unless something is worth doing. To decide that something is worth doing involves making an ethical judgment.

Here we have the flaw in Richard Taylor's subjectivist view that what matters in the life of Sisyphus is not the nature of the task he must perform, but whether he wants to do it. For Taylor the task can be as absurd as we like – and few are more absurd than rolling the same stone up the hill and never quite getting it to the top before it rolls down again – yet if that is what Sisyphus desires to do, then he is living the best possible life. Similarly, the Gestalt therapist I quoted earlier would no doubt have said, when confronted with the fate of Sisyphus:

> The question 'Is rolling the stone right or wrong for Sisyphus?' becomes 'Is this going to work for him now?' He must answer it in the light of his own wants.

And if, halfway through eternity, Sisyphus were to experience a mid-life crisis, Gail Sheehy could reassure him that no 'external valuations and accreditations' need trouble him, as long as he has his own 'inner validation'.

Among psychotherapists, Viktor Frankl is exceptional in his insistence on the need to find meaning in something outside the self. Frankl became aware of the importance of the need for meaning in the most desperate possible circumstances. As a Viennese Jew, he spent much of World War II in Nazi concentration camps. There, he saw that 'The prisoner who had lost faith in the future – his future – was doomed'.[28] These prisoners, who had nothing to live for, allowed themselves to decay, physically and mentally. Some committed suicide; some would no longer work, and were shot or beaten to death. The remainder succumbed to infections and diseases. To have a chance of survival, one needed something to live for. That something might be the prospect of reunion with a child or lover who had fled to safety before the war. Frankl knew a scientist who was kept going by the thought that he must finish his interrupted scientific research. The goal might even be the need to survive in order to bear witness to the unbelievable reality of the Holocaust. For Frankl himself, it was the thought of being able to recreate the manuscript of his first book, confiscated on the day of his arrival in Auschwitz. Frankl quotes Nietzsche: 'He who has a *why* to live for can bear almost any *how*'.[29]

Obsession with the self has been *the* characteristic psychological error of the generations of the seventies and eighties. I do not deny that problems of the self are vitally important; the error consists in seeking answers to those problems by focusing on the self. The mistake is akin to the one you would make if you were so dedicated to writing your autobiography that from an early age you decided to do nothing except write the autobiography. What would there be to write about? You could sit down at your computer and type: 'I am now writing my autobiography'. You could describe your thoughts about writing your autobiography, and maybe manage to carry on for a while in this mode, but unless you have some other experiences to write about, beyond the experience of writing itself, the book will be thin and the contents uninteresting. Similarly, if you were to invest all your time and energy into 'finding yourself' by looking inward, the self that you found would lack substance. It would be an empty self. Of course, no-one invests *all* his or her time and energy in looking inwards in this way; but many spend too much time doing it, and their lives are diminished as a result.

There are many reasons why people may be self-obsessed. Of those who seek the solution in psychotherapy, many are simply unhappy, and have come to believe that the fault must lie in their own head. Others, however, are persuaded by the ethos of the consumer society, reinforced in a thousand ways every day, that the only worthwhile aim is the pursuit of one's own pleasure or happiness. The mistake they make is an ancient one, known to philosophers as the 'paradox of hedonism'. The hedonist is dedicated to seeking pleasure; yet those who deliberately set out in search of pleasure rarely find it, except perhaps fleetingly. The modern version of this approach to life is superbly portrayed in Bret Easton Ellis's first novel *Less Than Zero*.

The young, rich, Los Angeles set he describes turn from alcohol to sex, to drugs, to endless televised rock video clips, to violence, and then back to alcohol, without finding much pleasure – let alone fulfillment – in any of it. The roots of Ellis's later, more shocking, *American Psycho* are already to be found in the aimlessness of such an existence. The British philosopher F. H. Bradley would have seen in Ellis's work a convincing illustration of what he wrote about the search for pleasure, more than a century earlier:

> Pleasures [are] a perishing series. This one comes, and the intense self-feeling proclaims satisfaction. It is gone, and *we* are not satisfied . . . another and another do not give us what we want; we are still eager and confident, till the flush of feeling dies down, and when that is gone there is nothing left. We are where we began, as far as the getting happiness goes; and we have not found ourselves, and we are not satisfied.
>
> This is common experience, and it is the practical refutation of Hedonism, or of seeking happiness in pleasure.[30]

The affluent consumer society puts the search for our own pleasure at the centre of our lives; and it leads to precisely the experience Bradley describes, even down to the very term he uses: we say that we are not satisfied and that we need to 'find ourselves'. We have forgotten the old wisdom that the way to find happiness or lasting satisfaction is to aim at something else, and try to do it well. As Henry Sidgwick wrote, in his measured Victorian way: 'Happiness is likely to be better attained if the extent to which we set ourselves consciously to aim at it be carefully restricted'.[31] At what, though, are we to aim?

A transcendent cause

In *Habits of the Heart*, Robert Bellah and his colleagues recognize and warn against the modern tendency to turn inwards in search of meaning. While they document this tendency, they also present another option. They talk to people who are politically active, like Wayne Bauer, who is involved in helping poor immigrant tenants in his neighbourhood. Bauer went through some difficult times in sorting out his own life, he says. Then:

Morality became a question to me. It's sort of like I wanted to put everything back together again with more durable material, one that would stand the strain . . . Watching politics is watching civilization struggle and evolve, and it's very exciting, but it's also much more personal because it's your struggle to evolve into this picture, into this historic picture somehow . . . I feel good about what I do. I feel that the work I'm involved in is directly affecting other people in beneficial ways. It's again this value question. You can spend all your time in seeing how many material goods you can get together and how much money you can make or you can spend it helping one another and working together . . . it's very beautiful to see and very exciting to be a part of because what you're seeing is kind of an evolution of consciousness.[32]

Marra James is involved in the environmental movement in a Southern California suburb. She says:

I sometimes describe myself as a rubber ball. I've been pushed down sometimes to where I've almost been pressed flat, but I've always been able to bounce back . . . I feel very much a part of the whole – of history. I live in a spectrum that includes the whole world. I'm a part of all of it. For what I do impacts the whole.[33]

In trying to explain why they find fulfillment in what they do, both Bauer and James mention involvement in a larger cause, being part of 'an evolution of consciousness', or part of history. The authors of *Habits of the Heart* note that while the American quest for purely private fulfillment 'often ends in emptiness', many people find that 'private fulfillment and public involvement are not antithetical' because they draw the content of their fulfillment from 'an active identification with communities and traditions'.[34]

Two very different authors agree with this view of what is needed to give meaning to our lives. Earlier in this chapter we saw how well Betty Friedan described the lack of purpose that women felt with the roles allocated to them. She saw the solution to 'the problem that has no name' in women developing a 'Life Plan', some 'lifetime interests and goals'. A job could be part of that, but then:

> . . . it must be a job that she can take seriously as part of a life plan, work in which she can grow as part of society.[35]

Thirty years after *The Feminine Mystique* was published, a new bestseller appeared that might well have been entitled *The Masculine Mystique*. Instead, its author, Robert Bly, called it *Iron John*. The difference between the two books is that while Friedan criticizes the feminine mystique, Bly wallows in it. He has run weekend retreats in which men go off into the woods in groups to read ancient legends about warriors who perform heroic deeds. Then these twentieth century American males whirl swords above their heads, and watch the sunlight glint on the shining blade. They hope, by these means, to rediscover the 'warrior' in themselves, but probably all they do is vindicate women's complaints that men never do grow up. *Iron John*, which spent a year on the bestseller lists, retells Grimm's fairy tale of 'Iron Hans', a Wild Man who emerges from a pond and initiates a young prince into manhood. Buried among its rambling commentary on episodes in the fairy story, however, *Iron John* contains a saving passage that reads as follows:

> When a warrior is in service, however, to a True King – that is to a transcendent cause – he does well, and his body becomes a hardworking servant, which he requires to endure cold, heat, pain, wounds, scarring, hunger, lack of sleep, hardship of all kinds. The body usually responds well. The person in touch with warrior energy can work long hours, ignore fatique, do what is necessary, finish the Ph.D. and all the footnotes, endure obnoxious departmental heads, live sparsely like Ralph Nader, write as T.S. Eliot did under a single dangling light bulb for years, clean up shit and filth endlessly like St Francis or Mother Teresa, endure contempt, disdain, and exile as Sakharov did. A clawed hand takes the comfort-loving baby away, and an adult warrior inhabits the body.[36]

Here is something fundamental on which Robert Bly, Betty Friedan, Wayne Bauer, Marra James, the authors of *Habits of the Heart*, and Viktor Frankl all agree: the need for commitment to a cause larger than the self, if we are to find genuine self-esteem, and to be all we can be. In sharp contrast to Richard Taylor's idea that any activity is as good as any other, as long as it is what we want to do, this suggests that some causes are more suitable than others for putting meaning into our lives.

But what is a 'True King', or a 'transcendent cause' as Bly variously calls it? If it is not all a matter of whatever we happen to want, how do we find causes that add meaning to our lives? Richard Taylor denied that it would add meaning to the life of Sisyphus if, instead of the stone always rolling down the hill, he were able to push it and other stones to the top, and then use them to construct a temple. The idea that Sisyphus could find meaning in building a temple appears to presuppose that at least some of our achievements could be objectively valuable. In response, Taylor points out that no matter how solidly the temple is built it will, in time, decay into rubble. Here he touches a chord that is given its classic resonance in Shelley's poem *Ozymandias*:

> I met a traveller from an antique land
> Who said: Two vast and trunkless legs of stone
> Stand in the desert . . . Near them, on the sand,
> Half sunk, a shattered visage lies, whose frown,
> And wrinkled lip, and sneer of cold command,
> Tell that its sculptor well those passions read
> Which yet survive, stamped on these lifeless things,
> The hand that mocked them, and the heart that fed:
> And on the pedestal these words appear:
> 'My name is Ozymandias, king of kings:
> Look on my works, ye Mighty, and despair!'
> Nothing beside remains. Round the decay
> Of that colossal wreck, boundless and bare
> The lone and level sands stretch far away.[37]

Bertrand Russell was fond of making a similar point, emphasizing our cosmic insignificance by pointing out that our entire world is only one planet circling around one star in a galaxy that contains about 300,000 million stars, and is itself only one among several million galaxies. The sun will eventually grow cold, and life on earth will come to an end, but the universe will continue, utterly indifferent to our fate.[38]

Such images might well give pause to Sisyphus if, gripped by the arrogance of Ozymandias, he imagines that his temple will last for eternity. But if Sisyphus were to read further into Russell's work he would come across a passage saying that while 'the realization of the minuteness of man and all his concerns' may at first strike us as oppressive, and even paralyzing, 'this effect is not rational and should not be lasting. There is no reason to worship mere size'.[39] Then Sisyphus would see that to create a temple that lasts as long as the Parthenon has lasted, and is as justly admired for its beauty and the skill of its construction, is an accomplishment in which he could take justifiable pride. Reflecting more deeply on his place in the universe, he would resume his labours.

So the fact that the most beautiful and enduring of human artefacts will eventually turn into dust is not a reason for denying that its creation was a worthwhile and meaningful task. Taylor does, however, have another reason for holding that the meaningfulness of what Sisyphus does depends on how he feels about it, rather than on the nature of the task itself. Even if Sisyphus were to complete his temple, and could rest and contemplate its beauty forever, what would that signify? Taylor says: only infinite boredom. Instead of 'the nightmare of eternal and pointless activity', we have 'the hell of its eternal absence'. Then Sisyphus would see that all his labours had been pointless after all.

Here too, Taylor makes a mistake that vitiates his account of how a human life could be made meaningful. He overlooks a special feature of the life of Sisyphus that does not apply to any human being. The gods have condemned Sisyphus to push his rock up the hill for all eternity. Therefore Sisyphus must be immortal. So he will outlive all human beings, and once his temple is finished, he still has an infinite amount of time ahead of him. No wonder that he should get bored contemplating his temple! We mere mortals are not like that. We will die before we perfect our temple. There is always more work to do.

If we are to find meaning in our lives by working for a cause, that cause must be, as Bly suggests, a 'transcendent cause', that is, a cause that extends beyond the boundaries of our self. There are many such causes. Footballers are constantly reminded that the club is larger than the individual; so are employees of corporations, especially those that work for corporations that foster group loyalty with songs, slogans and social activities, in the Japanese manner. To support one's Mafia 'family' is to be part of a cause larger than the self. So is being a member of a religious cult, or of the Nazi Party. And so too is working against injustice and exploitation in one of its many specific forms, as Marra James and Wayne Bauer, among many others, have done. No doubt a commitment to each of these causes can be, for some people, a way of finding meaning and fulfillment. Is it after all arbitrary, then, whether one chooses an ethical cause or some other cause? No; living an ethical life is certainly not the only way of making a commitment that can give substance and worth to your life; but for anyone choosing one kind of life rather than another, it is the commitment with the firmest foundation. The more we reflect on our commitment to a football club, a corporation, or any sectional interest, the less point we are likely to see in it. In contrast, no amount of reflection will show a commitment to an ethical life to be trivial or pointless. This is probably the most important claim in this book, but also the most contentious. In the final chapter I shall suggest that living an ethical life enables us to identify ourselves with the grandest cause of all, and that to do so is the best way open to us of making our lives meaningful.

CHAPTER 11

The good life

Pushing the peanut forward

Henry Spira left home as a teenager and went to work on merchant ships. As a seaman and member of the National Maritime Union he was part of a group of reformers challenging corrupt union bosses. In the McCarthy era, while working on an automobile assembly line in New Jersey, he wrote for leftist publications and earned himself a fat FBI file. In the sixties he was marching for civil rights in Mississippi. I met him in 1973 when he enrolled for a continuing education course on animal liberation that I was giving at New York University. He first heard of animal liberation when he came across an article about it in a Marxist magazine. The article dismissed the idea as the latest absurdity of the radical chic set associated with the *New York Review of Books*. Spira was able to discern, through the ridicule, the outline of an idea that might be worth learning more about. When the course finished and I had returned to Australia, Spira investigated experiments carried out on animals at the American Museum of Natural History, only a few blocks from where he lived. He found out that researchers there were mutilating cats, eliminating their sense of smell, for instance, in order to discover what effect this had on their sex lives. Spira called some other former members of my class, and together they organized a campaign to stop the experiments. The campaign grew; there were constant pickets outside its doors, and occasional larger demonstrations. Eventually the Museum announced that the experiments would cease. That may well have been the first time that a campaign against experiments on animals achieved its objective. Then Spira set his sights on bigger targets. He confronted Revlon over their testing of cosmetics on the eyes of fully conscious, immobilized rabbits. At first he was ignored, but he kept up the pressure; ten years later Revlon announced that they had ceased to test their products on animals. Several other cosmetics companies followed suit. As I write this, Spira is tackling Frank Perdue, America's best-known producer of factory-farmed chickens, publishing advertisements that accuse him not only of cruelty to the chickens he raises, but also of producing an unhealthy product, exploiting his workers, and seeking the aid of mobsters to prevent his workers unionizing. Moreover, Spira documents his accusations so well that the *New York Times* has accepted Spira's anti-Perdue advertisements.

Asked for the rationale behind a lifetime of activism on behalf of diverse causes, Henry Spira replies that he begins with the question: 'Where can I do the most to reduce the universe of pain and suffering?' Being constantly reminded of the pain and suffering that still needs to be eliminated may seem depressing, but Spira has kept his sense of humour. (One of the advertisements he has used in his campaign against Perdue was headed: 'There is no such thing as safe chicken'. Under the heading was a large photograph of a chicken carcass inside a condom.) In any case, Spira has too much to do to be depressed. In one interview, when asked what his epitaph should be, he replied: 'He pushed the peanut forward'. When, on my occasional visits to New York, I stay with him and his cat in his Upper Westside rent-controlled apartment, I always find him thinking about strategies for getting things moving ahead, and relishing the next challenge. I leave in good spirits.

In the midst of writing this book I received a letter from another longstanding friend from the animal liberation movement. Christine Townend founded the first organization in Australia to advocate an animal liberation ethic. Together with her husband Jeremy, a lawyer, she lived in a beautiful house on a large block of land in a leafy Sydney suburb. Some years ago, on a trip to India, she saw the desperate situation of animals in that country, where despite Hindu and Buddhist traditions that are kinder to animals than our own, the poverty of the people causes animals to have miserable lives and worse deaths. She began to spend a month or two each year in India, helping a struggling voluntary group based near Jaipur, in Rajahstan. The problems there were more clear-cut than in Australia, where the animal movement had entered a phase in which every reform became the subject of patient negotiation through interminable meetings of government committees. Now, Christine's letter was telling me, she and Jeremy had decided that since their children had grown up and left home, they could and should do more for the Indian organization. They were selling their home, Jeremy was giving up his law practice, and they were going to India to work as volunteers for at least the next five years. When I phoned Christine to express my admiration for her courageous decision, her voice was confident and filled with happiness. She was looking forward to doing something exciting and worthwhile. There was no sense of sacrifice, because she valued what she was doing more than the more comfortable lifestyle she was leaving.

Henry Spira and Christine Townend think in the manner so well expressed by the woman Carol Gilligan quotes in *In a Different Voice*. I have already quoted the passage once, in Chapter 9, but it is worth quoting again:

> I have a very strong sense of being responsible to the world, that I can't just live for my enjoyment, but just the fact of being in the world gives me an obligation to do what I can to make the world a better place to live in, no matter how small a scale that may be on.

This could have been said by many people I have known, people working for greater overseas aid to poor nations, to allow farm animals the elementary freedom of being able to turn around and stretch their limbs, to free prisoners of conscience, or to bring about the abolition of nuclear weapons. It may underlie the actions of those who show concern for strangers in the ways that I described in Chapter 8. Recall, too, how, as we saw in the previous chapter, Wayne Bauer and Marra James express their sense of being part of a larger whole, and the way in which this brings a strongly positive element into their lives.

These people take the broader perspective that is characteristic of an ethical life. They adopt – to use Henry Sidgwick's memorable phrase – 'the point of view of the universe'. This is not a phrase to be taken literally, for unless we are pantheists, the universe itself cannot have a point of view at all. I shall use Sidgwick's phrase to refer to a point of view that is maximally all-embracing, while not attributing any kind of consciousness or other attitudes to the universe, or any part of it that is not a sentient being. From this perspective, we can see that our own sufferings and pleasures are very like the sufferings and pleasures of others; and that there is no reason to give less consideration to the sufferings of others, just because they are 'other'. This remains true in whatever way 'otherness' is defined, as long as the capacity for suffering or pleasure remains.

People who take on the point of view of the universe may be daunted by the immensity of the task that faces them; but they are not bored, and do not need psychotherapy to make their lives meaningful. There is a tragic irony in the fact that we can find our own fulfillment precisely because there is so much avoidable pain and suffering in the universe, but that is the way the world is. The task will not be completed until we can no longer find children stunted from malnutrition or dying from easily treatable infections; homeless people trying to keep warm with pieces of cardboard; political prisoners held without trial; nuclear weapons poised to destroy entire cities; refugees living for years in squalid camps; farm animals so closely confined that they cannot move around or stretch their limbs; fur-bearing animals held by a leg in a steel-jawed trap; people being killed, beaten or discriminated against because of their race, sex, religion, sexual preference or some irrelevant disability; rivers poisoned by pollution; ancient forests being cut to serve the trivial wants of the affluent; women forced to put up with domestic violence because there is nowhere else for them to go; and so on and on. How we would find meaning in our lives if all avoidable pain and suffering had been eliminated is an interesting topic for philosophical discussion, but the question is, sadly, unlikely to have any practical significance for the foreseeable future.

People like Henry Spira or Christine Townend, or any of the millions of others working to reduce the many causes of misery that now afflict our planet, can justifiably find fulfillment in the work they do. They know that they are on the right side. This may sound smug. Today we are so tolerant of every possible point of view, that merely to talk of the 'right' side is already to risk appearing to be self-righteous. But to tolerate someone else's opinion is not to think that it is as valid as any other opinion. If we take a sufficiently long-term perspective, it is not difficult to see that on many issues, there *has* been a right side. There was a right side in the struggle against slavery. There was a right side in the workers' battles for the right to unionize, for limited working hours, and minimum working conditions. (No-one wants to return to the days in which children worked twelve-hour days in stifling factories or down coal mines.) There was a right side in the long campaign for votes for women, and for women to be admitted to universities, and to have the right to own property after they were married. There was a right side in the fight against Hitler. When Martin Luther King led marches so that African-Americans could sit on buses and in restaurants alongside white Americans, there was a right side. Today, there is a right side on issues that involve helping the poorest citizens in developing countries, promoting the peaceful resolution of conflicts, extending our ethical concern beyond the boundaries of our own species, and protecting our global environment.

On each of these issues there will be uncertainties about exactly how to go about achieving the objective, and how far to pursue it. We may support equal opportunity for racial minorities, but argue over whether affirmative action programs are a good way of bringing equal opportunity about. There is room for debate over whether equality for women carries with it the implication that they should always be free to decide whether to continue a pregnancy. That young calves should be confined in individual crates for months and kept deliberately anemic so that gourmets can eat 'white veal' is clearly wrong; but there can be reasonable differences of opinion about the desirability of retaining zoos. We should work towards a world without wars – but how best do we do that? There can be no ethical justification for the failure of most of the affluent nations – the United States, Germany, Britain, Japan, Australia – to meet even the miserly United Nations target for overseas aid of 0.7 percent of Gross National Product; but what is a reasonable level for overseas aid, and how that aid is best distributed, are questions needing further consideration. The perplexing questions arise only when we are close enough to the issue to discern its details. From far enough above, the broadest outlines are all we see. It is with that elevated level that I am here concerned. From there we can see that the issues I listed in the previous paragraph were not disagreements between two groups of people taking their stands on the highest principles of ethics, but struggles between those who are committed to ethical principles and those who are not. The former group were working for equal consideration for those without wealth or power, the latter were defending their own wealth, privileges and power.

Granted, the efforts of those working to extend the boundaries of ethical concern can go tragically astray. Marx and Lenin were genuinely trying to bring about a better life for the great mass of propertyless workers, but Marx's vision of how socialism was to be achieved had a fatal flaw: he believed that the abolition of private property would bring about a transformation of human nature, so that conflicts over power and privilege would not be a problem. (On this, the anarchist Bakunin showed himself to be far wiser.)[1] Lenin's conviction that Marx was right, combined with his authoritarian style of leadership, led him to seek coercive solutions to the problem created by the fact that at the time of the Bolshevik Revolution, most Russians did not want socialism. Thus the ethical commitment of Marx, Lenin and countless early Marxists led only to the nightmare of Stalinism. Fanaticism and authoritarianism in the name of ethical principle may well do as much harm as the selfish defence of sectional privileges. That is a good reason for rejecting fanaticism and authoritarianism, and for insisting on the retention of those basic civil liberties that restrain government and protect individuals from those who think they know best. If history can teach anything at all, it teaches us that our democratic freedoms are just as much in peril from those who are ethically motivated as they are from those who are driven by greed and personal ambition. In fact since we are more on guard against the latter, the danger from the former may be the greater. We should also be wary of those who offer us grand theories, claiming to know the cause of all our woes, and the only way of overcoming them.

None of this, however, is a reason for turning away from an ethical life in which we accept our own fallibility and do what we can, in immediate and practical ways, to make the world a better place. Voting for the right politician is not enough. When we put ethics first and politics second, we can judge people by what they are doing, now, rather than by who they vote for or what they would like to happen. Are you opposed to the present division of resources between the wealthy nations and the poor ones? If you are, and you live in one of the wealthy nations, what are you doing about it? How much of your own surplus income are you giving to one of the many organizations that is helping the poorest of the poor in the developing nations? Do you believe, perhaps, that there is no solution to world hunger without a solution to the problem of our growing global population? Fine, but what support do you give to organizations that promote population control? Are you indifferent to forests being turned into woodchips? If not, are you recycling your waste paper? Are you against confining farm animals so that they cannot walk around, or stretch all their limbs? But do you support the agribusiness corporations that keep animals this way by buying the bacon and eggs that they produce? Living an ethical life is more than having the right attitudes and expressing the right opinions.

The escalator of reason

In earlier chapters we saw that it is possible to explain, consistently with our nature as an evolved being, why it is that we are concerned for our kin, for those with whom we can establish reciprocal relationships, and to some extent for members of our own group. Now we have seen that some people help strangers, both in heroic circumstances and in more everyday ways. Does this not break the bounds of our evolved nature? How can evolutionary theory explain a sense of responsibility to make the entire world a better place? How could those who have such a sense avoid leaving fewer descendants, and thus, over time, being eliminated by the normal workings of the evolutionary process?

Here is one possible answer. Human beings lack the strength of the gorilla, the sharp teeth of the lion, the speed of the cheetah. Brain power is our specialty. The brain is a tool for reasoning, and a capacity to reason helps us to survive, to feed ourselves, and to safeguard our children. With it we have developed machines that can lift more than many gorillas, knives that are sharper than any lion's teeth, and ways of travelling that make a cheetah's pace tediously slow. But the ability to reason is a peculiar ability. Unlike strong arms, sharp teeth or flashing legs, it can take us to conclusions that we had no desire to reach. For reason is like an escalator, leading upwards and out of sight. Once we step upon it we do not know where we will end up.[2]

A story about how Thomas Hobbes became interested in philosophy illustrates the compelling way in which reason can draw us along. Hobbes was browsing in a library when he happened to come across a copy of Euclid's *The Elements of Geometry*. The book lay open at the Forty-seventh Theorem. Hobbes read the conclusion and swore that it was impossible. So he read the proof, but this was based on a previously proved theorem. He then had to read that; and it referred him to another theorem, and so on, until eventually the chain of reasoning led back to Euclid's set of axioms, which Hobbes had to admit were so self-evident that he could not deny them. Thus reasoning alone led Hobbes to accept a conclusion that, at first sight, he had rejected. (The episode so impressed him that in his greatest work, *Leviathan*, he attempted to apply the same deductive method of reasoning to the task of defending the right of the sovereign to absolute obedience.[3])

Reason's capacity to take us where we did not expect to go could also lead to a curious diversion from what one might expect to be the straight line of evolution. We have evolved a capacity to reason because it helps us to survive and reproduce. But if reason is an escalator, then although the first part of the journey may help us to survive and reproduce, we may go further than we needed to go for this purpose alone. We may even end up somewhere that creates a tension with other aspects of our nature. In this respect, there may after all be some validity in Kant's picture of a tension between our capacity to reason, and what it may lead us to see as the right thing to do, and our more basic desires. We can live with contradictions only up to a point. When the rebelling American colonists declared that all men have the right to life, liberty and the pursuit of happiness, they may not have intended to bring about the abolition of slavery, but they laid the foundation for a process that, over almost a century, brought about that result. Slavery might have been abolished without the Declaration of Independence, or despite the Declaration, abolition might have been staved off for another decade or two; but the tension between such universal declarations of rights and the institution of slavery was not difficult to see.

Here is another example, from Gunnar Myrdal's classic study of the American race question, *An American Dilemma*. Although this book was published in 1944, long before the civil rights victories of the sixties, Myrdal described the process of ethical reasoning that was making racist practices difficult to sustain:

> The individual . . . does not act in moral isolation. He is not left alone to manage his rationalizations as he pleases, without interference from outside. His valuations will, instead, be questioned and disputed . . . The feeling of need for logical consistency within the hierarchy of moral valuations – and the embarrassed and sometimes distressed feeling that the moral order is shaky – is, in its modern intensity, a rather new phenomenon.[4]

Myrdal goes on to say that the modern intensity of this need for consistency is related to increased mobility and communication, and the spread of education. Traditional and locally-held ideas are challenged by the wider society, and cannot withstand the appeal of the more universal values. This factor would, Myrdal predicted, lead to wider acceptance of universal values. He was thinking of the universal application of moral principles to all within the human species; but if he were writing today, he might well consider, as a further instance of the tendency he described, the view that the interests of nonhuman animals should also receive equal consideration.[5]

Curiously, when Karl Marx wrote about the history of class revolutions, he pointed to much the same tendency:

> Each new class which displaces the one previously dominant is forced, simply to be able to carry out its aim, to represent its interest as the common interest of all members of society, that is, ideally expressed. It has to give its ideas the form of universality and represent them as the only rational, universally valid ones . . . Every new class, therefore, achieves dominance only on a broader basis than that of the previous class ruling.[6]

Marx thought that reason was here merely providing a cloak for the class interests of those making the revolutions. Given his materialist view of history, he could hardly say anything else. Yet he also pointed out that because capitalism needed to concentrate workers in industrial centres and give them at least a minimum level of education, it contributed to raising the workers' awareness of their own situation. The same events can be seen in a different way: as the working out of the inherently universalizing nature of reasoning in societies that increasingly consist of educated and self-aware people, gradually freeing themselves from the constraints of parochial and religious beliefs. Since the general level of education and ease of communication are still increasing throughout the world, we have some grounds for hoping that this process will continue, eventually bringing with it a fundamental change in our ethical attitudes. (As I write, for example, we are seeing, in Somalia, a global reaction to human suffering that could not have taken place without the instant communication provided by television, the possibility of response provided by air transportation, and an international forum like the United Nations.)

Our ability to reason, then, can be a factor in leading us away from both arbitrary subjectivism, and an uncritical acceptance of the values of our community. The idea that everything is subjective, or more specifically, relative to our community, seems to go in and out of vogue with each generation. Like its predecessors, the current post-modernist mode of relativism fails to explain how it is that we can conduct coherent discussions about the values our community should hold, or maintain that our own values are superior to those of communities that accept slavery, the genital mutilation of women, or death sentences for writers who are deemed disrespectful of the prevailing religion. In contrast, the view I have defended accounts for the possibility of this kind of discussion on the basis of two simple premises. The first is the existence of our ability to reason. The second is that, in reasoning about practical matters, we are able to distance ourselves from our own point of view and take on, instead, a wider perspective, ultimately even the point of view of the universe.

Reason makes it possible for us to see ourselves in this way because, by thinking about my place in the world, I am able to see that I am just one being among others, with interests and desires like others. I have a personal perspective on the world, from which my interests are at the front and centre of the stage, the interests of my family and friends are close behind, and the interests of strangers are pushed to the back and sides. But reason enables me to see that others have similarly subjective perspectives, and that from 'the point of view of the universe' my perspective is no more privileged than theirs. Thus my ability to reason shows me the possibility of detaching myself from my own perspective, and shows me what the universe might look like if I had no personal perspective.

Taking the point of view of the universe as the basis of an ethical point of view does not mean that one must act impartially at all times. Some forms of partiality are themselves capable of impartial justification. For example, it is probably best for children generally if parents are regarded as having a much stricter duty to take care of their own children than they have to take care of the children of strangers. In this way society takes advantage of the natural ties of love between parents and children, which in normal circumstances is always to be preferred to the benevolence of a department of child welfare, no matter how well-intentioned the bureaucrats and social workers who make up the department may be. Love for one's children is a force that can be used for the good of all, but it does sometimes lead people to choose what is, from an impartial view-point, a lesser good. If the school your child attends is on fire, and you must choose between breaking open the door of the room in which she alone is trapped, and the door of another room in which twenty children are trapped – you have no time to get both doors open – most parents would probably rescue their own child. The parents of the other children might blame them for doing so, but if they were fair, they would probably recognize that in similar circumstances they would have done the same. If we weigh up the rescue of one's own child directly from an impartial standpoint, we will judge it to be wrong; but if we consider, firstly, the desirability of parental love for children, and then secondly that this act was motivated by that love, we will be more ready to accept it.[7]

Consistently with the idea of taking the point of view of the universe, the major ethical traditions all accept, in some form or other, a version of the Golden Rule that encourages equal consideration of interests. 'Love your neighbour as yourself', said Jesus. 'What is hateful to you do not do to your neighbour', said Rabbi Hillel. Confucius summed up his teaching in very similar terms: 'What you do not want done to yourself, do not do to others'. The *Mahabharata*, the great Indian epic, says: 'Let no man do to another that which would be repugnant to himself'.[8] The parallels are striking. Although Jesus and Hillel drew on a common Jewish tradition, Confucius and the *Mahabharata* appear to have reached the same position independently of each other and of the Judeo-Christian tradition. In each case, moreover, the words are offered as a kind of summary of all the moral law. Although the way in which Jesus and Hillel put the rule might be taken to limit it to members of one's own group, the parable of the good Samaritan firmly dispels this reading of whom Jesus thought one's neighbour to be.[9] Nor should Hillel, Confucius or the *Mahabharata* be interpreted as promoting, at least in these passages, anything less than a universal ethic.

The possibility of taking the point of view of the universe overcomes the problem of finding meaning in our lives, despite the ephemeral nature of human existence when measured against all the aeons of eternity. Suppose that we become involved in a project to help a small community in a developing country to become free of debt and self-sufficient in food. The project is an outstanding success, and the villagers are healthier, happier, better educated, economically secure, and have fewer children. Now someone might say: 'What good have you done? In a thousand years these people will all be dead, and their children and grandchildren as well, and nothing that you have done will make any difference'. That may be true, or it may be false. The changes we make today could snowball and, over a long period of time, lead to much more far-reaching changes. Or they could come to nothing. We simply cannot tell. We should not, however, think of our efforts as wasted unless they endure forever, or even for a very long time. If we regard time as a fourth dimension, then we can think of the universe, throughout all the times at which it contains sentient life, as a four-dimensional entity. We can then make that four-dimensional world a better place by causing there to be less pointless suffering in one particular place, at one particular time, than there would otherwise have been. As long as we do not thereby increase suffering at some other place or time, or cause any other comparable loss of value, we will have had a positive effect on the universe. In the previous chapter I suggested that Sisyphus might find meaning in his life, if, instead of rolling the same stone endlessly up the hill, he could roll many stones to the top and build a beautiful temple with them. If the temple Sisyphus might build is a metaphor for all possible goals, then by making the world a better place, we will have made a small contribution to the beauty of the greatest of all temples.

I have been arguing against the view that value depends entirely on my own subjective desires. Yet I am not defending the objectivity of ethics in the traditional sense. Ethical truths are not written into the fabric of the universe: to that extent the subjectivist is correct. If there were no beings with desires or preferences of any kind, nothing would be of value and ethics would lack all content. On the other hand, once there are beings with desires, there are values that are not only the subjective values of each individual being. The possibility of being led, by reasoning, to the point of view of the universe provides as much 'objectivity' as there can be. When my ability to reason shows me that the suffering of another being is very similar to my own suffering and (in an appropriate case) matters just as much to that other being as my own suffering matters to me, then my reason is showing me something that is undeniably *true*. I can still choose to ignore it, but then I can no longer deny that my perspective is a narrower, and more limited one, than it could be. This may not be enough to yield an objectively true ethical position. (One can always ask: what is so good about having a broader and more all-encompassing perspective?) But it is as close to an objective basis for ethics as there is to find.

The perspective on ourselves that we get when we take the point of view of the universe also yields as much objectivity as we need if we are to find a cause that is worthwhile in a way that is independent of our own desires. The most obvious such cause is the one mentioned by Henry Spira, at the beginning of this chapter: the reduction of pain and suffering, wherever it is to be found. This may not be the only rationally grounded value, but it is the most immediate, pressing, and universally agreed upon one. We know from our own experience that when pain and suffering are acute, all other values recede into the background. If we take the point of view of the universe we can recognize the urgency of doing something about the pain and suffering of others, before we even consider promoting (for their own sake rather than as a means to reducing pain and suffering) other possible values like beauty, knowledge, autonomy or happiness.

Does the possibility of taking the point of view of the universe mean that the person who acts only from a narrow perspective – for the sake of self, family, friends, or nation, in ways that cannot be defended even indirectly from an impartial perspective – is necessarily acting irrationally? Not, I think, in the full sense of the term. In this respect practical reasoning – that is, reasoning about what to do – is different from theoretical reasoning. If Hobbes had accepted Euclid's axioms, and been unable to find any flaw with the chain of reasoning that led from them to Euclid's Forty-seventh Theorem, but had nevertheless continued to hold that the theorem was 'impossible' we could rightly have said that he had failed to grasp the nature of Euclid's reasoning process. He would simply have been in error – and if, for example, he had applied this belief to some practical problem of measurement or construction, he would have got the wrong answer, and this would have handicapped him in reaching whatever goal he intended the measurement or construction to achieve. If, on the other hand, I act in a way that shows less concern for the suffering of strangers than for the suffering of my family or friends, I do not show that I am incapable of grasping the point of view of the universe, but only that this perspective does not motivate me as strongly as my more personal perspective. If to be irrational is to make a mistake, there is no mistake here; my pursuit of the more limited perspective will not lead me to a wrong answer that will prevent me reaching my own limited objectives. For instance, I argued in Chapter 5 that we have evolved as beings with particularly strong desires to protect and further the interests of members of our family. To disregard this side of our nature altogether is scarcely possible. The most that the escalator of reason can require is that we keep it in check, and remain aware of the existence of the wider perspective. So it is only in an extended sense of the term that those who take the narrower perspective might be said to be acting less rationally than those who are able to act from the point of view of the universe.

It would be nice to be able to reach a stronger conclusion than this about the basis of ethics. As things stand, Sidgwick's 'old immoral paradox', the clash between self-interest and generalized benevolence, has been softened, but it has not been dissolved.

Toward an ethical life

In a society in which the narrow pursuit of material self-interest is the norm, the shift to an ethical stance is more radical than many people realize. In comparison with the needs of people starving in Somalia, the desire to sample the wines of the leading French vineyards pales into insignificance. Judged against the sufferings of immobilized rabbits having shampoos dripped into their eyes, a better shampoo becomes an unworthy goal. The preservation of old-growth forests should override our desire to use disposable paper towels. An ethical approach to life does not forbid having fun or enjoying food and wine, but it changes our sense of priorities. The effort and expense put into buying fashionable clothes, the endless search for more and more refined gastronomic pleasures, the astonishing additional expense that marks out the prestige car market from the market in cars for people who just want a reliable means of getting from A to B – all these become disproportionate to people who can shift perspective long enough to take themselves, at least for a time, out of the spotlight. If a higher ethical consciousness spreads, it will utterly change the society in which we live.

We cannot expect that this higher ethical consciousness will become universal. There will always be people who don't care for anyone or anything, not even for themselves. There will be others, more numerous and more calculating, who earn a living by taking advantage of others, especially the poor and the powerless. We cannot afford to wait for some coming glorious day when everyone will live in loving peace and harmony with each other. Human nature is not like that at present, and there is no sign of it changing sufficiently in the foreseeable future. Since reasoning alone proved incapable of fully resolving the clash between self-interest and ethics, it is unlikely that rational argument will persuade every rational person to act ethically. Even if reason had been able to take us further, we would still have had to face the reality of a world in which many people are very far from acting on the basis of reasoning of any kind, even crudely self-interested reasoning. So for a long time to come, the world is going to remain a tough place in which to live.

Nevertheless, we are part of this world and there is a desperate need to do something *now* about the conditions in which people live and die, and to avoid both social and ecological disaster. There is no time to focus our thoughts on the possibility of a distant utopian future. Too many humans and nonhuman animals are suffering now, the forests are going too quickly, population growth is still out of control, and as we saw in Chapter 3, if we do not bring greenhouse gas emissions down rapidly, the lives and homes of 46 million people are at risk in the Nile and Bengal delta regions alone. Nor can we wait for governments to bring about the change that is needed. It is not in the interests of politicians to challenge the fundamental assumptions of the society they have been elected to lead. If 10 percent of the population were to take a consciously ethical outlook on life and act accordingly, the resulting change would be more significant than any change of government. The division between an ethical and a selfish approach to life is far more fundamental than the difference between the policies of the political right and the political left.

We have to take the first step. We must reinstate the idea of living an ethical life as a realistic and viable alternative to the present dominance of materialist self-interest. If, over the next decade, a critical mass of people with new priorities were to emerge, and if these people were seen to do well, in every sense of the term – if their co-operation with each other brings reciprocal benefits, if they find joy and fulfillment in their lives – then the ethical attitude will spread, and the conflict between ethics and self-interest will have been shown to be overcome, not by abstract reasoning alone, but by adopting the ethical life as a practical way of living, and showing that it works, psychologically, socially and ecologically.

Anyone can become part of the critical mass that offers us a chance of improving the world before it is too late. You can rethink your goals, and question what you are doing with your life. If your present way of living does not stand up against an impartial standard of value, then you can change it. That might mean quitting your job, selling your house and going to work for a voluntary organization in India. More often, the commitment to a more ethical way of living will be the first step of a gradual but far-reaching evolution in your lifestyle and in your thinking about your place in the world. You will take up new causes, and find your goals shifting. If you get involved in your work, money and status will become less important. From your new perspective, the world will look different. One thing is certain: you will find plenty of worthwhile things to do. You will not be bored, or lack fulfillment in your life. Most important of all, you will know that you have not lived and died for nothing, because you will have become part of the great tradition of those who have responded to the amount of pain and suffering in the universe by trying to make the world a better place.

NOTES

———◆———

CHAPTER 1 *The ultimate choice*

1 Information in this and the following paragraphs on Ivan F. Boesky is taken in part from Robert Slater, *The Titans of Takeover*, Prentice-Hall, Englewood Cliffs, NJ, 1987, ch. 7.

2 *Wall Street Journal*, June 20, 1985; quoted in Slater, p. 134.

3 Ivan F. Boesky, *Merger Mania*, Holt, Rinehart and Winston, New York, 1985, p. v. The earlier quotations are from pp. xiii–xiv.

4 Mark Brandon Read, *Chopper From the Inside*, Floradale Productions, Kilmore, Vic, 1991, pp. 6–7.

5 Plato, *The Republic*, Book II, 360, 2nd ed., trans. Desmond Lee, Penguin Books, Harmondsworth, Middlesex, 1984.

6 Robert Slater, *The Titans of Takeover*, p. 132; Adam Smith, *The Roaring '80s*, Penguin Books, New York, 1988, p. 209.

7 Michael Lewis, *Liar's Poker*, Penguin Books, New York, 1990, pp. 9, 81.

8 Donald J. Trump, with Charles Leerhsen, *Surviving at the Top*, Random House, New York, 1990, p. 13.

9 *Time*, April 8, 1991, p. 62.

10 Oliver Stone, dir./prod., *Wall Street*, CBS/Fox, Los Angeles, 1987.

11 Karl Marx, *Economic and Philosophical Manuscripts*, quoted in D. McLellan, ed., *Karl Marx: Selected Writings*, Oxford University Press, Oxford, 1977, p. 89.

12 See Francis Fukuyama, *The End of History and the Last Man*, Hamish Hamilton, London, 1992.

13 See Daniel Bell, *The End of Ideology*, 2nd edn., with a new Afterword,

Harvard University Press, Cambridge, Mass., 1988.

14 See Bill McKibben, *The End of Nature*, Random House, New York, 1989.
15 Derek Parfit, *Reasons and Persons*, Clarendon Press, Oxford, 1984, p. 454.
16 For a defence of this statement, see my *Practical Ethics*, 2nd edn., Cambridge University Press, Cambridge, 1993, ch. 6.
17 *The Independent*, London, March 20, 1992; I said something very similar in my book, *Practical Ethics*, 1st edn., Cambridge University Press, Cambridge, 1979, pp. 1–2.
18 Robert J. Ringer, *Looking Out for # 1*, Fawcett Crest, New York, 1978, p. 22.
19 Todd Gitlin, *Inside Prime Time*, Pantheon, New York, 1983, pp. 268–9.

CHAPTER 2 *'What's in it for me?'*

1 Joelle Attinger, 'The Decline of New York', *Time*, Sept. 17, 1990.
2 *New York Times*, March 2, 1992, p. B3.
3 *Time*, Sept. 17, 1990.
4 Richard Brooks, 'Dreamland Now Third World Capital', *The Observer*, London, May 3, 1992.
5 *Time*, Sept. 17, 1990.
6 Robert N. Bellah, Richard Madsen, William M. Sullivan, Ann Swidler and Steven M. Tipton, *Habits of the Heart: Individualism and Commitment in American Life*, University of California Press, Berkeley, 1985, p. 16.
7 *New York Times*, Oct. 10, 1991.
8 *New York Times*, Feb. 11, 1991.
9 Joseph Nocera, 'Scoundrel Time', *GQ*, Aug. 1991, p. 100.
10 Graef S. Crystal, *In Search of Excess: The Overcompensation of American Executives*, W. W. Norton & Co., New York, 1991, p. 205, *The Age*, Nov. 11, 1991.
11 *New York Times*, May 8, 1991.
12 *New York Daily News*, Feb. 3, 1992.
13 *Time*, Aug. 26, 1991, p. 54; *New York Times*, April 10, 1991, p. A22; May 10, A14; July 30, p. A1; *The Animals' Agenda*, July/Aug. 1991.
14 *Sunday Age*, Dec. 27, 1992.
15 Nancy Gibbs, 'Homeless, USA', *Time*, Dec. 17, 1990.
16 *Time*, Dec. 17, 1990.
17 Robert N. Bellah et al, *Habits of the Heart*, pp. 57, 82, 194; the quotation is from Alexis de Tocqueville, *Democracy in America*, J. Mayer, ed., trans. G. Lawrence, Doubleday Anchor, New York, 1969, p. 508.
18 Frances Fitzgerald, *Cities on a Hill*, Picador, London, 1987, pp. 241–2.
19 Raoul Naroll, *The Moral Order*, Sage Publications, Beverly Hills, Calif., 1983.

20 Thomas Hobbes, *Leviathan*, J. M. Dent, London, 1973, ch. 11, p. 49.
21 Thomas Hobbes, *Leviathan*, ch. 13, pp. 64–5.
22 *New York Times*, Dec. 25, 1990, p. 41.
23 *Democracy in America*, J. Mayer, ed., p. 508; quoted by Robert N. Bellah et al, *Habits of the Heart*, p. 37.
24 G. Hofstede, *Culture's Consequences*, Sage Publications, Beverly Hills, Calif., 1980, cited in H. Triandis, C. McCursker and H. Hui, 'Multimethod Probes of Individualism and Collectivism', *Journal of Personality and Social Psychology*, 1990, vol. 59, no. 5, p. 1010.
25 Quoted in Daniel Coleman, 'The Group and the Self: New Focus on a Cultural Rift', *New York Times*, Dec. 25, 1990.
26 D. McLellan, ed., *Karl Marx: Selected Writings*, pp. 223, 226.
27 P. R. Mooney, 'On folkseed and life patents' in *Advances in Biotechnology: Proceedings of an International Conference Organized by the Swedish Council for Forestry and Agricultural Research and the Swedish Recombinant DNA Advisory Committee, 11–14 March 1990*, Swedish Council for Forestry and Agricultural Research, Stockholm, 1990.
28 *E Magazine*, vol. 3, no. 1, Jan./Feb. 1992, p. 9.
29 Robert N. Bellah et al, *Habits of the Heart*, p. 163.
30 Andrew Stephen, 'How a burn-up ended in flames on the streets of LA', *The Observer*, London, May 3, 1992.
31 Martin Walker, 'Dark Past Ambushes the "City of the Future"', *Guardian Weekly*, May 10, 1992.
32 Richard Schickel, 'How TV Failed to Get the Real Picture', *Time*, May 11, 1992.
33 Andrew Stephen, 'How a burn-up ended . . .'.

CHAPTER 3 *Using up the world*

1 R. H. Campbell & A. S. Skinner, eds., *The Wealth of Nations*, Clarendon Press, Oxford, 1976, p. 24.
2 For Locke, it was a king in America, not Africa: 'And a king of a large and fruitful territory there feeds lodges, and is clad worse than a day labourer in England'. (John Locke, *Second Treatise on Civil Government*, introduction by W. S. Carpenter, J. M. Dent, London, 1966, ch. 5, para. 41.) See also Bernard Melville, *The Fable of the Bees*, pt.i.181: 'If we trace the most flourishing Nations in their Origin, we shall find that in the remote Beginnings of every Society, the richest and most considerable Men among them were a great while destitute of a great many Comforts of Life that are now enjoy'd by the meanest and most humble Wretches'. I owe this reference to R. H. Campbell and A. S. Skinner's *The Wealth of Nations* (ibid.). One hundred and twenty years later, the same argument was still at work in the thought of Andrew Carnegie; see page 73 of this book.
3 Jean-Jacques Rousseau, *Discourse on Inequality*, J. M. Dent, London, 1958, p. 163.
4 Adam Smith, *A Theory of the Moral Sentiments*, Oxford University

Press, Oxford, 1976, vol. IV, ch. 1, p. 10. I owe these references to Michael Ignatieff, *The Needs of Strangers*, Chatto and Windus, London, 1984, pp. 108 ff.

5 *Genesis*, I 24–28.

6 Sandra Postel and Christopher Flavin, 'Reshaping the Global Economy', in Lester R. Brown, ed., *State of the World, 1991: The Worldwatch Institute Report on Progress Towards a Sustainable Society*, Allen & Unwin, Sydney, 1991, p. 186.

7 Alan Durning, 'Asking How Much is Enough', in Lester Brown, ed., *State of the World, 1991: The Worldwatch Institute Report on Progress Towards a Sustainable Society*, Allen & Unwin, Sydney, 1991, pp. 154, 157.

8 For full documentation, see Sandra Postel and Christopher Flavin, 'Reshaping the Global Economy', p. 170.

9 'Ozone Hole Gapes Wider', *Time*, Nov. 4, 1991, p. 65.

10 See especially my *Animal Liberation*, 2nd edn., A *New York Review* Book, New York, 1990.

11 Jeremy Rifkin, *Beyond Beef*, E. P. Dutton, New York, 1992, p. 152. On the environmental costs of animal production, see also Alan B. Durning and Holly B. Brough, *Taking Stock: Animal Farming and the Environment*, Worldwatch Paper 103, Worldwatch Institute, Washington, DC, 1991.

12 Sandra Postel and Christopher Flavin, 'Reshaping the Global Economy', p. 178.

13 Fred Pearce, 'When the Tide Comes in . . .', *New Scientist*, Jan. 2, 1993, p. 23.

14 '"Don't Let Us Drown", Islanders Tell Bush', *New Scientist*, June 13, 1992, p. 6.

15 See Jodi L. Jacobson, 'Holding Back the Sea' in Lester Brown et al, *State of the World, 1990: The Worldwatch Institute Report on Progress Towards a Sustainable Economy*, Worldwatch Institute, Washington, DC, 1990.

16 '"Don't Let Us Drown". . .', p. 6.

17 Anil Agarwal and Sunita Narain, *Global Warming in an Unequal World: A case of environmental colonialism*, Centre for Science and the Environment, New Delhi, 1991, quoted in Fred Pearce, 'Ecology and the New Colonialism', *New Scientist*, Feb. 1, 1992, pp. 55–6.

18 Adam Smith, *A Theory of the Moral Sentiments*, vol. IV, ch. 1, p. 10.

19 See, for example, E. J. Mishan, *Costs of Economic Growth*, Staples, London, 1967, and D. H. Meadows et al, *The Limits to Growth*, Universe Books, New York, 1972. For an account of the development of the case for growth as well as anti-growth ideas in this period, see H. W. Arndt, *The Rise and Fall of Economic Growth*, Longman Cheshire, Melbourne, 1978.

20 Sandra Postel and Christopher Flavin, 'Reshaping the Global Economy', pp. 186–7.

21 Lester Brown, 'Picturing a Sustainable Society' in Lester Brown et al,

eds., *State of the World, 1990: The Worldwatch Institute Report on Progress Towards a Sustainable Society,* Worldwatch Institute, Washington, DC, 1990, p. 190.

22 The study is by Jose Goldemberg et al, *Energy for a Sustainable World,* Worldwatch Institute, Washington, DC, 1987, cited by Alan Durning, 'Asking How Much is Enough', p. 157.

23 Paul Wachtel, *The Poverty of Affluence,* Free Press, New York, 1983, p. 11.

24 Alan Durning, 'Asking How Much is Enough', p. 154.

25 Alan Durning, 'Asking How Much is Enough', p. 156, citing a personal communication from Michael Worley of the National Opinion Research Center, University of Chicago, Illinois, Sept. 1990.

26 Paul Wachtel, *The Poverty of Affluence,* pp. 22–3.

27 D. Kahneman and C. Varey, 'Notes on the Psychology of Utility', in J. Elster and J. Roemer, eds., *Interpersonal Comparisons of Well-Being,* Cambridge University Press, Cambridge, 1991, pp. 136–7. (I owe this and the following reference to Julian Savulescu, personal communication.)

28 P. Brickman, D. Coates and R. Janoff-Bulman, 'Lottery Winners and Accident Victims – is Happiness Relative?', *Journal of Personality and Social Psychology,* 1978, vol. 36, no. 8, pp. 917–927.

29 John Greenwald, 'Why the Gloom?', *Time,* Jan. 13, 1992.

30 R. A. Easterlin, 'Does Economic Growth Improve the Human Lot: Some Empirical Evidence', in P. A. David and M. Abramovitz, eds., *Nations and Households in Economic Growth,* Academic Press, New York, 1974, p. 121.

31 Alan Durning, 'Asking How Much is Enough', p. 157.

CHAPTER 4 *How we came to be living this way*

1 Max Weber, *The Protestant Ethic and the Spirit of Capitalism,* trans. T. Parsons, Unwin, London, 1930, p. 56.

2 Max Weber, *The Protestant Ethic,* pp. 71–2.

3 Aristotle, *Politics,* Book II (trans. B. Jowett), intro. H. W. C. Davis, Clarendon Press, Oxford, 1905, p. 61.

4 Aristotle, *Politics,* pp. 62–3.

5 Aristotle, *Politics,* pp. 43–4.

6 Aristotle, *Politics,* p. 46.

7 Deuteronomy, 23: 19–20.

8 Luke 6:35.

9 Matthew 21:12–13.

10 Mark 10:17–25.

11 W. E. H. Lecky, *History of European Morals from Augustus to Charlemagne,* Longman, London, vol. II, p. 81, 1899.

12 Gregory's remark is cited by Nicole Oresme, *Traictie de la Premiere Invention des Monnoies,* first published c. 1360, ch. 17, reprinted iA. E. Monroe, ed., *Early Economic Thought: Selections from economic literature prior to Adam Smith,* Harvard University Press, Cambridge,

Mass., 1965 (first published 1924), p. 96; Oresme gives no source and I have been unable to trace the original in Gregory.

13 Lester K. Little, *Religious Poverty and the Profit Economy in Medieval Europe*, Cornell University Press, Ithaca, NY, 1978, p. 38.

14 John T. Noonan, Jr., *The Scholastic Analysis of Usury*, Harvard University Press, Cambridge, Mass., 1957, p. 1.

15 Jacques Le Goff, 'The Usurer and Purgatory' in Center for Medieval and Renaissance Studies, University of California, Los Angeles, *The Dawn of Modern Banking*, Yale University Press, New Haven, Conn., 1979, pp. 28–30.

16 Jacques Le Goff in *The Dawn of Modern Banking*, pp. 32–43.

17 Lester K. Little, *Religious Poverty . . .* , pp. 36–7.

18 Lester K. Little, *Religious Poverty . . .* , p. 34.

19 Thomas Aquinas, *Summa Theologica*, II–II, Question 32, art. 5, trans. Fathers of the English Dominican Province, Benziger Brothers, New York, vol. II, p. 1328.

20 Thomas Aquinas, *Summa Theologica*, II–II, Question 67, art. 7, pp. 1479–1480.

21 On the natural law doctrine of property, and what became of it, see Stephen Buckle, *Natural Law and the Theory of Property: Grotius to Hume*, Clarendon Press, Oxford, 1990.

22 John T. Noonan, Jr., *The Scholastic Analysis of Usury*, p. 365–7.

23 Richard Huber, *The American Idea of Success*, McGraw-Hill Book Company, New York, 1971, p. 15, referring also to Louis B. Wright, *Middle-Class Culture in Elizabethan England*, Huntington Library Publications, Chapel Hill, North Carolina, 1935, pp. 165–200.

24 Andre Siegfried, *America Comes of Age: A French Analysis*, trans. H. H. and Doris Hemming, Jonathan Cape, London, 1927, p. 36.

25 Cotton Mather, *A Christian at His Calling*, Boston, 1701, quoted from Richard Huber, *The American Idea of Success*, p. 12.

26 William Penn, *The Advice of William Penn to His Children*, also quoted in Richard Huber, *The American Idea of Success*, p. 14.

27 Richard Huber, *The American Idea of Success*, pp. 20–21.

28 Nathaniel Hawthorne, *Tales, Sketches, and Other Papers, The Works of Nathaniel Hawthorne*, Houghton Mifflin, Boston and New York, 1883, vol. XII, p. 202; Paul Ford, *A List of Books Written by or Relating to Benjamin Franklin*, Brooklyn, NY, 1889, p. 55; I owe both items to Richard Huber, *The American Idea of Success*, p. 21.

29 Max Weber, *The Protestant Ethic*, p. 56.

30 Quoted without source by Peter Baida, *Poor Richard's Legacy*, William Morrow, New York, 1990, p. 25.

31 Peter Baida, *Poor Richard's Legacy*, p. 78; other quotations which follow this one are drawn from Chapter 4 of this book.

32 Richard Huber, *The American Idea of Success*, p. 25.

33 W. J. Ghent, *Our Benevolent Feudalism*, Macmillan & Co., Ltd., New York, 1902, p. 29, quoted by Richard Huber, *The American Idea of Success*, p. 66.

34 Quoted in Richard Hofstadter, *Social Darwinism in American Thought*, Beacon Press, Boston, 1966, p. 31.

35 Lochner v. New York, 198 US 45 (1905); quoted by Richard Hofstadter, *Social Darwinism*, p. 47.

36 Andrew Carnegie, *Autobiography*, Houghton Mifflin, Boston, 1948, p. 321; 'Wealth', *North American Review*, 391, June 1889, pp. 654–7.

37 Alexis de Tocqueville, *Democracy in America*, pp. 54, 615.

38 Quoted in Max Weber, *The Protestant Ethic*, p. 51.

39 Thomas L. Nicholls, *Forty Years of American Life*, London, 1964, vol. 1, pp. 402–4, quoted by Richard Huber, *The American Idea of Success*, p. 116.

40 Andre Siegfried, *America Comes of Age*, pp. 348, 353.

41 Harold Laski, *The American Democracy*, New York, 1948, pp. 165, 172, quoted by Richard Huber, *The American Idea of Success*, p. 35.

42 Friedrich Engels, 'The Labor Movement in the United States', in Lewis Feuer, ed., *Marx & Engels: Basic Writings on Politics and Philosophy*, Doubleday Anchor, New York, 1959, p. 496.

43 Vance Packard, *The Hidden Persuaders*, Penguin Books, Harmondsworth, Middlesex, 1957, p. 22.

44 Charles Reich, *The Greening of America*, Allen Lane, The Penguin Press, London, 1971, p. 1.

45 Peter Weiss, *The Persecution and Assassination of Jean-Paul Marat as Performed by the Inmates of the Asylum of Charenton Under the Direction of the Marquis de Sade*, Pocket Books, New York, 1966, p. 31, cited in Todd Gitlin, *The Sixties*, Bantam Books, New York, 1987, p. 424.

46 Michael Rossman, 'The Only Thing Missing was Sufis', *Creem*, Oct. 1972, reprinted in Michael Rossman, *New Age Blues*, E. P. Dutton, New York, 1979, p. 5.

47 Michael Rossman, *New Age Blues*, pp. 15–8.

48 Michael Rossman, *New Age Blues*, p. 20.

49 Jerry Rubin, *Growing (Up) at Thirty-Seven*, M. Evans, New York, 1976, p. 20; quoted by Christopher Lasch, *The Culture of Narcissism: American Life in an Age of Diminishing Expectations*, W. W. Norton & Co., New York, 1978, p. 14.

50 The 'Jacuzzi' comment is from Todd Gitlin, *The Sixties*, p. 433; Gitlin cites Charles Krauthammer, 'The Revolution Surrenders: From Freedom Train to Gravy Train', *Washington Post*, April 12, 1985, p. A25, but his own view is that the media focus on a few conspicuous cases distorted the reality, which was that many former radicals continued to work, in more structured and conventional ways, for peace and justice.

51 Kitty Kelley, *Nancy Reagan: An Unauthorized Biography*, Bantam Books, New York, 1991, p. 267.

52 Kelley, *Nancy Reagan*, pp. 274–5.

53 *Los Angeles Times*, Feb. 6, 1982; quoted by Robert Bellah, et al, *Habits of the Heart*, University of California Press, Los Angeles, 1985, p. 264.

54 *Time*, Aug. 3, 1987.

55 Frances Fitzgerald, *Cities on a Hill*, Picador, London, 1987, pp. 143, 195; John Taylor, *Circus of Ambition*, Warner Books, New York, 1989, p. 3; *Time*, Aug. 3, 1987.

56 *Time*, Aug. 3, 1987.

57 Frances Fitzgerald, *Cities on a Hill*, pp. 248, 375.

58 John Taylor, *Circus of Ambition*, p. 107.

59 John Taylor, *Circus of Ambition*, ch. 4.

60 George Gilders, *Wealth and Poverty*, Basic Books, New York, 1981, p. 118.

61 *New York Times*, March 5, 1992; *Wall Street Journal*, April 8, 1992. For further statistics on how the rich grew richer and the poor grew poorer in the eighties in America, see Donald L. Bartlett and James B. Steele, *America: What Went Wrong?*, Andrews and McMeel, Kansas City, Missouri, 1992, ch. 1.

CHAPTER 5 *Is selfishness in our genes?*

1 The story is told, unfortunately without further references, by John M. Darley and Bibb Latane, 'Norms and Normative Behavior: Field Studies of Social Interdependence' in J. Macaulay and L. Berkowitz, *Altruism and Helping Behavior*, Academic Press, New York, 1970, p. 86.

2 Richard D. Alexander, *The Biology of Moral Systems*, Aldine de Gruyter, New York, 1987, p. 159. Alexander was objecting to what I said about blood donors in *The Expanding Circle*, Farrar, Straus & Giroux, New York, 1981.

3 E. O. Wilson, *On Human Nature*, Harvard University Press, Cambridge, Mass., 1978, p. 165.

4 P. L. van den Berghe, 'Bridging the paradigms: biology and the social sciences', pp. 32–52 in *Sociobiology and Human Nature*, M. S. Gregory, A. Silvers and D. Sutch, eds., Jossey-Bass, Inc., Publishers, San Francisco, 1978. I owe this reference to Joseph Lopreato, *Human Nature and Biocultural Evolution*, Allen & Unwin, London, 1984, p. 209.

5 G. Hardin, *The Limits of Altruism: An Ecologist's View of Survival*, Indiana University Press, Bloomington, Ind., 1977.

6 Sources for the instances of altruism given in this paragraph—and details of additional examples—can be found in *Sociobiology: The New Synthesis*, pp. 122–9, 475, 495 and in Felicity Huntingford, 'The Evolution of Cooperation and Altruism', in Andrew M. Colman, ed., *Cooperation and Competition in Humans and Animals*, Van Nostrand Reinhold, London, 1982, pp. 3–5.

7 The example of the wolf's restraint comes from Konrad Lorenz, *King Solomon's Ring*, Methuen, London, 1964, pp. 186–9.

8 Dimity Reed, 'My Kidney for My Son', *Canberra Times*, Oct. 14, 1989.

9 Peter Hillmore, 'Kidney Capital', *The Age*, Aug. 17, 1991.

10 David Gilmore, *Manhood in the Making: Cultural Concepts of Masculinity*, Yale University Press, New Haven, Conn., 1990, pp. 42, 105, 149.

11 J. S. Mill, *On the Subjection of Women*, 1869, ch. 2; reprinted in J. S. Mill, *On Liberty, Representative Government, On the Subjection of Women*, J. M. Dent, London, 1960, p. 469.

12 Pat Shipman, 'Life and death on the wagon trail', *New Scientist*, July 27, 1991, pp. 40–42; Donald K. Grayson, 'Donner party deaths: A demographic assessment', *Journal of Anthropological Research*, Fall 1990, vol. 46, no. 3, pp. 223–242.

13 Plato, *Republic*, V, 464.

14 See Yonina Talmon, *Family and Community in the Kibbutz*, Harvard University Press, Cambridge, Mass., 1972, pp. 3–34.

15 John Lyons, 'The Revenge of the Mommy', *The Good Weekend*, Melbourne, Sept. 28, 1991.

16 Douglas Adams and Mark Carwardine, *Last Chance to See*, Heinemann, London, 1990, p. 134. The views of the New Zealand conservation officer resemble, and may derive from, a controversial theory developed by V. Wynne Edwards in *Animal Dispersion in Relation to Social Behaviour*, Oliver and Boyd, Edinburgh, 1962, and popularized by Robert Ardrey in *The Social Contract*, Collins, London, 1970. This theory now commands virtually no support among researchers in the biological sciences.

17 See J. Maynard Smith, *The Theory of Evolution*, Penguin Books, London, 1975; and Richard Dawkins, *The Selfish Gene*, Oxford University Press, Oxford, 1976, pp. 74, 200.

18 David Hume, *A Treatise of Human Nature*, Book III, pt. 2, sec. i., Ernest C. Mossner, ed., with an introduction by the editor, Penguin Books, Harmondsworth, Middlesex, 1984.

19 Sydney L. W. Mellon, *The Evolution of Love*, W. H. Freeman, Oxford, 1981, p. 261.

20 Robert Edgerton, *Rules, Exceptions and Social Order*, University of California Press, Berkeley, 1985, p. 147.

21 Joseph Lopreato, *Human Nature and Biocultural Evolution*, Allen & Unwin, London, 1984, pp. 225–235.

22 Richard D. Alexander, *The Biology of Moral Systems*, p. 160.

CHAPTER 6 *How the Japanese live*

1 The view presented here is the dominant one in both Japanese and Western writing about Japanese society. For a forceful critique of this dominant view, and the presentation of an alternative, see Ross Mouer and Yoshio Sugimoto, *Images of Japanese Society: a study in the social construction of reality*, KPI, London, 1986.

2 See, for example, the account of the hours worked at a Japanese bank

in Thomas P. Rohlen, *For Harmony and Strength: Japanese White-Collar Organization in Anthropological Perspective*, University of California Press, Berkeley, 1974, pp. 94–100, 111. Rohlen estimates that the employees at the bank he studied worked an average of fifty-six hours a week in the office, and spent another four to six hours a week socializing with fellow employees.

3 Jack Seward and Howard Van Zandt, *Japan: The Hungry Guest*, Yohan Publications, Tokyo, revised edn., 1985, p. 97.

4 B. H. Chamberlain, quoted in Thomas Crump, *The Death of an Emperor*, Oxford University Press, Oxford, 1991, p. 57.

5 Jack Seward and Howard Van Zandt, *Japan: The Hungry Guest*, p. 102.

6 See Herbert Passin, 'Japanese Society', in David Sills, ed., *International Encyclopedia of the Social Sciences*, Macmillan and The Free Press, New York, 1968, vol. 8, p. 242.

7 Thomas P. Rohlen, *For Harmony and Strength*, pp. 38–45.

8 Thomas P. Rohlen, *For Harmony and Strength*, p. 36.

9 See Mark Zimmerman, *How to do Business with the Japanese*, Random House, New York, 1985, pp. 12–3.

10 Jack Seward and Howard Van Zandt, *Japan: The Hungry Guest*, pp. 95–6.

11 Jack Seward and Howard Van Zandt, *Japan: The Hungry Guest*, p. 97.

12 Thomas P. Rohlen, *For Harmony and Strength*, pp. 79, 148–9.

13 Thomas P. Rohlen, *For Harmony and Strength*, 1974, p. 47.

14 Thomas P. Rohlen, *For Harmony and Strength*, pp. 97–100.

15 George W. England and Jyuji Misumi, 'Work Centrality in Japan and the United States', *Journal of Cross-cultural Psychology*, 1986, vol. 17, no. 4, pp. 399–416.

16 Robert Cole, *Work, Mobility and Participation: A comparative study of American and Japanese industry*, University of California Press, Berkeley, 1979, pp. 252–3, cited in Robert J. Smith, *Japanese Society: Tradition, Self and the Social Order*, Cambridge University Press, Cambridge, 1983, p. 60.

17 Robert Whiting, 'You've Gotta Have "Wa"', *Sports Illustrated*, Sept. 24, 1979, pp. 60–71, cited by Robert J. Smith, *Japanese Society*, p. 50.

18 John David Morley, *Pictures from the Water Trade: An Englishman in Japan*, Fontana, London, 1985, p. 185.

19 V. Lee Hamilton et al, 'Group and Gender in Japanese and American Elementary Classrooms', *Journal of Cross-Cultural Psychology*, 1991, vol. 22, no. 3, pp. 317–46, especially pp. 327, 336.

20 Jeremiah J. Sullivan, Teruhiko Suzuki and Yasumasa Kondo, 'Managerial Perceptions of Performance', *Journal of Cross-cultural Psychology*, 1986, vol. 17, no. 4, pp. 379–98, especially p. 393.

21 John David Morley, *Pictures from the Water Trade*, p. 53.

22 Jack Seward and Howard Van Zandt, *Japan: The Hungry Guest*, p. 54.

23 Thomas P. Rohlen, *For Harmony and Strength*, pp. 48–9, 175.

24 See Chapter 2, p. 26 of this book.

25 John David Morley, *Pictures from the Water Trade*, p. 38.

26 Robert J. Smith, *Japanese Society*, p. 81.

27 Tomosaburo Yamauchi, *Aite no Tatiba oi tatu – Hare no Dotoku Tetugaku*, Keiso Shobo Publishing Company Ltd., Tokyo, 1991. For more on the philosophy of R. M. Hare, see Chapter 9 of this book.

28 Thomas P. Rohlen, *For Harmony and Strength*, p. 52.

29 See, for example, Ross Mourer and Yoshio Sugimoto, *Images of Japanese Society*, pp. 196–7.

30 *Time*, Nov. 4, 1991, p. 7.

31 Thomas P. Rohlen, *For Harmony and Strength*, p. 252.

32 *Time*, Feb. 10, 1992, p. 11.

33 John David Morley, *Pictures from the Water Trade*, p. 184.

34 See Mary Midgley, 'On Trying Out One's New Sword', in Mary Midgley, *Heart and Mind: The varieties of moral experience*, Harvester Press, Brighton, 1981.

35 John David Morley, *Pictures from the Water Trade*, p. 121.

36 For details see Dexter Cate, 'The Island of the Dragon', in Peter Singer, ed., *In Defence of Animals*, Basil Blackwell Ltd., Oxford, 1985.

CHAPTER 7 *Tit for Tat*

1 Tony Ashworth, *Trench Warfare, 1914–1918: The Live and Let Live System*, Holmes and Meier, New York, 1980; cited by Robert Axelrod, *The Evolution of Cooperation*, Basic Books, New York, 1984, ch. 4.

2 This account is taken from the work of Peter Munch, as summarized by Raoul Naroll in *The Moral Order*, Sage Publications, Beverly Hills, Calif., 1983, pp. 125–7. See Peter Munch, *Crisis in Utopia*, New York, Crowell, 1971; the quotation is from Peter Munch, 'Economic Development and Conflicting Values: A Social Experiment in Tristan da Cunha', *American Anthropologist*, 1970, vol. 72, p. 1309.

3 Robert Axelrod, *The Evolution of Cooperation*, pp. 27–54.

4 The terminology of 'suckers' and 'cheats' comes from R. Dawkins, *The Selfish Gene*, Oxford University Press, Oxford, 1976.

5 Robert Axelrod, *The Evolution of Cooperation*, p. 99.

6 Richard Christie and Florence Geis, *Studies in Machiavellianism*, Academic Press, New York, 1970, pp. 318–320, citing studies by A. de Miguel and S. Guterman.

7 E. Westermarck, *The Origin and Development of the Moral Ideas*, vol. 2, Macmillan Publishing Company, London, 1906.

8 Cicero, *de Officiis*, J. M. Dent, ed., Everyman, London, 1955, vol. 1, par. 47.

9 See Chad Hansen, 'Classical Chinese Ethics' in Peter Singer, ed., *A Companion to Ethics*, Basil Blackwell Ltd., Oxford, 1991, pp. 72.

10 Alvin Gouldner, 'The Norm of Reciprocity', *American Sociological Review*, vol. 25, no. 2, 1960, p. 171.

11 Polybius, *History*, Book VI, sec. 6, quoted by E. Westermarck, *The*

Origin and Development of the Moral Ideas, vol. 1, p. 42.

12 Gerald A. Larue, 'Ancient Ethics' in Peter Singer, ed., *A Companion to Ethics*, p. 32.

13 Such feuds are common in many societies; see Jacob Black-Michaud, *Cohesive Force: Feud in the Mediterranean and Middle East*, Basil Blackwell Ltd., 1975; or Altina L. Waller, *Feud: Hatfields, McCoys and Social Change in Appalachia*, 1860–1900, University of North Carolina Press, Chapel Hill, North Carolina, 1988.

CHAPTER 8 *Living ethically*

1 For details on Wallenberg's life, see John Bierman, *The Righteous Gentile*, Viking Press, New York, 1981.

2 See Thomas Kenneally, *Schindler's Ark*, Hodder and Stoughton, London, 1982.

3 Samuel and Pearl Oliner, *The Altruistic Personality: Rescuers of Jews in Nazi Europe*, Free Press, New York, 1988. The cases mentioned earlier in the paragraph are taken from Kristen R. Monroe, Michael C. Barton and Ute Klingemann, 'Altruism and the Theory of Rational Action: Rescuers of Jews in Nazi Europe', *Ethics*, Oct. 1990, vol. 101, no. 1, pp. 103–123. See also Perry London, 'The Rescuers: motivational hypotheses about Christians who saved Jews from the Nazis', in J. Macaulay and L. Berkowitz, eds., *Altruism and Helping Behavior*, Academic Press, New York, 1970; Carol Rittner and Gordon Myers, eds., *The Courage to Care – Rescuers of Jews During the Holocaust*, New York University Press, New York, 1986; Nehama Tec, *When Light Pierced the Darkness – Christian Rescuers of Jews in Nazi-Occupied Poland*, Oxford University Press, New York, 1986; and Gay Block and Malka Drucker, *Rescuers – Portraits of Moral Courage in the Holocaust*, Holmes and Meier, New York, 1992.

4 Primo Levi, *If This is a Man*, trans. Stuart Woolf, Abacus, London, 1987, pp. 125, 127–8.

5 The story of Corti and Delaney is the subject of Jonathan Kwitny's *Acceptable Risks*, Poseidon Press, New York, 1992.

6 The Blockaders, *The Franklin Blockade*, The Wilderness Society, Hobart, 1983, p. 72.

7 *Conservation News*, vol. 24, no. 2, April/May 1992.

8 Maimonides, *Mishneh Torah*, Book 7, ch. 10, reprinted in Isadore Twersky, *A Maimonides Reader*, Behrman House, New York, 1972 , pp. 136–7.

9 R. M. Titmuss, *The Gift Relationship*, Allen & Unwin, London, 1971, p. 44.

10 These figures were obtained from correspondence received from the relevant bone marrow registries during June/July 1992.

11 Alfie Kohn, *The Brighter Side of Human Nature*, Basic Books, New York, 1990, p. 64.

12 B. O'Connell, 'Already 1,000 Points of Light', *New York Times*, Jan. 25, 1989, A23. (I owe this reference to Alfie Kohn, *The Brighter Side of Human Nature*, p. 290.) See also *Time*, April 8, 1991.

13 Aerosol production of personal care products in 1989 declined 11 percent from 1988 levels, according to the Chemical Specialty Manufacturers Association, *The Rose Sheet*, Federal Department of Conservation Reports, Chevy Chase, Maryland, vol. 11, no. 50, Dec. 10, 1990.

14 'Doing the Right Thing', *Newsweek*, Jan. 7, 1991, pp. 42–3.

15 The quotations are taken from R. M. Titmuss, *The Gift Relationship*, pp. 227–8.

16 E. Lightman, 'Continuity in social policy behaviors: The case of voluntary blood donorship', *Journal of Social Policy*, 1981, vol. 10, no. 1, pp. 53–79; J. A. Piliavin, D. E. Evans and P. Callero, 'Learning to "give to unnamed strangers": The process of commitment to regular blood donation', in E. Staub et al, eds., *Development and Maintenance of Prosocial Behavior: International Perspectives on Positive Morality*, Plenum Press, New York, 1984, pp. 471–491; J. Piliavin, 'Why do they give the gift of life? A review of research on blood donors since 1977', *Transfusion*, 1990, vol. 30, no. 5, pp. 444–459. For Aristotle's views on virtue, see his *Nicomachean Ethics*, trans. W. D. Ross, World Classics, Oxford University Press, London, 1959. I take the point made in this paragraph from 'Giving Blood: The Development of Generosity', an unsigned article in *Issues in Ethics*, 1992, vol. 5, no. 1, published by the Santa Clara University Center for Applied Ethics, Calif.

CHAPTER 9 *The nature of ethics*

1 For an account of the history of its exposure see A. N. Prior, *Logic and the Basis of Ethics*, Oxford University Press, Oxford, 1949.

2 Some philosophers have tried to show this, dismissing the very question we are discussing as incoherent. See, for example, Stephen Toulmin, *The Place of Reason in Ethics*, Cambridge University Press, Cambridge, 1961, p. 162. For the reasons given, this is a mistake. Nothing substantive can hang on the definition of a word. For further discussion see my 'The triviality of the debate over "Is–Ought" and the definition of "moral"', *American Philosophical Quarterly*, 1973, vol. 10, pp. 51–6.

3 See Rabbi Hillel's saying in the Babylonian Talmud, Order Mo'ed, Tractate Sabbath, sec. 31a; Confucius: Lun Yu XV: 23 and XII: 2, quoted from E. Westermarck, *The Origin and Development of the Moral Ideas*, vol. 1, p. 102; Marcus Aurelius, *Commentaries*, vol. IV, no. 4, trans. A. S. L. Farquharson, Oxford University Press, Oxford, 1944, p. 53.

4 This is obviously a very brief summary; the interested reader should consult R. M. Hare, *Freedom and Reason*, Oxford University Press, Oxford, 1965, and R. M. Hare, *Moral Thinking*, Oxford University Press, Oxford, 1981.

5 Jean-Jacques Rousseau, *Emile*, tr. Barbara Foxley, J. M. Dent, London, 1974, p. 345.

6 Jean-Jacques Rousseau, *Emile*, pp. 340, 349.

7 Sigmund Freud, 'Some Psychical Consequences of the Anatomical Distinction between the Sexes', *The Standard Edition of the Complete Psychological Works of Sigmund Freud*, James Strachey, ed., Hogarth Press, London, 1964, vol. XIX, p. 257.

8 Cited by Jean Grimshaw, 'The Idea of a Female Ethic' in Peter Singer, ed., *A Companion to Ethics*, p. 496.

9 Carol Gilligan, *In a Different Voice: Psychological Theory and Women's Development*, Harvard University Press, Cambridge, Mass., 1982. For Kohlberg's original discussion of the dilemma, see Lawrence Kohlberg, 'Continuities and Discontinuities in Childhood and Adult Moral Development Revised' in *Collected Papers on Moral Development and Moral Education*, Moral Education and Research Foundation, Cambridge, 1973. See also Lawrence Kohlberg, *The Philosophy of Moral Development*, Harper and Row, San Francisco, 1981.

10 Nel Noddings, *Caring: A Feminine Approach to Ethics and Education*, University of California Press, Berkeley, 1984, pp. 153–9.

11 For a brief criticism of the basis on which Gilligan reached her conclusions, see Susan Faludi, *Backlash*, Chatto & Windus, London, 1992, pp. 361–6.

12 Alison Jaggar, 'Feminist Ethics: Projects, Problems, Prospects' in Claudia Card, ed., *Feminist Ethics*, University Press of Kansas, Lawrence, 1991, pp. 79–103, especially pp. 92, 94. For another general account of feminist ethics, see Jean Grimshaw, 'The Idea of a Female Ethic', in Peter Singer, ed., *A Companion to Ethics*.

13 Carla Bennett, People for the Ethical Treatment of Animals, personal communication, May 15, 1992.

14 Carol Gilligan, *In a Different Voice*, p. 21.

15 Matthew 16:28; see also Matthew 10:23 and 24:34; Mark 9:1 and 13:30; Luke 9:27.

16 Matthew 24:44.

17 Matthew 6:2–4.

18 See Matthew 5, 6 and 7: Jesus also talks about reward and punishment in Matthew 19:27–30 and 25:31–46; Mark 3:29, 8:34–38, 9:41–8, and 10:21; and Luke 9:24–5, 12:4–5 and 14:7–14.

19 Immanuel Kant, *The Moral Law: Kant's Groundwork of the Metaphysic of Morals*, trans. H. J. Paton, Hutchinson, London, 1966, p. 10. Kant scholars will no doubt protest that in other writings Kant said other things that give his moral philosophy a softer face. No doubt he did. I make no claim about Kant's consistency; I claim only that Kant did hold the position described here, and advocated it in what many regard as his finest work in moral philosophy.

20 F. H. Bradley, *Ethical Studies*, 2nd edn., Oxford University Press, Oxford, 1959, p. 63.

21 H. Arendt, *Eichmann in Jerusalem*, Faber & Faber, London, 1963, pp. 120–3. Later Eichmann contradicted himself, saying that he ceased to live according to Kantian principles after being charged with

the administration of the Final Solution. This may refer to the idea of living according to a general law, or perhaps to Kant's further formulation of the categorical imperative requiring that we treat other people always as ends, and never as means. I am not suggesting that Kant's ethics, properly understood, lead to mass murder; only that the idea that we should do our duty for duty's sake, without asking for further justification, is misconceived and dangerous.

22 R. Hilberg, *The Destruction of the European Jews*, Quadrangle, Chicago, 1961, pp. 218–9.

23 Soren Kierkegaard, *Fear and Trembling: Dialectical Lyric* (1843), trans. Howard V. Hong and Edna H. Hong, Princeton University Press, Princeton, NJ, 1983, p. 15.

24 F. P. Ramsey, 'Epilogue' in R. B. Braithwaite, ed., *The Foundations of Mathematics and Other Logical Essays*, Routledge & Kegan Paul, London, 1931, p. 289.

25 *The Gilgamesh Epic* has been reprinted in various places, including James B. Pritchard, ed., *The Ancient Near East*, Princeton University Press, Princeton, NJ, 1958. The passage quoted is from Tablet X (iii), p. 64.

26 Roshi Philip Kapleau, *To Cherish All Life*, The Zen Center, Rochester, NY, 1981, pp. 27–30.

27 See Anthony Ashley Cooper, 3rd Earl of Shaftesbury, *Characteristics of Men, Manners, Opinions and Times*, Bobbs-Merrill, New York, 1964 (first published 1711); Joseph Butler, *Fifteen Sermons preached at the Rolls Chapel and A dissertation of the Nature of Virtue*, T. A. Roberts, ed., S. P. C. K., London, 1970. David Hume, *A Treatise of Human Nature*, ed. with an introduction by Ernest C. Mossner, Penguin Books, Harmondsworth, Middlesex, 1984.

CHAPTER 10 *Living to some purpose*

1 Albert Camus, *The Myth of Sisyphus and Other Essays*, trans. Justin O'Brien, Alfred A. Knopf, Inc., New York, 1969, p. 3.

2 Albert Camus, *The Myth of Sisyphus and Other Essays*, pp. 121, 123.

3 Richard Taylor, *Good and Evil*, Prometheus, Buffalo, NY, 1984 (first published Macmillan, New York, 1970).

4 Betty Friedan, *The Feminine Mystique*, Penguin Books, Harmondsworth, Middlesex, 1965, p. 19.

5 Richard Gould, *Yiwara Foragers of the Australian Desert*, Collins Publishers, London, 1969, p. 90.

6 Donald Trump, *Surviving at the Top*, p. 5.

7 Thorstein Veblen, *The Theory of the Leisure Class*, Unwin Books, London, 1970 (first published 1899), pp. 35, 37.

8 Thorstein Veblen, *The Theory of the Leisure Class*, pp. 77–8.

9 Thorstein Veblen, *The Theory of the Leisure Class*, p. 111.

10 Thorstein Veblen, *The Theory of the Leisure Class*, p. 39.

11 Michael Lewis, *Liar's Poker*, p. 203.

12 John Taylor, *Circus of Ambition*, pp. 176–7.
13 Tom Wolfe, *Bonfire of the Vanities*, Farrar, Straus & Giroux, New York, 1987, pp. 329–330.
14 Michael Maccoby, *The Gamesman: The New Corporate Leaders*, Bantam Books, New York, 1978, p. 111.
15 Connie Bruck, *The Predators' Ball*, pp. 302, 314.
16 Alfie Kohn, *No Contest: The case against competition*, Houghton Mifflin, Boston, 1986, p. 111.
17 Alfie Kohn, *No Contest*, pp. 112–3.
18 ABC News, *20/20*, Transcript #1221, ABC Television, New York, May 15, 1992, p. 5.
19 Joseph Veroff, Richard Kulka and Elizabeth Douvan, *Mental Health in America: Patterns of Help-Seeking from 1957 to 1976*, Basic Books, 1981, cited by Robert N. Bellah et al, *Habits of the Heart*, p. 121.
20 Peter Brown and Henry Shue, 'Introduction' in Peter Brown and Henry Shue, eds., *Food Policy: The Responsibility of the United States in the Life and Death Choices*, Free Press, New York, 1977, p. 2.
21 V. Frankl, *Man's Search for Meaning: an introduction to logotherapy*, trans. Ilse Lasch, Hodder & Stoughton, London, 1964, pp. 103–4.
22 Robert N. Bellah, et al, *Habits of the Heart*, p. ix.
23 M. Scott Peck, *The Road Less Travelled*, Arrow Books, London, 1990, pp. 58–9.
24 Robert N. Bellah et al, *Habits of the Heart*, p. 127, 130.
25 Robert N. Bellah et al, *Habits of the Heart*, p. 129.
26 Robert J. Ringer, *Looking Out for # 1*, pp. 20–1.
27 Gail Sheehy, *Passages: Predictable Crises of Adult Life*, Bantam Books, New York, 1977, p. 251.
28 V. Frankl, *Man's Search for Meaning*, p. 74.
29 V. Frankl, *Man's Search for Meaning*, p. 76.
30 F. H. Bradley, *Ethical Studies*, Oxford University Press, Oxford, 1959 (first published 1876), p. 96.
31 H. Sidgwick, *The Methods of Ethics*, 7th edn., Macmillan, London, 1907, p. 405.
32 Robert N. Bellah et al, *Habits of the Heart*, p. 18.
33 Robert N. Bellah et al, *Habits of the Heart*, p. 158.
34 Robert N. Bellah et al, *Habits of the Heart*, p. 163.
35 Betty Friedan, *The Feminine Mystique*, p. 300.
36 Robert Bly, *Iron John*, Element Books Ltd., Longmead, Shaftesbury, 1990, p. 151.
37 Reprinted in Thomas Hutchinson, ed., *The Poetical Works of Shelley*, London, 1904, p. 550.
38 See Bertrand Russell, 'The Expanding Mental Universe' in Robert Egner and Lester Dononn, eds., *The Basic Writings of Bertrand Russell*, Allen & Unwin, 1961, pp. 392–3; see also 'What I Believe' in the same book, p. 371.
39 Robert Egner and Lester Dononn, eds., *The Basic Writings of Bertrand Russell*, p. 393.

CHAPTER 11 *The good life*

1 On this, see Peter Singer, *Marx*, Oxford University Press, Oxford, 1980, pp. 75–76.

2 I used the metaphor of 'the escalator of reason' in my book, *The Expanding Circle*, p. 88; some parts of this section draw on that work. Colin McGinn put essentially the same argument in 'Evolution, Animals and the Basis of Morality', *Inquiry*, 1979, vol. 22, p. 91.

3 John Aubrey, *Brief Lives*, ed., A. Clark, Oxford University Press, Oxford, 1898, vol. 1, p. 332.

4 Gunnar Myrdal, *An American Dilemma*, Harper & Row, New York, 1944, app. 1.

5 See my *Animal Liberation*, 2nd edn., for an account of the basis of this view, and of the movement to which it has given rise.

6 Karl Marx, *The German Ideology*, International Publishers, New York, 1966, pp. 40–1.

7 For more detailed discussion of these points, see my book, *Practical Ethics*, 2nd edn., pp. 232–4.

8 The sources are, respectively: *The Gospel According to St Matthew*, 22:39; *Babylonian Talmud*, Order Mo'ed, Tractate Sabbath, sec. 31a; Lun Yu XV:23 and XII:2, quoted by E. Westermarck, *The Origin and Development of the Moral Ideas*, vol I, p. 102; and *Mahabharata*, XXIII:5571

9 Luke, 10:29–37.

INDEX

---

abortion as ethical issue 16, 163-4
acquisition 17-18, 203
   Acquisitive Societies 73-4
   see also consumerism; consumption
Adams, Douglas 98
   Hitchhiker's Guide to the Galaxy 188
affluence
   adaptation level 50-1
   not related to happiness 50-1, 54
   obligations of 16
Agarwal, Anil 47
Akers, John 26
Alexander, Richard 85, 86, 104-5
Allsop, David 163
altruism 20, 85-6, 103-5
   among animals 87
   assistance to persecuted 104, 154-60,
      167-8
   blood donors 85, 164-5, 168-9, 183-4
   bone marrow registries 165
   indirect reciprocity 104-5
   mothers' sacrifice for children 88-9
   not inherited 99-100
   voluntary work and donations 166
   see also co-operation; group, caring
      for
ambition, personal, as ideal 19
animals
   altruism among 87
   animal liberation 160-2, 163, 219-21
      People for the Ethical Treatment of
         Animals 161, 178

   women in majority 178-9
   co-operation among 138, 141
   experiments on
      American Museum of Natural
         History 219-20
      for cosmetics 167, 219-20, 233
      Revlon 220
   exploitation by law 34-5
   factory farming 16, 44, 162, 198-9,
      220
   failure of Marine Mammal Protection
      Act 35
   need for purpose 198-9
   number of domestic 45
   patenting 34-5
   production of methane gas 45
   social 138
   submission in defeat 87
   treatment in Japan 190-1
   treatment in Third World 221
Aquinas, Thomas
   on Aristotle 63
   on private property 63-4
Araskog, Rand 25-6
Aristotle
   on the art of making money 56-8
   Calvin's attitude to 66
   doctrine of sterility of money 58
   and Judeo-Christian teaching 63
   on Plato 191
   on practice of virtue 35, 169
   on trading 58

ACKNOWLEDGEMENTS

———•———

I owe thanks to many people. Di Gribble of Text Publishing suggested that the time was right for a book on this theme, and Michael Heyward of the same firm advised me after the book reached the draft stage. An Australian Research Council Grant made it possible for Margaret Parnaby to provide part-time research assistance, gathering materials, checking references and providing critical comments at every stage of the work. Her work has helped to put flesh on the bare bones of the outline I had planned. Various drafts were read by Aaron Asher, Stephen Buckle, Paola Cavalieri, Lori Gruen, Helga Kuhse, Shunici Noguchi, Renata Singer, Henry Spira and Tomasaburo Yamauchi. Each gave me helpful comments and, collectively, they have made the book – whatever faults it may still have – much better than it would have been otherwise.